PEOPLE of the
WETLANDS

Bryony and John Coles

PEOPLE of the WETLANDS

Bogs, Bodies and Lake-Dwellers

WITH 150 ILLUSTRATIONS

THAMES AND HUDSON

Ancient Peoples and Places
FOUNDING EDITOR: GLYN DANIEL

Title pages: Reconstruction of a heavy wooden roadway of the
European Neolithic, winding across a raised bog. All of the
vegetation, pools, timber and bird life are based on evidence
preserved in the waterlogged peats around this road, the Abbot's
Way in Somerset, England.

First published in the USA in 1989 by
Thames and Hudson Inc., 500 Fifth Avenue
New York, New York 10110

Library of Congress Catalog Card Number 89-50546

Printed and bound in the German Democratic Republic

Contents

Preface

IT IS THE PURPOSE of this book to set out some of the trials and
achievements of wetland archaeology since its beginnings 150 years ago
and to acknowledge the great contribution that wetlands can make to our
understanding of the past.

Glyn Daniel, the founder and editor of Ancient Peoples and Places, first asked
us to undertake this work about 10 years ago, but it is only now that we have been
able to assemble information from many parts of the world, and to begin to see
the nature and potential of modern wetland archaeology. We think that he would
like to have the story of his bog body dinner recounted here (Chapter 7).

Although the archaeology of wetlands has a long and eventful history, it is only
in recent years that the development of scientific techniques has allowed a full
examination of many drowned and waterlogged sites. In addition, the pressures
of modern society have caused and are causing the loss of many of the most
important wetlands in the world. An active, some would say frantic, episode of
wetland archaeology has been underway for the past 20 or 30 years, and its
results are only now being made available. The recognition of the precision in
dating, and the outstandingly good preservation, offered by wetlands has now
started to augment and in some cases to re-write the prehistory of human
societies.

We have received help and encouragement in the preparation of this book
from many wetland archaeologists and others, and we hope that our colleagues in
the Wetland Archaeology Research Project will approve of our compilations of
some of their work. We are particularly grateful to a number of archaeologists
and museum curators who have supplied photographs and other illustrations.
Acknowledgment of the source of all the illustrations appears elsewhere in the
text. We also thank Mike Rouillard who has drawn many of the maps and other
illustrations. Mrs Jennifer Warren kindly typed most of the manuscript. We
espcially thank the following for kindness and assistance on our several wetland
tours gathering material for the book: Søren Andersen, Wil Casparie, Dale
Croes, Michel Egloff, Hajo Hayen, Barbara Purdy, Barry Raftery, Joachim
Reichstein, Ulrich Ruoff, Haio Zimmermann, and our many colleagues in the
United Kingdom.

Maillezais, September 1988

NOTE: All dates in this book are expressed in calendar years, based on tree-ring
and calibrated radiocarbon dating.

1 Reconstruction of the Bronze Age village at Cortaillod-Est, Switzerland, *c.* 1000 BC.

1·The decades of discovery

Few things can be more interesting than the spectacle of an ancient, long-forgotten people, thus rising, as it were, from the waters of oblivion.

THE WORDS OF JOHN LUBBOCK, in his *Prehistoric Times* of 1865, sum up the fascination of those ancient peoples whose villages lie submerged by sea, lake or bog, and whose lives were bounded by the peculiar qualities of wetland environments. In our book the dwellers of wetlands will be discussed, their settlements and artifacts described, their economic activities assessed, and their life and death portrayed (*ill. 1, ill. 2*). The story is partial, incomplete and fragmentary, like all archaeological evidence, but the advantages of a wetland environment will become apparent as the narrative unfolds. Because not all wet places are the same, it is sometimes difficult to find a form of words to describe every wetland; raised bog, swamp, marsh, fen, mud-flat, lake-edge and riverside are all different environments, linked only by a proximity to and a dependence upon water. The term wetland or waterland seems to us to be appropriate, and wetlanders will be used as a general term to describe those many ancient communities of people who lived upon or beside the variety of water-dominated landscapes from at least 10,000 years ago up to the present. Each of the different environments will be described in its relevant section.

The history of research into the ancient wetlanders of Europe, and other parts of the world, is a combination of economic, geological and opportunistic events which culminated in the winter months of 1853–4. By this time, archaeology was becoming established as a discipline, and had a long if not very distinguished history of discovery and excavation in Europe, the Near East, Egypt and other regions. The Three Age System of prehistory was accepted in Europe, and objects of the Stone Age, Bronze Age and Iron Age were eagerly sought in barrows, hillforts and other sites. Major agricultural improvements, including drainage, were underway, and artifacts of stone, bronze and gold were being retrieved from land newly-taken under cultivation. Land was being cleared and worked elsewhere, too, and colonization and settlement of former wilderness in America was in progress. Rural life was in general difficult, with few amenities and services, yet the development of industry elsewhere had already led, in many countries, to the emergence of a wealthy middle class; the landed gentry had not yet succumbed to the pressures of population and economy. The opening-up of many regions of the world to European explorers, missionaries, exploiters and settlers had unveiled a dazzling array of life-styles and adaptations to different environments, and the scientific communities of Europe were energetic in the

2 A 2,000-year-old bog body from Rendswühren, Germany, preserved in waterlogged peat.

collection and study of newly-discovered plants and animals. All of these events played a part in the explosion of wetland archaeology in the decades 1855–1875, an explosion which could have been foreseen.

Early warnings

Well before 1855, the archaeological community had ample notice of the possibilities of watery environments for the preservation of unusual evidence. On St John's Day, 24 June 1450, a group of peasants from Bönsdörp in Germany came to their parish priest and said that in cutting peat they had come upon a dead man stuck fast in the peat up to his neck. What was to be done with him? The priest advised them to leave the man alone, as the bog was inhabited by elves who had lured him to his death, and so burial in the churchyard was unthinkable. The man was never seen again. Such was the fate of many bodies, abandoned through fear or superstition. More detail emerges from a body found in 1773 in a peatbog at Ravnholt in Denmark. A peasant, digging peat 'one and a half ells' (1 m) below the surface suddenly chopped off a human foot with his spade. The local judge was called and made a full report on the discovery:

A fully preserved male body was found, which was seen by me, the undersigned (Judge Fogh) and two others who observed the following: the body lay stretched on its back with both arms crossed behind the back as if they had been tied together, although there was no trace of bindings. The body was entirely naked except for the head, which was encased in a sheepskin cap, on the removal of which it could be clearly seen that the man had a reddish beard and very short hair, which would have been compatible with the wearing of a wig. The skin was intact over the whole body except under the chin, where one could see right down to the bone, and the front teeth seemed to have been driven into the mouth. The body was otherwise whole and intact, and all the limbs were clearly visible, except for the one foot that had been struck off by the peat-spade.

This body was probably of the Iron Age, based on the skin cap and the likelihood that the man's throat had been cut. A set of branches laid over the body also suggests that it falls within the group of Iron Age sacrifices or executions (Chapter 7).

It was not only north Germany and Denmark where bodies from the bog were noted. In 1821 a tall man was discovered in County Galway, Ireland, submerged under 9 ft (3 m) of peat; he was clad in a deerskin tunic and had a short beard and dark reddish hair. And from England, records before 1700 noted 'sometimes in mosses are found human bodies entire and uncorrupted'. A few seem unlikely:

> Most shudderingly entrancing of all was the Ancient Briton, who suddenly emerged from the peat in Burwell Fen, when the turf-diggers were at work. He stood upright in his dug-out canoe. His lank black hair drooped to his shoulders. The peat-dark skin was still stretched over the bones of his face. The eyes had gone but the eye-sockets were dark with mystery. He was clad in a long leather jacket, belted, with garters round his legs and the right arm was raised as though about to cast a spear. That body of the unknown hunter, the nameless warrior, had been preserved in the peat for uncounted aeons of time. It crumbled to dust in the sharp Fen air. (J. Wentworth Day)

That of course was just the problem. Material, whether flesh and blood, or wood, could not sustain its condition once exposed to air and almost all of the early waterlogged objects were soon lost. In 1823, peat-diggers in Kragehul Fen in Denmark came upon a rich burial with objects of metal and a 'whole waggon with wheels which fell to pieces when exposed to the air'; this was an Iron Age sacrificial or ritual deposit, lost here, but nonetheless serving as a warning to the antiquaries of the time. Other vehicles, or parts of them, sometimes survived for future examination. In the Netherlands, a one-piece disc wheel was discovered at Gasselterboerveen in 1838; its crude nature aroused such curiosity that it was saved, only to be identified later as of Roman origin, and then as a giant lid or table-top, before modern studies resolved the artifact as a Neolithic wheel (*ill. 4*). From Scotland, a tripartite disc wheel found *c*.1830 was published as a shield and was only identified as a wheel 120 years later. From wheels to roads; here too the records existed to indicate the potential of boglands, yet nowhere in the abundant literature of bog roads in Ireland, Germany and the Netherlands is there much astonishment at the existence or quality of the ancient wooden paths and roads that lay submerged beneath the peat. Wooden trackways were in use as roads well into the historic period; in 1619, for example, a description was published of a heavy wooden roadway in northern Russia, made to help the

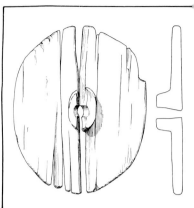

3, 4 **Early discoveries in the peatbogs of the Netherlands**
(*Left*) Wooden roadway of 500 BC, the Valtherbrug, discovered in 1818, and seen here in an 1892 photograph.
(*Above*) Neolithic disc wheel found in 1838 at Gasselterboerveen.

Dutch merchants and court ambassadors on their journey from Narva to Novgorod. The road was wide and heavy enough to support a coach and horses. Its illustration is remarkably like that of the Valtherbrug (the Valthebridge) in Drenthe, the Netherlands. This was a wide roadway made of logs and planks placed transversely along the line, and was not only seen in 1818 but was traced through the moorland by ditch observations and peat-cutting for a total distance of 12 km. The road was eventually photographed in 1892 (*ill. 3*) and later dated to about 500 BC. A year later, 1819, a heavy roadway was encountered in the peat in north Germany, near Lohne; the planks were so tightly packed and finely-carpentered that no opening could be seen on the surface.

In Ireland, the rural population of the Midlands in the early 19th century had greatly increased, and the use of peat as fuel, and the hauling out of the bogs of any ancient wood, whether bogoaks or other timbers, led to more discoveries of the multitude of roadways that had once traversed the quaking bogs. The ancient Irish records provided antiquaries with many a reference to the building of such roadways, and gave an historic context to the discoveries as well as a sense of *déjà vu* so that little was done to investigate the constructions. In the Life of St Brigid by Cogitosus, possibly of the 7th century, a king summoned his subjects to make a wide firm road through a deep and almost impassable fen (*grunna*), and through swamps (*in paludibus*) with tree branches (*ramis arborum*) and other firm road materials (*munitionibus firmissimis*).

Where lakes and rivers barred the passage of ancient wetlanders, rafts, logs, bridges and dugouts were used, and some of these too were recorded well before the advent of wetland archaeology. In 1780 in Scotland,

> the first recorded discovery of one of the primitive canoes of the Clyde was made by workmen engaged in digging the foundations of Old St Enoch's Church. It was found at a depth of twenty-five feet from the surface, and within it there lay a no less interesting and eloquent memorial of the simple arts of the remote era when the navies of the Clyde were hewn out of the oaks of the Caledonian forests. This is a beautifully-finished stone celt, doubtless one of the simple implements of its owner, if not, indeed, one of the tools with which such vessels were fashioned into shape; though it is undoubtedly more adapted for war than for any peaceful art. (Daniel Wilson)

And there were more, both here and elsewhere. By 1847, many canoes had been found along the Clyde at Glasgow and the locals were getting blasé:

> At a depth of seventeen feet below the surface, and about 130 feet from the river's original brink, the workmen uncovered an ancient canoe, hewn out of the trunk of an oak, with pointed stem, and the upright groove remaining which had formerly held in its place the straight stern. The discovery was made in the autumn of 1847; and the citizens of Glasgow having for the most part a reasonable conviction that boats lose their value in proportion to their age, the venerable relic lay for some months unheeded, until at length the Society of Antiquaries of Scotland made application for it to the Trustees of the River Clyde, and the rude precursor of the fleets that now crowd that noble river is safely deposited in their museum. (Daniel Wilson)

Well before 1850, the association of dugouts with other wetland monuments had been established in Scotland and Ireland. Lakes, loughs and lochs were known through both historical references and antiquarian observation to contain artificial islands, some submerged but others exposed, which held ancient dwellings (*ill. 6*). Some of these crannogs, as they were often called, remained elusive and were never examined. A probable crannog at Ardbrin, Co. Down, was identified in 1809 on the basis of a stratum of burnt oak, a canoe and four paddles, all dug from the peat. A century before, the bog had been open water, and from its silts was recovered a large and perfectly-curved bronze horn of the Iron Age, one of the treasures of Ireland and perhaps the finest musical instrument of prehistoric Europe. This, and the fragments of harps from other bogs, suggested to some that 'in time of peace, the sweet sound of the harp, and in war, the hoarse bray of the trumpet, resounded over the waters of the lakes' in which the crannogs stood.

The crannogs of Ireland and Scotland in particular were soon to become closely identified with the pile-dwellings of other regions of the world, and to become objects of great interest, but before 1850 they were barely acknowledged in the literature, and none was properly excavated or understood.

'The Crannoge of which I am now to give an account was discovered by me in the summer of 1812', so wrote John Mackinlay:

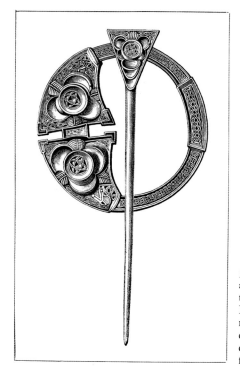

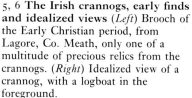

5, 6 **The Irish crannogs, early finds and idealized views** (*Left*) Brooch of the Early Christian period, from Lagore, Co. Meath, only one of a multitude of precious relics from the crannogs. (*Right*) Idealized view of a crannog, with a logboat in the foreground.

There is a small mossy lake, called Dhu-Loch, situated in a narrow valley in the middle of that strong tract of hill-ground extending from the Dun-hill of Barone to Ardscalpsie Point, to which valley, it is said, the inhabitants of Bute were wont to drive their cattle in times of danger. I remember, when a schoolboy, to have heard that there were the remains of some ancient building in that lake, which were visible when the water was low; and happening to be in that part of the island last summer, I went to search for it. I found a low green islet about twenty yards long, which was connected with the shore, owing to the lowness of the water, after a continuance of dry weather. Not seeing any vestiges of stone foundations, I was turning away, when I observed ranges of oak piles, and on examination it appeared that the edifice had been thus constructed.

The walls were formed by double rows of piles, $4\frac{1}{2}$ feet asunder, and the intermediate space appears to have been filled with beams of wood, some of which yet remain. The bottom had been filled up to the surface of the water with moss or turf, and covered over with shingle, or quarry rubbish, to form a floor. The ground-plan was a triangle, with one point towards the shore, to which it had been connected by a bridge or stage, some of the piles of which are still to be traced.

Earlier still was a crannog discovered at Roscrea, Co. Tipperary, in 1810 when the waters of Lough Nahinch (the lake of the island) were lowered by drainage. It was not until 1840 that the great wealth, in both artifacts and information, to be found in crannogs was revealed by work at Lagore, Co. Meath; this crannog is now known to have been the seat of some kind of chieftain in the later first millennium AD. The founder of Irish archaeology George Petrie was puzzled by the regular appearance in Dublin of a dealer, 'bringing for sale objects of

archaeological interest, which he stated had been found near Dunshaughlin. Struck by the frequency of the dealer's calls, Petrie decided to unravel the mystery by visiting the place; he reached Lagore House, and there, carelessly thrown on the floor of a barn, he saw a large and miscellaneous collection of antiquities, consisting chiefly of weapons composed of iron – swords, daggers, spear- and axe-heads, saws, chains, shears, small culinary vessels, etc. etc; pins and brooches of bronze (*ill. 5*), articles of bone, and even of wood, all of which had been found by labourers engaged in making a drain through the ancient lake bed. Petrie endeavoured to procure some of these for his collection, but the steward, or caretaker, in the absence of his employer, would not part with any.

For some years after the drainage operations, the soil of Lagore remained unturned by the spade; but in 1846, 1847 and 1848, the site of the crannog was reopened by men engaged in the process of turf-cutting, and, as on the previous occasion, quantities of bones were exhumed, and with them a surprising number of antiquities, together with the remains of the ancient stockading, and the ruins of several structures evidently used as huts; one of them is thus described by W. F. Wakeman:

> Let the reader imagine a foundation formed of four roughly-squared planks of oak, each about twelve feet in length (so arranged as to enclose a quadrangle), the ends of which were carefully fitted together. From the angles of this square rose four posts, also of oak, to the height of about nine feet. In these grooves were cuts, into which roughly-split planks of oak had been slipped, so as to form the sides of the house; the irregularities between the boards were tightly caulked with moss; a low and narrow opening in one of the sides had evidently served as an entrance. There were no traces of window or chimney.' (Wood–Martin)

15

7 The wooden 'house' from Inver, Co. Donegal, Ireland, found in 1833 under 25 ft (8 m) of peat. It may have been a mortuary house.

The wealth of detail available from sites such as Lagore was in effect too great for the antiquaries of the day, and the abundance of portable artifacts must have discouraged those like Petrie who sought structural evidence; the looting of the site would not have allowed much careful observation. Yet the seeds of wetland archaeology were here, and also in Co. Donegal in 1833, scene of an extraordinary discovery, 'the most perfectly preserved primitive dwelling of (wooden) material yet brought to light in Ireland' (*ill. 7*). Investigated by a Captain W. Mudge, RN, the hut was surrounded by a fence with a gate, and there were traces of a substructure of logs beneath; the site was probably a crannog. The hut

was nearly square, twelve feet wide, and nine feet high, formed of rough logs and planks of oak, apparently split by wedges, the interstices filled with a compound of grease and fine sea sand. One side of the hut, supposed to be the front, was left entirely open. The framework consisted of upright posts and horizontal sleepers, mortised at the angles, the end of each post being inserted into the lower sleeper of the frame, and fastened with a large block of wood. The discoverer states that the mortises were very rough, as if made with a kind of blunt instrument, the wood being bruised rather than cut, and it may be inferred that a stone celt found lying upon the floor of the house was the identical tool with which the mortises had been formed. By comparing the chisel with the marks of the tool used in making the mortises and grooves, it was found to correspond exactly with them, even to the slight curved surface of the chisel; but the logs had evidently been hewn with a larger instrument in the shape of an axe, undoubtedly of stone, as the marks, though larger than those the chisel would have made, are of the same character, being somewhat hollow and small cuts, not presenting the smooth surface produced by a common iron axe.

The interior of the structure was divided into two stories, each about four feet in height; its flat roof was sixteen feet beneath the original surface; therefore, nearly twenty-five feet of bog must have grown around it since its first erection; a piece of a leather sandal, a flint arrow-head and wooden sword were found.

The depth at which the hut was buried, and the flint and stone implements found in it, seem to prove unquestionably its extreme antiquity; added to which, upon the level of the floor, and extending all around, were the corkers of a forest of hard wood trees that had co-existed with the occupation of this structure. (Wood-Martin)

Corkers may refer either to the bark of oak, or to lichens formerly growing on the forest floor. In the light of recent discoveries in wetlands (as at Haddenham in the Fens), this structure might have been a wooden tomb rather than a dwelling – a house for the dead.

It will be clear, we hope, that most of the virtues of archaeological work in wetland of whatever sort were revealed well before 1855. Structures and artifacts and bodies, still in their original shapes, and mostly undecayed, offered possibilities for interpretation and understanding that antiquaries could never hope for on their dryland sites. Yet the interest in material culture, fostered in the minds of the gentry by the development of 19th-century industry, as well as by the interest engendered by the 'Grand Tours' of the Classical world of Greece and Rome, and by the rewards offered by collectors to those employed in working the land, meant that structures and organic objects were often ignored, or abandoned, or wilfully destroyed, in the efforts to retrieve valuables for display cabinets or for sale to dealers. It was only a major climatic event, revealing a mass of structural evidence in Switzerland, that persuaded the scientific world at least of the importance of wetlands for an understanding of past human communities.

Two fruitful decades: 1855–1875

The landscape of Switzerland is most often thought of as a series of impressive and unending mountains, with glaciers and upland meadows overlooking the narrow valleys which carry the meltwaters away. Yet the northern half of the country, called the Foreland and the Jura to the west, contains a series of lakes some of which are both long and wide. Among these are Lakes Geneva and Neuchâtel in the west, and the narrower Lake Zürich farther east. It was in these lakes that wetland archaeology developed through the discovery of the lake-dwellings (ill. 9).

In 1829 a small clearance was made in the harbour of the town of Meilen, which lies on the north shore of Lake Zürich. In the dredging, some wooden piles were dragged up, as well as some artifacts of Neolithic type. No antiquary was present, and the material was mostly put into barges and dumped in the

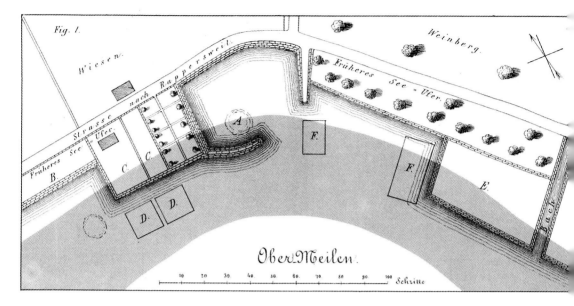

8 The harbour at Meilen, Switzerland, and the first recognition of the 'pile-dwellers'. Dredging in 1829 (A) yielded some relics but the lowering of the lake level exposed the piles in 1851 (B) and 1854 (C). Further discoveries were made in later years (D-F).

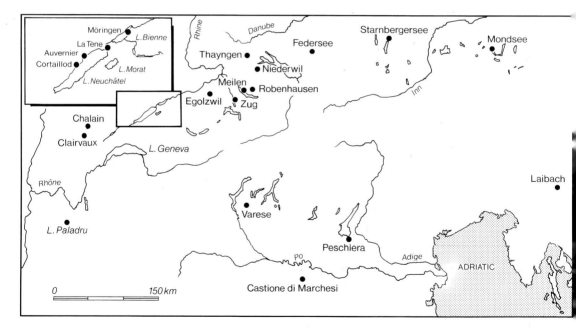

9 Map of the Alpine region, showing the location of pile-dwellings and other sites discovered in the 19th century in Switzerland, and parts of France, Germany, Austria, Yugoslavia and Italy.

deepest part of the lake. Twenty-four years later, however, conditions had changed. In the winter of 1853–4, a long drought and extreme cold caused the rivers feeding the lake to shrink, and the lake waters to recede to their lowest recorded level (*ill. 8*). A contemporary account reads:

> In January 1854, Mr Aeppli of Ober Meilen informed the society at Zürich, that remains of human industry, likely to throw unexpected light on the primaeval history of the inhabitants of the country, had been found near his house in that part of the bed of the lake then left dry by the water.
>
> The discovery of these antiquities was made in the following manner: The inhabitants were making use of the low state of the water to recover from the lake a certain portion of land, which they had enclosed with walls, and were filling in the space with mud, excavated from the shore a little in front. This was done at two places in the little bay between Ober Meilen and Dollikon. The workmen, as soon as they began to excavate, found to their great astonishment the heads of piles, and a great number of stag's horns, together with several implements, an account of which will be given in the detailed description of this settlement . . . (F. Keller)

Early on the scene was Dr Ferdinand Keller, President of the Antiquarian Association of Zürich. He observed an upper layer of yellowish mud with pebbles, being a modern deposit, overlying a blackish mud some 2 to $2\frac{1}{2}$ ft (*c*.0.75 m) thick in which the tops of wooden piles appeared and also an abundance of relics; below this was a brownish mud, free of relics, but with the piles deeply penetrating. The piles were of oak, beech, birch and fir, and were mostly split halves or quarters of tree stems, sometimes more slender complete stems. They were about $1\frac{1}{2}$ ft (0.5 m) apart and were in rows parallel to the shore. A few piles were pulled up and exhibited ends roughly pointed, exactly as could be created by the stone axes found in the relic bed. Keller made an interpretation based on the descriptions of dwellings set upon piles, and thus raised over the open waters, of many areas of the world then being explored and reported. He decided that the Swiss piles (*ill. 11*) had also probably held platforms upon which huts had been erected, the people thus living over the water, dropping their debris into the lake muds, and eventually abandoning their homes and platforms due to fire, flood or famine. At Meilen, they left behind the lower parts of the piles, deeply embedded in the muds, as well as stone axes still in their antler sleeves, perforated axe-hammers, flint tools, bone points, clubs, pottery and spindle-whorls. Keller wrote:

> The piles were from the commencement driven into the actual bed of the lake; and they were so long that their heads stood a few feet above the water, whatever might be its level. They stood in close rows, and when covered with horizontal timbers and boards formed a scaffolding, making a firm foundation for the erection of the dwellings. These abodes were therefore like the fishermen's huts which were found in earlier times. We know, indeed, very little as to the shape of these ancient huts, except that they were built of poles and hurdlework, coated on the outside with clay. In or near the huts there was room enough for all the operations of daily life to be carried on, as well as the manufacture of every implement used in household economy. Here they cooked, and here they spun; here clothes, string, and all manner of hunting

and fishing tackle were made; here serpentine, stag's horn, and bones of various animals were worked up into tools; here the pottery was manufactured. In short, this was the place where every craft or art known to the settlers was brought into play. All the refuse of burnt wood, the remains of animals used for food, and useless or broken utensils were thrown into the water, where they sank into the mud. (*ill. 12*).

As soon as the finds at Meilen were made known, there was an 'irruption of activity' in Switzerland, with the appearance of a crop of lacustrine explorers who combed the lakes for sites. Local fishermen had fouled their nets for decades on the piles of numerous sites in the bays of the lakes of Zürich, Neuchâtel, Bienne, Geneva and others, and they rapidly identified sites to antiquaries and collectors alike, often aiding the latter. By the end of 1854, Keller published his first report, the first of many, on 'Die Keltischen Pfahlbauten in den Schweizerseen', and in this he could already record sites other than Meilen. By 1866, six reports had appeared, and in that year an English translation of the reports was prepared and published by J. E. Lee. More reports emerged thereafter, and another edition of the book in 1878. By then, there was a multitude of sites to record. Some lay beneath the waters, others were buried by the silts or peats of former lakes, and these latter were more easily explored. But a majority of the sites were still submerged by water, less clearly now that the extraordinary low lake levels of 1853–4 had risen; the sites had in effect reverted to their underwater positions. Their yield of artifacts, once antiquarian interest had been aroused, was seized by a variety of ingenious techniques.

In Lake Geneva, the first underwater excavation was conducted by a geologist, Adolphe von Morlot (*ill. 13*). Donning a bucket with a glass-window, and supplied by air from a small pump in a rowboat operated by Professors Troyon and Forel, he stalked the bottom of the lake, armed with a net and a pick, retrieving objects from among the piles protruding from the lake bed. Morlot wrote: 'It was strikingly poetical to stand amid those ancient posts in the bluish twilight.' Other sites lay under such clear water that artifacts could be seen from boats, and pairs of long-handled forceps were used to pick them from the bottom. Where buried by mud, a trenching rake was used, pressed down from above by wooden handles, and sometimes a steam-driven mud engine, or dredger, was used to bring to the surface vast heaps of mud and broken artifacts (*ill. 10*). Stratigraphical considerations were clearly of little concern in such operations.

By 1860, many settlements of the lake-dwellers were known. In Lake Geneva (Lac Léman), twenty-six stations were identified, and in Lake Neuchâtel (Neuenburgersee) dozens more; in the lakes of Zürich, Bienne (Biel) and Morat, more sites were identified and explored. Some were of the Neolithic, others were of the later Bronze Age and these latter excited the greater curiosity and pillage. Explorations extended outwards, to the French Alpine lake of Bourget where by 1862, eight settlements of the Bronze Age were identified and explored by the Count de Beauregard.

Other lakes and sites followed suit. In 1860, the French prehistorian Gabriel de Mortillet suggested that the North Italian lakes might hold lake-dwellings, and the naturalist Bartolomeo Gastaldi at once identified a site at Mercurago. In 1863 de Mortillet and Edouard Desor visited Lombardy in the company of the

10 Forceps and trenching rake used for extracting relics from the lake muds of Switzerland.

11-13 **Early discoveries of the pile-dwellings** (*Top*) Exposure of wooden piles at Bevaix-Treytel, Switzerland, in 1885, one of the many Neolithic settlements discovered by lowered lake levels. (*Above*) Idealized 19th-century view of a pile-dwelling, positioned in a lake with bridges to the shore. (*Right*) The first underwater archaeologist – Adolphe von Morlot, 1854, armed with pick and butterfly net.

Italian archaeologist Stoppani. On their first day, 21 April, they found two settlements in Lake Varese, and by the end of the year there were six sites identified (*ill. 14*).

Earlier still, in 1851, the harbour of Peschiera on Lake Garda had been dredged and bronzes and piles were noted, to little avail. In 1860 the process was repeated and Keller was informed of the finds; this inspired an antiquarian inspection and recording of the site, to be followed by further discoveries in the lake of other sites. The artifacts from all these Bronze Age sites went to museums outside the region, particularly to Rome, until De Stefani, a local inspector, was induced to begin work again at Peschiera in 1881. The relics were deposited in the museum at Verona, to form the basis of the Bronze Age collections of the north of Italy.

In the Po valley, terremare sites had for long been known; these consisted of wide low mounds of clay, ash and sand, used as fertilizer for decades. During the quarrying, many implements of stone, horn, metal and clay were often encountered but little notice was paid to them. In 1822 they were interpreted as cremation pyres for the Celtic Boii, and as late as 1861 – that is after the recognition of the Swiss lake-dwellings – Gastaldi considered the mounds to be the result of floods, washing down 'Roman graves, cremations and funeral feasts'. In the same year, however, the naturalist Strobel announced that he had found the remains of a pile-dwelling underneath a terremare at Castione dei Marchesi in Parma. The site consisted of about 11 ft (3.5 m) of deposits of marl, overlain by recent soils and underlain by the clay of the floodplain, into which latter the piles were driven. Strobel and his archaeologist collaborator L. Pigorini made the fundamental leap by writing:

> Man did not meet there only to arrange and devour the feast, but to employ himself besides in domestic avocations, in preparing implements and arms, to sew garments, and make nets – in a word, to inhabit them; besides, to exercise the practices of their religious worship, and, perhaps, also to burn their dead, and all these after the fashion of the barbarians, such as the people of the *marl-beds* must have been. These people, according to the place and time, were fishermen, hunters, shepherds, and even agriculturists.

The work of discovery and interpretation of the terremare proceeded apace, and the decade 1870–1880 was one of great activity. Castione dei Marchesi was excavated afresh in 1877 by Pigorini, and his acute observations laid the foundation for future work (*ill. 15*).

Meantime, work went on in the Alpine lakeland of the north, the east and the west. The site of La Tène, type-site for the later Iron Age of central Europe, was discovered at the north end of Lake Neuchâtel in 1858 by Friedrich Schwab and others, yielding a wealth of metalwork and some piles. In 1876, the lake waters were lowered, the site became dryland and was ready for extensive examination in 1880. The remains of bridges and houses were found, and a river channel packed with swords, spears, axes, chains, chariot pieces, wooden objects, and the bones of horse, oxen and humans. Since these early days, more artifacts have been recovered, particularly by work from 1907 to 1913, and parts of human brain preserved in the wet channel deposits have been recently reported.

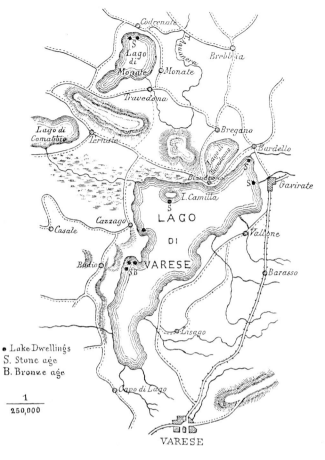

14, 15 Lake-dwellings in Italy
(*Right*) Keller's map of the lakes of
Varese and Monate, north Italy, where
lake-dwellings were discovered in
1863. (*Below*) View of the excavation
of Castione dei Marchesi, by Pigorini
1877. Note the great depth of
overburden and the prehistoric box-
frames of houses preserved.

• Lake Dwellings
S. Stone age
B. Bronze age

$$\frac{1}{250,000}$$

16   Drawing of the excavations in 1876 of the Neolithic settlement of Schussenried, Germany, with its 'confounding' horizons, the result of rebuildings and repairs.

To the west, Lake Paladru was explored by boat on 24 September 1864 and no less than six pile sites were found. There had been a legend in the area that the lake contained a drowned city, the catastrophe brought about by the maledictions of some neighbouring monks. Again, a lowering of the lake levels prompted excavations in 1870, and 1600 sq. yards (1340 sq. m) of piles could be seen, with the relic bed yielding masses of objects and the wooden frames of square houses clearly identifiable.

By 1870 matters were, essentially, in some chaos. Antiquaries, natural scientists, collectors, fishermen and peasants were all pursuing their aims over the Alpine region, and the destruction of sites and relics was unabated. The site of Wollishofen in Lake Zürich was basically dredged out, with huge amounts of wood collected for firewood by the locals, and a large array of Bronze Age objects for the dealers, swords, axes, knives, bracelets, pins and sheet metal, as well as fine and coarse pottery vessels and enigmatic clay crescents, probably symbols of particular families or segments of the community.

To the east, in Austria, the examination of the Neolithic settlement of Mondsee began in 1872, by the ubiquitous mud machine, and that of Laibach Moor was started in 1875. The Moor had been drained already and peat was being dug from the drying sediments. The piles of the settlement were for once carefully measured, and the horn and bone artifacts, outnumbering those of stone, formed an unusual collection in which bones of red deer, elk, beaver, boar and aurochs were abundant. Domestic animals were present, as well as enormous quantities of the water chestnut.

To the north, Lake Starnberg in Bavaria revealed the piles of a lake-dwelling in 1864 and excavations of 1874 by mud machine during low water levels yielded prehistoric relics but, not surprisingly, little structural evidence. In Württemberg, the site of Schussenried in the basin of an ancient lake, the Federsee, was examined in 1876 but confounded the excavator, E. Frank, by the thickness of the relic bed and the complications of rebuilt pile structures (*ill. 16*); 'almost every square yard excavated was so varied in character that each day's work seemed to throw less light on the matter'. This is perhaps not so unusual a phenomenon in wetland archaeology even today.

In the region of the Jura lakes of Bienne, Neuchâtel and Morat there was a wide area called the 'Gross Moos', a peat-filled marshland, formerly perhaps a very large body of water joining the three lakes into one. In 1868 a correction to the lake levels was made, in order to prevent the regular flooding of the area, and the effect of this scheme was to lower the lake levels by 6–8 ft (2–2.5 m). As the lake levels declined – first the waters of Bienne, in 1872, then the others – harbours and jetties became land-locked, shoreland was left high and dry, and the lake beds were exposed (*ill. 17*). The 'harvest time of archaeology' had begun, but described by others as 'a chaotic treasure hunt'. Fishermen abandoned the fish and took to antiquity, and dealers abounded. The government finally stepped in and forbade any excavations or recovery of artifacts except by the Canton authorities. In Lake Neuchâtel, the largest of these lakes, 1878 was supposed to mark the end of the wholesale removal of objects from the dozens of sites now known to exist, but the sale of lacustrine artifacts continued. It was difficult to stop, as the correction of the waters continued until 1888, and sites became more accessible with time. In 1871–2, for example, the station of Mörigen in Lake Bienne was only 3 ft (1 m) below the waters, and there were a number of boats more or less constantly anchored over the site, searching for antiquities. In 1873, the boats were driven off and excavations began of the Bronze Age station which measured 550 × 350 ft (175 × 110 m). Wooden chambers, in effect cofferdams, were built so that the relic bed could be explored out of the water. Relics included bronzes, collected assiduously, and pottery, 'the major part of which was unfortunately of no value'. Later work was better, 'the quantity of broken pottery was prodigious. Some perfect vessels were found standing upright, others turned upside down, and, in fact, lying in all directions'. Large pieces of wattle-work of birch and alder, mortised planks, and posts notched at the top, represented supports, floors or walls. Much of the relic bed had been washed away by wave action, and the mud machine had wreaked havoc in places, but nonetheless the yield of later Bronze Age artifacts was immense. An important aspect of the work was the collection of plant remains, received by Uhlmann of Münchenbuchsee and sieved, floated and sorted patiently. The plants included unburnt sweepings as well as burnt grain and seeds, and among the long list provided by Uhlmann were edible wild fruits (crab apple, acorn, beech nuts, hazelnuts, sloe and *Rubus*), cultivated vegetables (bean, pea, lentil), cereals (barley, wheat, emmer wheat, oat, millet), other plants (flax, poppy, clematis) and various weeds (couch grass, Brome grass, mustard, shepherd's purse, goosefoot) and marsh plants (sedge, rush, buttercup). Also noted were burnt chrysalis shells of flies, fish-scales, sheep dung and cow dung.

Another Bronze Age station, at Auvernier, was also explored, but it lay under 14 ft (4 m) of water when first attacked and the hand scraper or rake was used extensively. Nonetheless, or perhaps as a result, the station was described in 1878 as 'unquestionably the richest and most considerable of all those hitherto examined in Switzerland. It has surpassed even the station at Mörigen'. The bronze artifacts from Auvernier litter many museums today, and their quality of workmanship is exceptionally high (*ill. 18*) (see Chapter 5).

Among all the stations investigated in this energetic period, that of Robenhausen perhaps best illustrated the potential of wetland archaeology. The lake of Pfäffikon had been reduced by 1858 to a small size, surrounded by encroaching peat beds (*ill. 19*). Within the peat were found the piles of a Neolithic settlement, examined by the owner of the site Jacob Messikomer on behalf of the Antiquarian Association of Zürich. It was speedily recognized that excavations in peat were much easier than those in the muds of the lake even if the latter were above water. The peat bed had:

> treasured up, as it were, in its bosom all the implements which fell into the water when the floorings gave way, and also the different relic beds belonging to the successive settlements, all in their regular order. Circumstances so favourable to the investigation are not to be found together in any other lake dwelling. (Keller)

The area covered by piles was almost 3 acres (1.5 ha), set about 2,000–3,000 paces from the former shores of the lake. Contact with the shore and dry ground was thought to be by a bridge or platform fully 3,000 paces long. The substructure of the settlement was made up of an estimated 100,000 piles of oak, beech and pine, 10–11 ft (3–3.5 m) long and driven into the lake muds and peats. Parts of the platforms, mostly cross-timbers with holes for wooden pins, were preserved as were elements of a palisade, consisting of hurdles fastened to the outer piles. The outlet of the lake of Pfäffikon ran through the site, and furnished Messikomer with sections and with plans of the piles. Further excavations were also made abutting the canalized brook and three distinct horizons were identified. A shell-marl beneath held the sharpened bases of the first pile-built settlement:

> Above this there is a bed about four or five inches thick, greasy and sticky to the touch, arising from decomposition of the remains of plants, and having the appearance of peat. Implements are found in this bed, but not abundantly. Above this lies a bed of charcoal arising from the conflagration of the first settlement; it contains grains of barley and wheat, also threads, and pieces of cloth, and fishing-nets, all in beautiful preservation from having been carbonised. From all appearances this first settlement was not of long duration.
>
> After the catastrophe which had happened to the first dwelling, the colonists erected new homes on the site of their old ones, for above the lowest bed of charcoal we find a bed of peat three feet thick, in which are embedded bones, pottery, etc, and also the material of an ancient flooring. Then follows again a bed of charcoal, with corn, apples, pieces of cloth, bones, pottery, and the usual implements of stone and bone. The huts of this *second* settlement were likewise destroyed by fire, as may be clearly seen by the burnt heads of the second series of piles. The settlement was erected more firmly than the

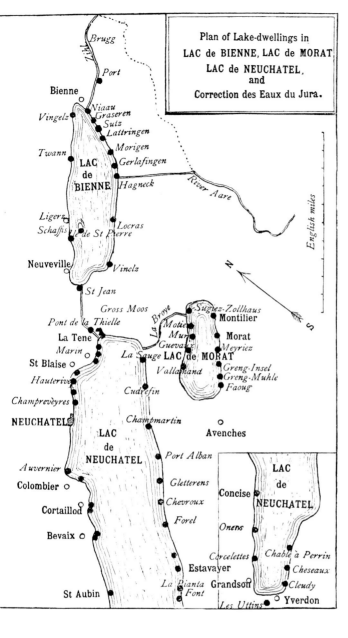

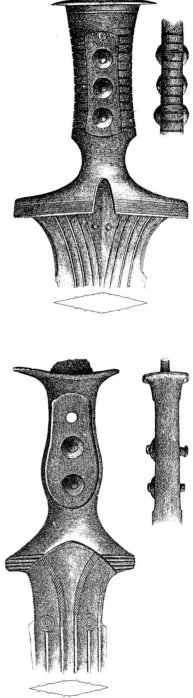

17, 18 **Swiss discoveries** (*Above*) Map of the Jura lakes, Switzerland, showing the numerous sites known to Robert Munro by 1882. The Gross Moos drained area is also indicated (centre). (*Above right*) Drawing of two sword handles of bronze from Auvernier, Lake Neuchâtel, Switzerland. The handles are *c.* 10 cm long.

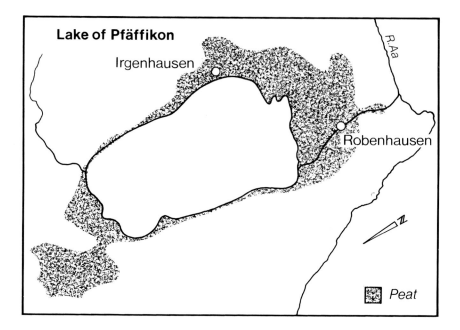

19, 20 **Robenhausen, the best-preserved settlement of Neolithic Europe**
(*Above*) Map of the small lake of Pfäffikon, Switzerland, showing the peat beds in
1858, the drainage network, and the two Neolithic settlements of Robenhausen and
Irgenhausen set near the shores of the original lake. (*Below*) Drawing of the split oak
piles of the latest settlement at Robenhausen, in 1865. Conditions for excavations
were difficult.

previous one, for the piles are so numerous that on the average they are three or four in every square foot. The length of time also that this settlement lasted was much greater, as the bed of peat formed during its existence was much thicker.

Above the second bed of ashes a new bed of peat is spread about three feet thick; in this there are also remains of a flooring, as well as a number of stone celts either broken, half finished, or in good preservation, some of them are of nephrite: pottery was also found here, as well as other things usually met with in lake dwellings. This settlement must have lasted a long time, but seems only to have extended over a part of the whole area. It is a singular fact that while the piles of the two first settlements reach down to the shell-marl, those of the third settlement were driven into the mass of ground or material arising from the two first settlements. The piles of the upper settlement also consist entirely of split trunks of oak, while those of the two lower ones are round stems of soft kinds of wood. It is also remarkable that in the remains of this third erection no signs of any catastrophe by fire are to be discovered, and we may therefore venture to conclude that the colonists, probably compelled by the increase of the peat, left these abodes of their own accord. (*ill. 20*).

The reason why no corn, apples, or manufactures of flax, are found in the upper layer, may probably be found in the fact that the latest erection was not burnt, for nearly all the specimens of the above descriptions which have come down to us are in a carbonised condition. (Jakob Messikomer)

North of the settlement, the peat layers contained abundant charcoal in a wide band about 200–300 yards wide, while elsewhere the peat had no such horizons. Much charcoal had been seen in the relic beds, and Messikomer interpreted these observations as showing that at least one of the settlements had been burnt down at a time when a strong wind from the south, called the *Fönwind*, had fanned the flames and spread burning straw and reeds out of the settlement and onto a broad stretch of the peat to the north.

Keller and his collaborators were ecstatic about Robenhausen, as the site seemed to confirm in all respects the view that the settlements had originally stood on piles in the open waters of the lake, and that due to extensive waterlogging and the effect of peat formation, the range of material culture preserved was unsurpassed. Messikomer found six dwellings, spaced equally apart, measuring 27 × 22 ft (8.5–6.5 m), each with its own hearth, grindstone, corn, cloth, raw flax, and clay loom weights. He also noted:

that in many cases objects are found together which have a certain mutual relation. In one place a considerable quantity of corn (wheat and barley) was found together with bread; in another locality these articles of food were found together with burnt apples and pears; in a third, flax and its different manufactures; and in a fourth, these very things were discovered together with the earthenware cones used for the loom. There can be no doubt that in the first-named two localities there were store-houses of different kinds of grain, and that in this very place the corn was bruised and ground, and afterwards either boiled in pots to a kind of porridge or made into dough with water without separating the bran, and then baked into a kind of cake or bread on hot rounded stones, and under the glowing embers. The large number of

granite slabs used for mealing or grinding stones, and found together with the objects last mentioned, prove that the manufacture of meal was carried on here to a considerable extent. The third and fourth localities indicate a large store of flax, which is found here sometimes in skeins, or hanks, sometimes spun, platted, or woven in the form of threads, cords, nets, mats, and cloth, just as in a linen-merchant's warehouse.

This is probably the first major site analysis anywhere in the world, based upon extraordinarily well-preserved evidence which could hardly be missed, but nonetheless only capable of interpretation by someone who was interested in the evidence of activities as well as the portable artifacts.

Between the huts were animal stalls, identified by thick layers of litter and manure.

A few of the faeces of goats had been found in a carbonised state, but they were taken for acorns or some other similar seeds. But a careful examination of them by Professor Heer soon revealed the true nature of these objects, so little pleasing in themselves, but so highly interesting when found in a lake dwelling. With respect to the excrements of cows and swine, we must look for their determination not so much to the eye of the naturalist as to the practised glance of the agriculturist, and we may rely with implicit faith on Mr Messikomer and his labourers when they assure us that this is the actual nature of these substances. The litter for the cows consisted chiefly of straw and rushes; that for the smaller animals was of sprigs of fir and twigs of brushwood. In these masses of excrement may be noticed the pupa-cases of the insects identical with those which are found so numerously at the present day in the manure of cattle-sheds.

Among other aspects of the economy of the settlement, both animal and plant remains were abundant.

The indigenous fauna is more largely represented here than in any other settlement: the bones are often found together in heaps of from fifty to one hundred pounds; from their weight some of them have sunk eight to ten inches into the mud at the bottom of the lake. As five tons of bones were gathered in the Aa brook canal alone, the mass of animal remains buried in the whole colony must be immense. Scales of fish are found everywhere in great abundance, a proof that fish formed a considerable portion of the food of the inhabitants; they also laid up stores of water-chestnut (*Trapa natans*), and apples dried for winter use. In one place 300, or half a peck [4.5 litres], were found together. Quantities of beech-nuts and acorns were also met with, which probably were intended as food for the swine. The whole weight of the pieces of bread found when the canal was deepened and altered, may be about eight pounds, and would probably correspond with newly-baked bread weighing about forty pounds. Of stone-fruit there are more sloe than cherry stones. The seeds of raspberries, strawberries, elderberries, and blackberries, are also met with, [and] different varieties of corn. Mealing-stones and grinding-stones are common, and so are the hearthstones or those used for baking. Burnt rushes, the remains of thatch, are found in abundance, and fragments of pottery with various kinds of ornamentation are met with in countless numbers. The well-known tools of stone, horn, and bone, were very common.

Also common were wooden artifacts, knives, ladles, clubs, axe handles, flail, bows, fishing gear, floats and hooks, tub, yoke, a decorated board, a door (*ill. 21*). Even more unusual, and perhaps only matched even now by sites such as Chalain, Hornstaad and Feldmeilen (see Chapter 4), were balls of string and twine, a willow or lime bast mat found with flax strips, and a number of pieces of textile, some of which survived exposure to the air and now rest in glass boxes in many European museums.

To us today, the variety and size of the collections of artifacts and the evidence of structures and economy from Robenhausen and the other sites seem exceptional. What is generally overlooked is the calm air with which such sites were received, by Keller, Gastaldi, Schwab and all the others. Excitement there was, in the discoveries and in the wealth of artifacts, but little emphasis was ever attached to the wetland elements of the evidence, to the wooden piles, cross-beams, flooring and wall hurdles of the settlements, or to the wide variety of plants, both wild and cultivated, or to the cushioning effect of peat and mud for preservation of fragile artifacts, or to the gentle waterlogging that preserved textiles. In recent years very considerable attention has been paid to such elements of the archaeological record, where they have survived and been recovered. But it seems that every time such an event occurs now, astonishment is expressed at the preservation of organic materials, and comment is made about how such materials fill out the record dominated for so long by the dry archaeology typified by the Three Age system: Stone, Bronze, Iron. The reason why Keller and his contemporaries did not dwell on the organic, waterlogged elements of the record from the lakes and peatbeds is probably because they had not yet become conditioned to a dryland mentality. They were also subjected to a flood of ethnographic observations from the later 19th-century explorers, traders and settlers, all of which naturally expressed the dominance of organic wood, plants and textiles in the material culture of the communities observed. In addition, their place in the late 19th-century industrial revolutions of Europe persuaded them of the importance of industry, whether of wood, pottery, stone or metal, and so artifacts of whatever material received equal treatment; in fact, due to the collecting mania of the time, Bronze Age sites were preferred to Stone Age sites as the Metal Age provided a closer link with the foundries of the 19th century than did the more primitive Stone Age. For these reasons, the (to us) quite extraordinary material culture of the lake-dwellings was only to be expected – it deserved attention but not exaggeration. The lesson was not lost on Keller's successors.

21 **Wooden artifacts from Neolithic Robenhausen** (*Opposite*) Stone axes in wooden hafts, length 30–50 cm. (*Above*) Whisks or stirrers, length 16 cm; a ladle, length 36 cm; and a wooden dagger. See ill. 78.

2 · Extending the search

THE PERIOD FROM 1855 to 1874 was one of profound importance for European prehistory and we have touched here only upon the discoveries in the lakes and moors of the Alpine area. As we have seen, earlier instances of the rewards of wetland sites were known in many parts of Europe well before 1855, but it was Keller's determination, persistence and domination of the Swiss work that persuaded others to look farther afield, to emulate the Alpine discoveries and to make their own mark upon the discipline.

Irish crannogs

Matters had not stagnated in Ireland or Scotland (*ill. 22*), for example, following the Lagore crannog revelations of 1840. The work of the Commission for the Arterial Drainage and Inland Navigation of Ireland had already uncovered over twenty crannogs before 1852, and excavations at Cloonfinlough and Ardnakillen continued to reveal details of past lives that prompted W. G. Wood-Martin (Lieutenant-Colonel of the 8th Brigade of the North Irish Division of the Royal Army) to say: 'To look back to antiquity is one thing; to go back to it is another.' He was referring to the discovery at Ardnakillen of

> a boat 40 feet in length and 4 feet across the bow, hollowed out of a single oak; and in which were a skull, a bronze pin, and a spear . . . The skull is perforated in the forehead, and has the mark of no less than twenty sword cuts on it, showing the murderous conflict in which its owner must have engaged; and near to it were found a neck-piece of iron and 20 feet of rude chain attached, that would do credit to the dungeons of Naples, and by which its unhappy victim was made fast.

From the crannog itself, about 50 tons of bones were said to have been quarried by the peasantry and sold for fertilizer, and doubtless also many of the richly decorated relics from the site.

From the Coal-Bog near Boho a remarkable house was preserved amidst a crannog but it was destroyed in 1880.

> In one place a wooden structure measuring 11 feet 10 inches, formed of rude wooden beams, with roughly-executed mortises, was found no less than 21 feet below the surface of the peat. Two flint implements, several fragments of hand-made pottery, devoid of ornamentation, broken hazel–nut shells, and in the vicinity, at the same depth in the peat, a few wooden dishes. The stool of a hugh (yew) tree, which, before its decay, must have measured 14 feet in diameter, was found 2 feet above the level of the floor of the hut, which sent its roots downwards. (Wood-Martin)

22 Map of British and
Irish wetland sites mentioned
in the text.

This sounds remarkably like the Inver house (Chapter 1).

There were many other crannogs examined or recorded in Ireland in the decades from 1870, and by 1886 Wood-Martin could prepare a book on *The Lake Dwellings of Ireland: or Ancient Lacustrine Habitations of Erin, commonly called crannogs*. This provided a clear expression of site and setting.

> Marshes, small loughs surrounded by woods, and large sheets of water, were alike suitable for the home of the Irish lake-dweller, his great and primary need being protection . . . Having decided on the position, the crannog builder set to work by driving stakes into the bottom of the lake in a circle of from sixty to eighty feet in diameter, a considerable length of the stake sometimes projecting above the water; these were in many instances joined together by horizontal beams, the interior filled up by branches of trees, stones, gravel, earth, and bracken. . . . piles are driven in various parts of the interior . . . to consolidate the mass . . . Next were placed one or two layers of round logs, cut into lengths of about six feet, generally mortised into the upright piles, kept in position by layers of stone, clay and gravel . . . Considerable ingenuity was displayed in the formation of these island homes, which were frequently constructed in a depth of twelve to fourteen feet of water; and, apart from having served in their day as secure retreats for large numbers of persons, they have proved their durability by resisting successfully the ravages of time, which may be reckoned by centuries.

Many of the difficulties in understanding the details of construction and dating of the Irish crannogs were not solved by their normal 'examination' by the local landowner or the peasantry. The Lisnacroghera crannog in Co. Antrim was submerged in a peatbog, and only in 1882 were its antiquities revealed by peat-cutting; this activity succeeded in removing the wooden structure without record, but the splendid artifacts were spread about the area and only after an energetic search was a collection made of iron swords and ornamented sheet bronze scabbards, iron spears with wooden handles, and bronze shield mountings, all in the Celtic Iron Age style.

Robert Munro and the Scottish crannogs

It was in Scotland that crannog investigations moved on from a period of relic collection to that of structural examination with a measure of stratigraphic control. The instigator of this work was Robert Munro, a medical doctor. By 1882 he had produced a book called *Ancient Scottish Lake-Dwellings or Crannogs* in which he brought together a record of old and new discoveries, most of them stimulated by Keller's widely-publicized reports on the Swiss lake-dwellings. All the early excavations of Scottish crannogs were in the south-west. The first was at Lochlee crannog in Ayrshire, 1878–79. Through a complicated series of events, Munro was told of the crannog and having just been to Zürich to see the Swiss lake-dwelling finds he was eager to excavate. On his first visit to the site, a small dugout canoe was hauled from the peat. A presumed palisade around the small island in the peat was exposed by trench (*ill. 23*). The interior of the site had heavy oak beams 6 ft (2 m) long with square-cut holes at each end, some with upright stakes driven through them. A log platform high in the structure was noted, with a number of hearths upon it and the tangled remains of flooring, possibly walling and general wood debris. Beneath was a thick deposit of roughly hewn logs, forming the substructure of the crannog.

> After considerable labour, when indeed the probability of total discomfiture in reaching the bottom was freely talked of, our most energetic foreman at last announced that . . . he could find no trace of further woodwork. The total depth of the excavation was about 16 feet.

The relics from the site included stone querns, bone points, wooden troughs, dishes, clubs and part of a canoe, a decorated board (*ill. 24*), some iron tools, bronze brooches and bridle bit, fragments of leather and a plait of moss. Lochlee remains one of the more enigmatic of Scottish crannogs in terms of structure but its early examination and careful recording mark a development in lake-dwelling research not matched by many contemporary investigations.

> The great value, however, of the investigations of the lake-dwellings, especially in the south-west of Scotland, depends on the quantity and variety of the remains of human industry discovered in and around their sites. It is from such fragmentary remains as food refuse, stray ornaments, broken weapons, useless and worn-out implements, and such-like waifs and strays of human occupancy, that archaeologists attempt to reconstruct the outlines of the social life and organisation of the prehistoric past.

23, 24 **Lochlee crannog, Scotland** (*Right*) Drawing of the excavation of the crannog in 1878–79. The site was trenched, here exposing part of a palisade around the crannog. (*Below*) Carved wooden board from the crannog, engraved with Celtic designs. Width 11 cm.

In his understanding of the nature of archaeological evidence and the uses to which it may be put, Munro was preparing himself for a brief but intensive introduction to the lake dwellings of Europe. In 1886 he was offered the Rhind lectureship in Archaeology for the year 1888 by the Society of Antiquaries of Scotland; his title was the *Lake dwellings of Europe*. He wrote of his predicament and his solution:

> My first and almost immediate step was a hasty run to the principal centres of lake-dwelling researches in Europe, so as to get a preliminary idea of the best and most practical way of carrying out this work. It was only then that the magnitude of the labours I had undertaken dawned upon me. The relics from the more important settlements, with few exceptions, were so widely scattered that, to form an intelligible notion of the civilisation and culture of their inhabitants from a study of their industrial remains, scores of museums and private collections had to be visited. . . . There is hardly any corner of the lake-dwelling area in Europe which has not yielded new materials.

Munro and his wife attempted to bring all this material together, by visiting the whole of Central Europe with notebook and sketch pad, seeing sites and museums and consulting libraries. The result was a series of six Rhind lectures in 1888 and the publication of *The Lake-Dwellings of Europe* in 1890. One can only applaud his energy and appreciate his scientific curiosity. Indeed, only a little more development of his ideas might have opened the door to the kind of understanding we have today of the lake dwellings, based in part upon absolute and precise chronologies. He wrote in 1882:

> But is there nothing in the local phenomena of these lake-dwellings to indicate, even approximately, the period of their existence, or the changes that have taken place since, by submergence, they have disappeared from the gaze of mankind? Dame Nature retains many agents in her service who faithfully keep tally of many passing events, though not always by days or years. The woody rings of a tree, water-worn channels, strata in rocks, and accumulated mud, are some of the piles of records which she freely places at our disposal – though often only to baffle our limited and feeble efforts to decipher them.

He was here on the edge of discovering a chronology based on tree-rings (the identification of annual growth variations) and a comprehension of the lake sediments which would have ended the preoccupation with the pile-dwelling theory; but he went no further than this.

A site visited by Munro in his travels was Lake Clairvaux in the low plateau of the Jura mountains of eastern France. Here, during drainage operations, antiquities had been found well before 1870, but the existence of a lake-dwelling was not suspected until Jules le Mire virtually stumbled over an oak pile during a period of low water. Excavations soon revealed the relic bed, full of Neolithic antler, horn, flint and wooden artifacts. In 1890 the Abbé Bourget published le Mire's work and in 1899 the Société d'Emulation du Jura organized further excavations, in order to enrich the collections of the Museum at Lons-Le-Saunier. A record exists of the society's visit to the site on 14 September.

Several trenches were already open, and our arrival did not interrupt the work. On the contrary, we all joined in, and, some taking picks, others shovels, and others searching the spoil heaps, each tried to be useful and to augment the heap of artifacts already discovered. There were found many antlers, some very beautiful, horns, flint, whetstone, numerous bones, teeth of ruminants and other animals, shells, charcoal and coarse pottery, burnt stones used no doubt as pot-boilers, and finally piles, well conserved in the lake marl. (Émile Monot)

The Clairvaux station has been the subject of many further excavations including modern work which has revealed many new facets of Neolithic life (see Chapter 4). Another site receiving comparable modern treatment is Chalain, suspected in 1879, and firmly identified in 1904 when the lake was lowered:

On the vast white surface of the lake marl showed a multitude of piles, sometimes still protruding by several decimetres, occasionally of fir, more often quarters of split oak, often very big; their presumed length varies from less than 2–3 metres to 6–7 metres, such that their original length must have been from 4–5 metres to 9–10 metres. (Louis-Abel Girardot)

Ehenside Tarn

In this period of expansion of wetland archaeology there was relatively little going on in England, yet there already existed not only the usual notices of individual organic artifacts from lakes and mosses, but also a report on a prehistoric settlement site. In 1870, a Reverend Mr Kenworthy described, and imaginatively interpreted, some remains exposed in Ehenside Tarn, Cumbria. The tarn was only one of a large number of small pools, which by 1870 were often reduced to peat-filled hollows in the low hills (*ill. 26*). Ehenside Tarn covered 5–6 acres of ground, set amidst hills only about 100 ft (32 m) above sea-level. The tarn was drained in 1869, leaving some stone and wooden artifacts exposed on the sides. They were described thus:

There was a very large quantity of charcoal, burnt wood, broken twigs, nuts, and leaves, and some few, but not many, broken and charred bones of wild cattle, and perhaps deer . . . The rude and primeval people whose existence these relics indicate were only in possession of implements of flint and stone. Fire they had, abundant proof of such remains in the ashes, charcoal, and refuse; and there are numerous fragments of broken earthen vessels, the outside of which has been burnt white, and has cracked while the pot has been simmering over the fire . . . Besides the flint and stone implements, the wood bespeaks the work of simple human intelligence. Some pieces of oak are cut in lengths, evidently from massive full-grown trees, such as have not grown in this locality for many ages. One piece of oak, some four feet in breadth, being half of a tree, has been hollowed out by stone chisels and fire. Another piece has been wrought in the shape of a bench; it bears the marks of blows from a roughly-sharpened axe. Considering the flint tools, some of the cuts are wonderfully clean. The whole of the oak is yet so fresh that handsome furniture might be made of it. Then there are at least two paddles shaped like the foot of a water-fowl, the web of which, once formed of skin, is now

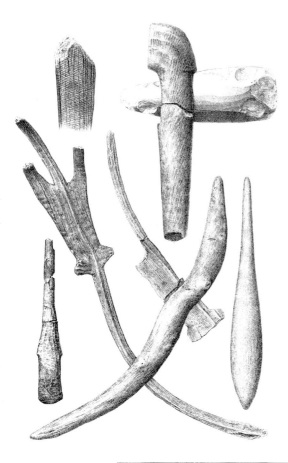

25, 26 **Ehenside Tarn, Cumbria, England** (*Left*) Artifacts from the Neolithic settlement. The stone axe is 29 cm long. The wooden clubs and fish spears are unique to the British Neolithic. (*Below*) Map of Ehenside Tarn in 1871 after drainage, with the Neolithic settlement sites marked.

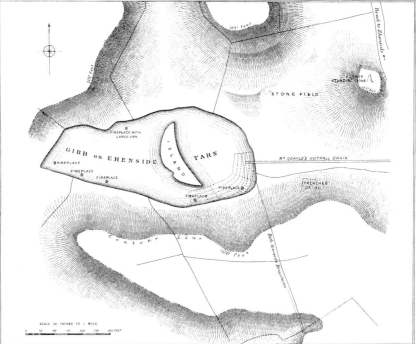

decayed . . . Let the reader now picture to himself a tarn almost oval-shaped, and four or five acres in extent, the centre ten or fifteen feet deep at the least, and steep at the sides. Let him imagine on the water rafts of oak bound and covered with trees, to form the foundation of cottages or huts. Let him conceive this, and he will realise the idea of a lake-dwelling of the earliest Britons. (Kenworthy)

The tarn was examined by R. D. Darbishire in 1871 who wrote a full and objective account of the site and relics. The tarn had already been reduced from a soft bog to a 'solid, heavy, peaty mass' containing layers of fallen trees, branches and leaves, underlain by mossy peat. From the forest bed were recovered stone axes and wooden clubs (ill. 25), and it is probable that the earlier relics also came from this horizon. Among them were a greenstone axe fitted with beechwood haft, wooden clubs, pronged fish spears or reed forks of oak, and other wooden artifacts. Efforts were made to preserve some of these pieces:

The wood of all these has suffered much loss of texture in the bog-water. Those which have been simply allowed to dry have cracked and shrunk so as scarcely to retain their figure. Several of oak have retained their longitudinal fibre, but have warped extremely in drying. The recent ones were brought home packed in wet bog-earth, washed clean, and soaked, according to the Danish method of M. C. F. Herbst in a hot saturated solution of alum, and then slowly dried. Owing to some inexperience in the mode of treatment, the smaller articles (having been, probably, too effectually soaked) were destroyed by the crystallization of the alum, suffering a sort of powdery dissolution. The others gave signs of similar injury, and, having been soaked again in warm water to remove surplus alum, are now preserved in a solution of glycerine (2/3) and water (1/3). [Needless to say, this is not now a normal practice, and freeze-drying or impregnation with wax is preferred treatment for waterlogged wood.]

Other notices were sent to Munro about crannogs and other wetland sites, but little excavation was possible. Perhaps interest in English crannogs was left unkindled by the occasional remark about the wetland occupants of the north and west:

Did it never strike you when Caesar talks of the Morini taking refuge in their marshes, and Dio Cassius of Severus pursuing the Caledonii into theirs, in which he lost 50,000 of his own troops, that such facts presuppose the existence of pile fortresses, or at least of crannogs in these morasses? For those Celts required a 'pied à terre' literally, to enable them to hold out any time in such situations; they could not squat for weeks like a flock of wild ducks upon the surface of morasses.

Glastonbury

In the late 19th century, there were other wetland sites being exposed in England, and mostly lost through lack of interest. In the Somerset Levels, however, one site was not forgotten. In 1834 a farmer uncovered a line of horizontal split alder planks near Westhay, but it was not until 1864 that the new owner of the land ordered its renewed exposure and invited the local Society to view the structure. In 1873 a further part of the track, for that is what it was, was excavated and finally published in 1880 by C. W. Dymond, and called the Abbot's Way, the name given to the track by early peat-cutters. The Abbot's Way was one of the key sites in the later development of archaeology in the Levels. However, the main impetus in England in the late 19th century for wetland sites was not the tracks of Somerset, the tarns of Cumbria, or the crannogs of Holderness and East Anglia, but a different Somerset discovery.

In 1888, Arthur Bulleid, a medical student born and raised in Glastonbury, Somerset, read Keller's book on *The Lake Dwellings of Switzerland*. He came to the opinion that similar sites might be preserved in the wet moors of the Somerset Levels, and so he decided to search the area.

> For four years as opportunities occurred, the moorlands were explored looking for probable sites, more particularly in the peat-cutting localities of the Shapwick and Edington Burtle Turbaries. On a Wednesday afternoon in March, 1892, when driving across the moor from Glastonbury to Godney, a field was noticed to be covered with small mounds, an unusual feature in a neighbourhood where the conformation of the land is for miles at a dead level. On the following Sunday afternoon the field was visited, and anticipations were agreeably realized by picking up from the numerous mole-hills a number of pottery fragments, a whetstone, and pieces of bone and charcoal . . . A week or two later tentative excavations took place by digging trenches into two of the mounds. The sections exposed clay floors with hearths, supported by massive timber substructures. Quantities of bone and antler, and a beautifully polished jet ring or bead, were among the relics discovered.

Bulleid began major excavations in 1893 and they continued, with one gap, until 1907. The site was a gigantic crannog, built on felled trees, brushwood and stone, and had over its period of life from about 300 BC to AD 100 supported as many as 80 houses or other buildings. The waterlogged character of the site had ensured the survival of wooden piles or posts, flooring and collapsed walls (*ill. 27*), a wide variety of artifacts of many materials, and a vast selection of plant and animal remains (see Chapter 5). During the work, many scientists and antiquaries came to see the site, among them Munro, who contributed materially to the organization of the work and to the publication reports of 1911 and 1917. The Glastonbury Lake Village featured in the *Illustrated London News*, and, suspiciously, was depicted as a classic Swiss pile-dwelling on the boxes of the Honiton Match Company. Bulleid never claimed that his site had been constructed on piles over open water. It may be worth the comment here that in the recording of the structures or artifacts, and in the use of natural scientists for specialist reports, Bulleid and his collaborator Harold St George Gray were in the forefront of archaeology at this period. They had the advantage of a period of scientific interest in the preserved remains of ancient environments and economies.

Terps: mounds of the north European coasts

Along the coasts of the Netherlands and north Germany, ancient settlements had been known for long, and indeed had been described by their contemporary, Pliny:

27 (*Opposite*) Excavations at Glastonbury Lake Village, England, in about 1895.

I have myself personally witnessed the condition of the Chauci, both the Greater and the Lesser, situate in the regions of the far north. In these climates a vast tract of land, invaded twice each day and night by the overflowing waves of the ocean, opens a question that is eternally proposed to us by Nature, whether these regions are to be looked upon as belonging to the land, or whether as forming a portion of the sea?

Here a wretched race is found, inhabiting either the more elevated spots of land, or else eminences artificially constructed, and of a height to which they know by experience that the highest tides will never reach. Here they pitch their cabins; and when the waves cover the surrounding country far and wide, like so many mariners on board ship are they; when, again, the tide recedes, their condition is that of so many shipwrecked men, and around their cottages they pursue the fishes as they make their escape with the receding tide. It is not their lot, like the adjoining nations, to keep any flocks for sustenance by their milk, nor even to maintain a warfare with wild beasts, every shrub, even, being banished afar. With the sedge and the rushes of the marsh they make cords, and with these they weave the nets employed in the capture of the fish; they fashion the mud, too, with their hands, and drying it by the help of the winds more than of the sun, cook their food by its aid, and so warm their entrails, frozen as they are by the northern blasts; their only drink, too, is rainwater, which they collect in holes dug at the entrance of their abodes; and yet these nations, if this very day they were vanquished by the Roman people, would exclaim against being forced to slavery! Be it so, then – Fortune is most kind to many, just when she means to punish them.

With the construction of the great sea-dykes in the 18th and 19th centuries, much of the flooded lands was made safe from the sea, and was gradually dried out. The lands were then intensively cultivated and the ancient settlements of the coastal inhabitants, consisting of low but extensive mounds, called *Terpen*, of turf, earth, charcoal, manure, and other debris, often became the sites of modern villages (*ill. 28*) (see Chapter 3). Where, however, such mounded areas were free of structures, they were a valuable source of fertilizer. When Munro visited the terp of Aalzum during his European tour he was led up an inclined road towards a church which crowned the summit of the mound:

> . . . . on each side the land was perfectly flat and bearing a splendid crop: here a field of magnificent beans, and there an equally promising one of wheat. These fields were formerly part of the terp-mound from which the fertilising stuff has already been removed, but this road was left undisturbed, so that we [were] actually walking on a portion of its surface . . . At last the actual workings were reached, and we found ourselves in front of a perpendicular section some 15 or 18 feet high, from which men and women were busily engaged in loading the boats. Uppermost in my thoughts was the paramount question of the existence of upright piles . . . Great was my delight when, at the very first glance, my eye detected an undoubted pile of oak just in face of the cutting.

Munro was informed that West Friesland alone had about 150 terps known to have existed, but some of them had already been totally quarried away. Elsewhere along the coastlands there were more, called *Warfen*, *Wurthen*, and

28 A terp (Ziallerns) in Lower Saxony, Germany. In the distance, the low terp mound is occupied now by a modern settlement, prominent in an otherwise featureless landscape.

Wierden in different regions. In East Friesland, mounds had been noted by 1879, and farther east there were many mounds known by 1883. The Fahrstedter Wurth, examined in 1881, was 21 ft (7 m) high with at least three distinct levels of wooden piles and horizontal timbers. Munro considered that these mounds had supported and become built up around pile-dwellings, a view not now if ever accepted. Dating from about 300 BC to AD 1100 (when the first dykes were built to protect the land) the *Terpen* and *Wierden* provided a rich source of evidence about the societies dismissed in so uncomplimentary a manner by Pliny. And not only him. In the *History of the Rise of the Dutch Republic*, Motley traced:

> the gradual development of what is now the kingdom of Holland, from a race of ichthyophagi who dwelt upon mounds which they raised like beavers above the almost fluid soil.

Farther to the east, a number of lake-dwellings had been reported from the north European plain, from near Wismar in Germany across to former Prussia and Poland. Indeed, the first notice of piles from a possible settlement was made in 1839 at the mouth of the river Wiek in Pomerania, and a few sites were examined by R. Virchow. In a small lake, the Persanzigersee near Neustettin, drainage in 1863 revealed a small island surrounded by a series of box frames 13 ft square, made of overlapped tree trunks, like log cabins, but with upright piles placed on both inside and outside 'walls'; the excavator Kasiski believed these to be the substructure of pile-dwellings but they may have been parts of a rampart. In 1881, piles and Bronze Age artifacts were recovered from Spandau near Berlin and, before that, a pile structure at Czeszewo in Poland was already well known, the locals having pulled out the piles for firewood.

Farther north, in Denmark in particular, the development of new railways and roads, and the growth of land improvements through drainage in particular, coincided with the emergence of an affluent middle class educated already in antiquarian interests. Museums were established for the many artifacts found by the workers of the land, and the bog finds of the Bronze and Iron Ages continued to emerge and dazzle with their richness of design and decoration, and sometimes of their material too. Gold objects sometimes went to dealers, or to the melting pot, and there was a brisk trade in antiquities looted from sites such as barrows and from the bog deposition places. The legislation enacted in Scandinavia for the protection of the relics of the past was firm but basically unenforceable, and it was supplemented in Denmark at least by the payment of rewards. The wetland settlements of the area remained hidden for the moment by the sea as well as by the moor and marshlands.

Along the eastern shores of the Baltic Sea, Keller's work also stimulated an interest in lake-dwellings. Around Lake Valgjärr in southern Estonia an ancient legend had for long existed, in which a brother and sister defied the rules and married one another. Their wedding feast was held in their manor house in a small valley, but was ended when first lightning struck and burnt the place, then rain came and turned the valley into a lake, drowning the couple and all the guests. By 1640 divers had retrieved some objects from the lake bottom, and in 1718 peasants cutting holes in the ice claimed to see the remains of the wooden building. Further sightings in the 19th century led to a revived interest when the theory of pile-dwellings emerged. The settlement beneath the lake, probably a crannog, was finally examined in 1958, by a team of divers, and turned out to be of the late first millennium AD. There was no sign of the bride and groom, but the timbers had been burnt.

The Court of the Pile-dwellers

The influence of the lake-dwellings of Switzerland, so widely spread throughout Europe in the last decades of the 19th century, was not confined to even this large area. The rapid publication in translation of Keller's reports in 1866 and 1878 created interest elsewhere, and in one place in particular led to an expedition unique in its character and in its achievement.

By 1875, the coastal middens and burial mounds of Florida were under examination by a wealthy Philadelphian, Clarence B. Moore. Equipped with a movable excavation house and living accommodation – namely a coal-fired steamboat called the Gopher – Moore travelled along the Florida coasts for 11 years in the winter months, excavating and collecting as he went. His records and publications were simple and clear, and from these a knowledge of the material culture and abundance of pre-European sites was available.

Along the southwestern coast of Florida are a multitude of islands, mostly low mangrove islands surrounded by reefs and shoal waters. Some are very small, with only a few trees or a rocky reef, others are large, and among the latter is Key Marco, or Marco Island, of about 6,000 acres (*ill. 40*). In 1895, the owner of a property on Key Marco began to dig garden muck from a wet peaty deposit between two low ridges composed almost entirely of shells. Such shell ridges and mounds were a regular feature on many of the islands along the coast (*ill. 29*). A few pieces of wood, rope and shell tools were found in the quarrying operation. News filtered through to a Colonel Durnford of the British Army who was exploring the area out of antiquarian interest. Durnford went to Key Marco and

29, 30   Florida shell mounds and the Court of the Pile Dwellers (*Above*)
Prehistoric shell bank and terrace on Demorey's Key, part of a prehistoric marina
and settlement on the Florida coast. The shells are of *Busycon* and *Fasciolaria*, piled
up to form banks and landing stages for canoes. The seawater would have originally
filled the foreground. (*Below*) Photograph of the 1895 excavations in the Court of
the Pile Dwellers at Key Marco, Florida. The waterlogged mucks held masses of
wooden and other artifacts, heaped in disarray.

excavated in the muck, recovering a heap of wooden objects, netting and rope, pottery and shell tools; these are now in the British Museum. Durnford went to Philadelphia to show his finds to the Museum there; by pure chance, Frank Cushing was present. He was employed by the Bureau of American Ethnology, and had already made his name by work in Arizona on the ancient Zuni culture. Cushing was a lively and colourful character, and upon seeing the relics from Key Marco and hearing of the site, he offered to investigate further. He wrote:

> I believed, indeed, that their condition and their occurrence beneath the peaty deposits of muck might even betoken some such phase of life in southern Florida as that of the Ancient Lake Dwellers of Switzerland.

In May 1895, Cushing travelled by steamship to Jacksonville in north-eastern Florida, then proceeded up the St Johns River, and across to Punta Gorda by rail and horseback. He hired a sloop, explored some of the islands and keys along the 90 miles (150 km) south to Key Marco, excavated for a day in the muck there, and returned to his base in Washington with sufficient relics to persuade his superiors to fund a major excavation. The story of this is best told in as many of Cushing's words as possible, although his interim and only published report is longer than this entire book (see Chapter 3 for site description).

The expedition took over a schooner, the Silver Spray, and used this as excavation base and home for the 3-month-long work at Key Marco. The site itself was a shell mounded area on the island, covering about 50 acres, and it had been in effect a prehistoric marina. Shells, including those of the large *Busycon* and *Fasciolaria gigantea* had been piled up and banked to form water courts, with shell benches or platforms like fingers providing embayments for canoes, in effect a

> veritable haven of ancient wharves and pile-dwellings, safe alike from tidal wave and hurricane within these gigantic ramparts of shell, where, through the channel gateways to the sea, canoes might readily come and go.

The court from which the relics had already come was a small area of about 12,000 sq. ft (c.1,100 sq. m).

> The entire court was thickly overgrown with mangrove trees, underneath which also thickly grew, to a uniform height of six or eight inches, bright green aquatic weeds and mangrove shoots. Since the interior of this artificial and filled-up bayou was still not above the level of the surrounding tide-swept mangrove swamps through which the canals led, it lay almost continually under water, and its excavation looked at first to be almost impossible, and at best a most formidable undertaking.

Cushing cleared a path for a sluice, and the team, consisting of Cushing and Mrs Cushing, two trained archaeologists, an artist-draughtsman called Wells Sawyer, and three 'Sailors and Excavators', bailed out the site; they repeated this operation at the start of almost every day, restricting the areas to be emptied thus by judicious sections or 'bins' (*ill. 30*). Even so, he vividly recalls:

> much of our search in the lower depths had to be made merely by feeling with the fingers. I deem it unnecessary to give further details of our operations, save to say that three or four of us worked side by side in each section, digging

inch by inch, and foot by foot, horizontally through the muck and rich lower strata, standing or crouching the while in puddles of mud and water; and as time went on we were pestered morning and evening by swarms and clouds of mosquitoes and sand-flies, and during the midhours of the day tormented by the fierce tropic sun heat, pouring down, even thus early in the season into this little shut-up hollow among the breathless mangroves.

Enough has perhaps been said already to indicate that Cushing was never one to minimize his task or to diminish the character of his environment in his writings. Sawyer also commented on the conditions:

The whole place was like a thick sponge saturated with water holding a great quantity of salt and a large variety of smells. We had brought a crew of work men from up the coast, but almost to a man they looked with absolute revolt upon the unpromising hole.

But they soon changed their minds once the mucks began to reveal the treasures of Key Marco. George Gause, the foreman, kept a diary and this reveals the excitement of the daily hunt for relics:

Friday the 6 went to work early soon found the most purfect painting ever found by an excibiter a pair of shells with Indian painted inside the I found a turtles head purfect then an Indian adz and 2 bowls 3 mallets 2 plumets 1 beautifull gorge found by Alfred Mr Clark found some nice thing such as pessell plummets and a head dress so we come in all well find 2 pleasure sch [schooners] anchored near had got 2 tarpons 2 sawfish 1 15 ft long 1 14 ft long then we play cards.

The waterlogged mucks of the court contained a vast hoard of artifacts in a bewildering array of materials and shapes. Almost all objects were of organic material, a majority of wood, with many pieces of cordage, and less fragile shell, bone and horn; there were only a small number of potsherds and stone objects. Some of the wooden artifacts had been painted with white, black, grey-blue and brown-red pigments.

Some of the things thus recovered could be preserved by very slow drying, but it soon became evident that by far the greater number of them could not be kept intact. No matter how perfect they were at first, they warped, shrunk, split, and even checked across the grain, like old charcoal, or else were utterly disintegrated on being exposed to the light and air if only for a few hours. Thus, despite the fact that after removing the surface muck from the sections, we dug only with little hand-trowels and flexible-pronged garden claws – and, as I have said before, with our fingers – yet fully twenty-five per cent. of these ancient articles in wood and other vegetal material were destroyed in the search; and again, of those found and removed, not more than one-half retained their original forms unaltered for more than a few days.

Unique to archaeology as these things were, it was distressing to feel that even by merely exposing and inspecting them, we were dooming so many of them to destruction, and to think that of such as we could temporarily recover only the half could be preserved as permanent examples of primitive art.

Mrs Cushing apparently took the brunt of the desperate attempts to preserve the relics, and it is due to her work that so many did indeed survive, even if in parlous

47

31–33 **Wooden artifacts from Key Marco, Florida** (*This page, clockwise from above left*) Carved and painted life-sized mask; engraved leaping dolphin, height of board *c.* 10 cm; carved kneeling feline, height 15 cm. (*Opposite, above left*) Photograph in the field of three life-sized wooden masks with shell inset eyes. (*Opposite, above right*) Engraved and painted kingfisher, height of board 45 cm.

states. The expedition eventually sent 11 barrels and 59 boxes of artifacts to
Philadelphia.

Among the artifacts recovered and well-recorded was (*ill. 33*),

a thin board of yellowish wood, a little more than sixteen inches in length, by
eight and a half inches in width, which I found standing slantingly upward
near the central western shell-bench. On slowly removing the peaty muck
from its surface, I discovered that an elaborate figure of a crested bird was
painted upon one side of it, in black, white, and blue pigments. Although
conventionally treated, this figure was at once recognizable as representing
either the jay or the king-fisher, or perhaps a mythologic bird-being designed
to typify both . . . To me, the remains that were most significant of all
discovered by us in the depths of the muck, were the carved and painted
wooden masks and animal figureheads. The masks were exceptionally well
modelled, usually in realistic representation of human features, and were life-
sized; hollowed to fit the face, and provided at either side, both above and
below, with string-holes for attachment thereto. Some of them were also
bored at intervals along the top, for the insertion of feathers or other
ornaments, and others were accompanied by thick, gleaming white conch-
shell eyes that could be inserted or removed at will, and which were concave –
like the hollowed and polished eye-pupils in the carving of the mountain-lion
god – to increase their gleam. Of these masks we found fourteen or fifteen
fairly-well preserved specimens, besides numerous others which were so
decayed that, although not lost to study, they could not be recovered.

The work of Sawyer, the artist-draughtsman, was without any doubt the saving grace of the Key Marco excavation. So much was lost on site, after recovery, and since transmission to the museums, that the drawings, watercolours and photographs (*ill. 32*) of the artifacts are in effect the basis of any real consideration of the material culture of Key Marco, a point ably brought out by Marion Gilliand's recent work. Cushing worked only in one court at Key Marco, the Court of the Pile Dwellers as he called it, perhaps 1 per cent of the shell mounded area. The whole site is now 'developed', and contains homes, hotels, apartments, a golf course and all the paraphernalia that obliterate a landscape.

Cushing was not hesitant in drawing upon ethnographic and historic references in his interpretations of the site and the relics. Having read Keller's theory of pile-dwellings, he was keen to demonstrate that the Court at Key Marco had held structures upon the wooden piles that he observed here and there in the muck and in the shell banks. A footnote to his lengthy interim report records a 17th-century observation of a Caribbean society:

> they plant themselves upon some little ascent, that so they may have better air and secure themselves against those pestilent flies which we have elsewhere called Mesquitos and Maringoins, which are extremely troublesome. . . . The same reason it is that obliges the Floridians . . . to lodge themselves for the most part at the entrance of the sea, in huts built on piles or pillars. (John Davides)

And among the heaps of worked wood there were toy canoes, two of which were found side-by-side, with thin sticks and twisted bark lying across them. Cushing thought these were representations of the sea-going craft of the people, possibly used as catamarans. He quoted from the narrative of Jonathan Dickinson (called *God's Protecting Providence Man's Surest Help and Defence . . .*), shipwrecked on the Florida coast *c*.1700, who observed his Indian captor returning home from an expedition:

> The Cacique came home in great state. He was nearly nude and triumphantly painted red, and sitting cross-legged on their ship's chest, that stood on a platform midway over two canoes lashed together with poles. He maintained a fierce expression of countenance and looked neither to the left nor to the right, but merely exclaimed 'wow' when they greeted him from the shore.

One could almost say the same of the Court of the Pile-Dwellers.

The importance of the collections from Key Marco rests on the fact that they are unique. Clarence Moore continued his searches along the coast until 1907 and excavated, like Cushing before him and others after him, in many shell courts. He wrote:

> search for objects of wood has been fruitless. . . . At all events that such objects are not general in the muck and marl of the keys makes Mr Cushing's collection more to be prized and more likely to remain unique.

And yet they did not lack a context in the prehistoric record of the Florida coast. Following Cushing's lecture on his work to the American Philosophical Society in 1896, one of the discussants said:

What I consider the most important point in Mr Cushing's discoveries is that he was able to bring out of this muck deposit on the Florida Keys a large number of objects which by being buried in the muck were preserved; whereas the same objects if buried in a sand mound or lost in a shell heap would have perished. It is important to note that the objects in this collection, made of imperishable material, such as stone, bone and shell, are of the same character as those already known from other parts of Florida. Thus it seems to me that Mr Cushing's discovery instead of indicating a new culture, has thrown a powerful light upon, and greatly extended our knowledge of, the old culture of Florida. (Putnam)

Reinterpreting the lake-dwellings

We have seen that the development in wet-site archaeology in the decades from 1854 to about 1900 was heavily influenced by the lake-dwelling images first propounded by Keller, and championed by many others. From the beginning, almost every site, whether in a lake, on a coast or a floodplain, or in a marsh or peatbog, was labelled a lake-dwelling, constructed on piles. There were exceptions, but these did not become apparent until work on the Alpine lakes had entered a new phase, and one concerned more with excavations in peatbogs and marshes than in lakes. Although much had been written about the houses set upon the platforms and piles, no indisputable house floors had been identified in the deeper lake sites, in part due to the methods of excavation but also to the heavy erosive power of water. The first unmistakable traces of floors were seen on sites sealed by peat, first at Niederwil (*ill. 34*) in the Egelsee, Switzerland, where the term *Packwerkbau* (houses built on top of wooden floors) was more or less invented. The site was originally examined by Messikomer of Robenhausen fame, and an 1862 photo shows a substructure of branches under two house floors, beside which were upright wall posts. Keller's insistence on pile-supported houses rather obscured the matter, and his own illustration of Niederwil clearly showed the problems. E. Frank began to question the evidence both here and in the Federsee as well, where further house floors had survived. Not only that, but from 1919 onwards R. Schmidt and then H. Reinerth worked in the Federsee and exposed wide areas of settlements such as Riedschachen and Aichbühl, and Reinerth went on to do the same in the marshland at Dullenried and Wasserburg-Buchau. Each site yielded detailed house plans, with floors, hearths and other elements quite clearly delineated by careful excavation. Through the application of scientific studies of soils, sediments, plant remains and the separation of different phases of occupation through stratigraphic control, Reinerth in particular could begin to demonstrate that the wetlands in which these settlements had been established had been subjected to fluctuating lake levels through time. This was a major innovative concept in the study of the lake-dwellings. All the evidence suggested that a reappraisal of Keller's dogma was required, and by the late 1930s Oscar Paret accepted Reinerth's theory of fluctuating lake levels, and Emil Vogt did too after the Egolzwil 3 excavations. Josef Speck then reinforced the new stand by showing at Zug-Sumpf that houses had been directly built on the earth and not on piles; the importance of this was that Zug was a real north Alpine lake and not a small marshland where conceivably the pile-dwelling concept need not have applied. Some

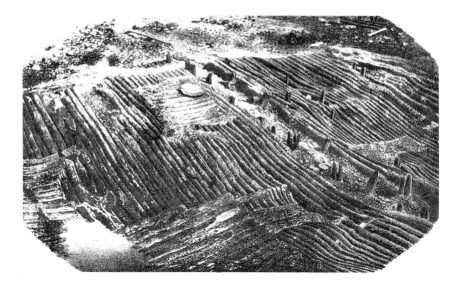

prehistorians, particularly the Germans, disowned the pile-dwelling theory quite early, but most of the Swiss clung stubbornly to the concept – after all, they had been brought up on it as children and all around could be seen the books, the relics and the reconstructions of the pile-dwellings. Yet the evidence against was growing with every new investigation. In 1954, the centenary of Keller's lake-dwelling discoveries and publication, almost all prehistorians finally abandoned the concept. An important paper by E. Vogt in the volume *Das Pfahlbauproblem* was the final nail, and it was a somewhat ironic exercise to celebrate the centenary of the pile-dwellings by denying their existence.

The new interpretation, put simply, was that the lake levels had fluctuated, both seasonally and, more importantly, climatically over time. Settlements had been established, not perched on piles in the lake waters but on the soft shores of lakes only recently exposed by the retreat of the waters (*ill. 35*). The house floors were set directly upon the ground, with the uprights to hold walling and roofing driven deeply into the underlying deposits to prevent the houses sinking into the soft subsoils. In due time, as lake levels rose, the settlements were abandoned, and the waters destroyed the structures, except for the lower parts of the long piles. The debris of abandonment and occupation was covered by lake silts and thus preserved in the relic beds. In assessing the relationship of these lake sites to those from the dryland, Oscar Paret wrote:

> The wealth of the marshes and lakes in archaeological traces and especially in elements of structure are not explained by different methods of construction, but only by the conditions of preservation (in the wet deposits) which are infinitely more favourable than on dry ground. Everywhere however, and at all times, man has sought a dry habitation. A dry soil, a dry bed is to him as precious as a hat is to a head. Prehistoric man was a man and not an amphibian. We see clearly, with his houses built on the ground itself, a settlement of peaceful cultivators and pastoralists, on a dried-out shore, limited on one side by the line of the shore where it fell away into the lake and on the other by the slope of the ancient shore.

34–36 **New ideas about the lake-dwellings** (*Opposite, above*) Drawing of the wooden flooring of Neolithic houses at Niederwil, Switzerland, exposed in 1862. (*Above*) Reconstruction of a Neolithic settlement at Aichbühl, Germany, showing the houses set on the dryland well away from the lake waters. (*Right*) The first aerial photograph of a submerged lake-dwelling, Cortaillod in Lake Neuchâtel, taken in about 1925.

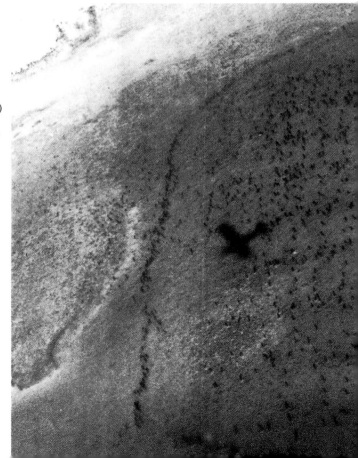

His book *Le Mythe des cités lacustres*, published in 1958, marked the end of the pile-dwelling theory. The relic beds had overwhelmed the early archaeologists with their wealth of artifacts and their exceptional preservation. The pioneers had never been able to study the deposits of occupation and of abandonment, and they could not work underwater and examine the sediments; they had also ignored the variety of ethnographic examples, picking only those that suited the pile-dwelling theory. It was the relic beds that had dominated the thinking, and together with the powerful arguments of Keller, Munro and others, they had prevented questions being asked for almost 100 years.

As an aside, two innovations in the examination of submerged lake-dwellings took place in Lake Neuchâtel in 1925–7. Here Paul Vouga made the world's first aerial photographic record of ancient sites through the still cold waters of the lake (*ill. 36*), and here he developed the idea of coffer-dam excavation. By sinking large cylindrical tubes 2–3 m long down onto the settlement at Cortaillod, then pumping out the water, he was able to descend by ladder to the relic bed and stand amidst the piles. His costume for this exercise was pin-stripe suit and hat.

Modern excavations of the Alpine settlements began with Walter Guyan's work at Thayngen-Weier and René Wyss at Egolzwil 5. Here a growing range of scientific studies could be applied, among them pollen analysis and studies of the trees which went to make up the structure of the sites. To these were soon added dendrochronological (tree-ring) studies, perhaps the most important of recent innovations. The second correction of the Jura lakes in the 1960s exposed more sites and put them within reach of the camera, now from the air, and of the underwater excavator, and changes in legislation in Switzerland supplied archaeology with the kind of support that major multidisciplinary excavations demanded. From these projects there now emerges the idea of a spectrum of environmental conditions under which ancient people determined to settle at or near the shores of lakes, or on the edges of marshes. And their structures can now be seen to reflect this variety of settings, with earth-fast houses, or pile-assisted houses, or indeed even pile-supported houses. Keller would be pleased with that.

New projects in northern Europe

Archaeologists in northern Europe pursued their own wetland studies. In 1908 excavations were initiated in a peatbog at Alvastra in southern Sweden, and work continued, with one gap, until 1930. The structural evidence consisted of a wooden platform and hundreds of piles or posts, basically comparable to that of the Swiss pile-dwellings but here there was neither evidence nor suggestion that the structures had rested above the ground. The platform covered about 1200 sq. m and there were fence lines of posts, over 100 hearths and all the indications of a Neolithic settlement built on the surface of a mire. The site yielded quantities of stone battle-axes, amber beads in battle-axe shapes, flint axes, arrowheads, bone chisels and awls, and pottery; more recent excavations have augmented these collections, and also increased the number of wooden objects (see Chapter 4). Alvastra is a good example of the basic contribution of a pioneering excavation, indicating the scale and general nature of the site, but only capable of interpretation through more modern work which included the latest techniques for recovery of fragile materials, and for the sampling of sediments and wood for environmental and chronological definition. In the case of Alvastra, there was one further complication in this process, namely, that the original excavations were never published.

At about the same time, from 1908 to 1913, another project got underway, in Scotland, where the early crannog excavations of Munro and others had not been followed further. The Reverend Odo Blundell took up, or down, the challenge and pursued his crannog interests in the Highlands, including diving amidst the ice-cold waters of a number of lochs. Not for him the free swimming techniques of today; he had to borrow the clanking gear of the divers of the Caledonian Canal. In Loch Bruiach he experienced a severe storm as he prepared to examine the planks of a crannog, and 'feared that the water kelpies were very angry at the intrusion' into their realm. The war in 1914 put an end to the wetland activities of both Blundell and Munro.

The terps of the Netherlands were examined and explained by the work of A. E. van Giffen in 1931–7 at Ezinge. He had first excavated on a terp in 1908. At Ezinge, he identified six major occupation levels, extending from 300 BC to the 13th century AD. The earliest settlement was on the flat inside a rectangular palisade where a house and barn were established. Immediately after this, an artificial mound was constructed over the dismantled remains, and a 6-ft (2-m) high area of turf and earth and other debris, 115 ft in diameter, was used to base four farmsteads. The terp was enlarged again to three times the area and almost twice the height, to support farmsteads arranged radially around a small square, and the process of enlargement and rebuilding went on until the sea-walls made it unnecessary to raise and protect the settlement. The importance of the Ezinge excavations lay in the recognition of the artificial character of the terp, the excellent quality of preservation of material, and the demonstration that pile-dwellings were neither necessary nor present. The detail revealed about the farmsteads in particular was a revelation. Who, even among the pioneers of wetland archaeology, could have foreseen a quality of evidence capable of describing a prehistoric farmstead holding 52 cows, individually stalled, standing with hindlegs on wattle matting and facing the outer walls, with a central passage leading from the stable area to a well-constructed and closely defined living area with hearth, sleeping places and storage areas? (cf Chapter 3). On reflection, perhaps Munro might have done so.

The study of other types of wetland sites, trackways for example, was not actively pursued during this time; the pioneers had retired, and the new generation had other interests. Yet discoveries continued, and none more unusual than the Boylston Street 'fish weir' in Boston, USA. In 1913 the construction of a subway through the Back Bay district had uncovered many piles or stakes set upright in a peat and clay deposit sealed by 5 m of silt (and 6 m of 19th-century fill). The stakes held brushwood 'wattling' and were interpreted as a fish weir in the ancient Charles River. Work in the 1930s and 1940s succeeded in identifying various lines or fences of these stakes, as well as other concentrations in ovals or oblongs. An estimated 65,000 stakes had existed, covering 2 acres; the wood was sassafras, oak, alder and many other species including beech, some at least felled in late spring. But what was the site, and what was its age? The matter is only now being investigated anew, and preliminary results suggest an age of about 4,000 years; the function of the structure remains a puzzle.

37, 38 **Excavations at the Iron Age settlement of Biskupin, Poland, in the 1930s** (*Above*) The collapsed palisade, roadway and other structures at Biskupin. (*Below*) Excavations amidst the timbers.

In 1933, in Lake Biskupin, Poland, a narrow peninsula was examined by a local teacher, W. Szwajcer, following earlier reports of wooden piles. He found sufficient timber to persuade the prehistorians Joseph Kostrzewski and Zdzislaw Rajewski of Poznan to begin excavations in 1934 (*ill. 38*). The flooring and lower walls of wooden houses were soon revealed, along with bone, horn, wood and stone artifacts. Appeals for funding and other help were met with donations from many sources and the work was greatly enlarged in the years that followed, until the war in 1939 suspended operations. Seven houses were found in 1934, and a palisade and parts of eight streets paved with logs were seen in 1935. Lake Biskupin was dammed off from the site and reconstructions were attempted, to encourage visitors and to instruct schoolchildren. Studies of pollen and peat, sediments and bones were established, in efforts to comprehend the place of the fortress in the environment of the middle first millennium BC. By 1939, half of the 2-hectare settlement was exposed and the excavation teams involved up to 200 labourers and many archaeologists. The quantity of portable material recovered was astounding, literally millions of objects and samples. The remains of wooden palisades, streets and houses were left *in situ* (*ill. 37*), requiring active conservation or slow drying by covering them with rushes, moss and soil. Aerial photographs were taken from 1935 with both aeroplanes and balloons. The lake bed was searched by divers who retrieved many artifacts, a dugout canoe and finally the remains of a bridge which had connected the site with the mainland. The settlement had been on an island, not a peninsula, and the 'lake-dwellers' once more came to prominence. In 1939, the main gate of the fortress, including both wings of the doors, was found. It is both interesting and important to note that the excavator Rajewski publicized the site as much as possible, by balloon flights distributing leaflets, by films, popular articles, and by the reconstructions. A total of 400,000 people visited the site in the years 1934–9, and the name Biskupin was installed on official maps of Poland.

In the war years 1939–45, much damage occurred, the reconstructions were destroyed and the site abandoned to decay. But in 1945 work began again, both excavations and reconstructions, and it still continues (Chapter 5); the work in the 1930s however was the time when the full implications of wet-sites were asserted – the potential for information, the multi-disciplinary studies required, and the realization of public interest.

These were innovations in wetland archaeology, and they were matched in importance by research elsewhere. Crannog excavations by Hugh Hencken in Ireland, at Ballinderry and Lagore, were not notable for their use of environmental studies, although the sites and finds demanded them. But in eastern England, the work of Hazzledine Warren and others was succeeded by a major project that got wetland archaeology out of the bog and into the light of mainstream archaeology.

Although a small number of antiquities, including bog bodies, had been recorded from the Fens of East Anglia in the 18th and 19th centuries, little work had been done on either the archaeology or the environmental evidence. The Fens consisted of about 4,000 sq. km (1 million acres) of former wetlands, much of it barely above sea-level, and had undergone severe drainage since the 17th century. With drainage, the surfaces of the fields subsided until they lay below the water courses, when pumps had to be installed. The landscape is now in effect upside down with rivers and drains raised above the land. And much of the

Fen is flat, so flat that the pollen analyst Harry Godwin commented on the flatness of the scenery to a resident of the Fens and was at once dismissed with the assertion, 'Any fool can appreciate mountain scenery. It takes a man of discernment to appreciate the Fens.' The rate of shrinkage of the peat was measured in one of the last surviving meres, at Whittlesey, in 1848. Wooden posts driven into the bedrock until their tops were flush with the ground were exposed for a full 2 m by 1860; a replacement iron post now stands 4 m above the uncut but shrunken peat surface, and taken together these posts show the rapid effects of drainage, and the slower long-term shrinkage of the deposits as the water is drawn from them by adjacent drainage channels, oxidation and degradation.

In 1932 the implications of drainage for buried archaeological remains, and of Fenland deposits for environmental studies, were recognized and a group of scientists mostly based in Cambridge undertook the investigation of the Fens. The Fenland Research Committee had botanists, geologists, geographers and archaeologists, working with drainage engineers and other local informants including Graham Fowler, manager for water transport at a sugar beet factory at Ely. Godwin recorded how the Committee was activated. Fowler

> was very widely known and few new discoveries failed to come to his notice. When a site he had visited seemed to merit closer attention telephone calls would inform the members of the committee most likely to be concerned and next day with gum-boots, spades and peat-indifferent clothing a small party would rendezvous at some agreed point, to be led to the site and there investigate, measure, photograph and sample it as seemed necessary.

Excavations by Grahame Clark were undertaken in the Fens at Shippea Hill where basal sands, stratified peats and clays, representing episodes of freshwater fen and the effects of seawater flooding, contained Mesolithic, Neolithic and Bronze Age material. For the first time, the relics could be put into an environmental context. Part of that context was supplied by Godwin, then developing the science of pollen analysis. Both Clark and Godwin were strongly influenced by palaeoecological work in Scandinavia, where multidisciplinary projects had investigated the late glacial and early post-glacial history of the region, using the evidence of glacial and meltwater deposits, fluctuations in sea-levels, the tilting of the land through ice-release, pollen analysis of peat, and the counting of varves (annually-deposited laminations in sediments of the lakes existing near the glaciers).

In 1936 the Fenland Research Committee extended its search to the mud flats of the East Anglia coast, where Hazzledine Warren had been working and where some of the pioneers of modern British archaeology (Clark, Stuart Piggott and Godwin) now investigated the structures and material culture of the Neolithic (Chapter 3). The Committee's activities came to an end in 1940 but its impact on archaeology was considerable, particularly so in its insistence that the natural sciences had to play a part in any real effort to comprehend archaeological sites and landscapes. The process of education was continued by Clark's major excavations at Star Carr in 1949–51, which mark the beginning of modern wetland archaeology in western Europe, and the remainder of this book is devoted to the modern work in Europe, America and elsewhere.

3 · Living by the sea

I N THE COLDEST PHASES of the last Ice Age, the surface of the earth was relatively dry and sea levels were low. Water was locked up in glaciers and snowfields, rendering some regions inhospitable and leaving others dry and open to human settlement. As temperatures rose at the end of the Ice Age, some 10,000 years ago, the glaciers released their water and over the next few thousand years sea levels crept up and up. Detailed research has shown that this was not necessarily a steady rise, more a case of two steps forward and one step back, and complicated in some regions by rising land levels as the surface of the earth was released from its overburden of ice and snow.

In many regions, therefore, the sea has encroached on the land. In northern Europe it submerged an area at least the size of present-day England, severing Britain from the continent and creating what we now call the North Sea and the English Channel. In the north Pacific the land mass of Beringia, which once lay between Alaska and Siberia, was likewise lost. In northern Scandinavia and in north Britain, however, land rise outran the rising sea and old coastlines now lie inland. Elsewhere, the coastline has fluctuated back and forth, as in the Fens of East Anglia and the Somerset Levels in England, and the Marais Poitevin in western France. These regions have changed from salt to freshwater and back again a number of times in the last 10,000 years. The present Baltic Sea has been at times a freshwater lake, and southern Sweden has been linked to Denmark rather than to its present northern lands. Denmark itself encapsulates the interplay of changing land and sea levels, with northern Jutland now higher in relation to the sea than 5,000 years ago, whereas southern Zealand and Fyn are lower.

The ecological zones that were shifted back and forth by changing water levels included some of the richest known. Mud–flats at low tide, endless reed–beds and brackish lagoons may not sound attractive, but coastal marshes, estuaries and deltas, sheltered bays and lagoons, and tidal creeks reaching far inland, all would shelter fish and wildfowl, many congregating daily with the ebb and flow of tides. Other species like geese or salmon would arrive as seasonal migrants. Mussels and crabs, shrimps and cockles were there for the picking, along with many other shellfish and crustacea. Edible plants included seakale and numerous species of seaweed, and their palatability is reflected in the number of present-day vegetables which have been developed from coastal plants, including the Brassicas or cabbage family. Another valuable coastal resource was salt, precious as a preservative in the days before refrigeration, as well as for its savour.

Of all the coastal ecosystems, estuaries are generally held to be the most productive, and they were clearly attractive to prehistoric peoples, who also favoured lagoons and tidal creeks. On many rivers, the intertidal zone once extended much further inland than today. Weirs and other barriers have been erected to control river traffic and flooding, particularly on major rivers such as the Thames, the Gironde and the Rhine. Most notably in the Netherlands, the incursions of the sea have been pushed back by man, and land reclaimed for settlement and agriculture. In the pages that follow we shall come across the first stages of control and reclamation, which have led to the drastic reduction of a once diverse and extensive habitat.

The preservation of archaeological sites in coastal zones has usually been due to a rise in sea-level. In those areas where, as we have noted, the land has risen in relation to the sea, the once-wet settlements of marsh-dwellers are today stranded inland, dry and often devoid of organic remains other than bone and shell. But where the sea has risen in relation to the land, coastal settlements have been submerged, and where this happened soon after occupation a variety of organic materials may well have been preserved, as at Tybrind Vig, a Mesolithic site from Denmark. Elsewhere, silting has contributed to preservation, and in the case of Key Marco in Florida this may have been the silting of an artificially deepened lagoon. In areas such as the East Anglian Fens and the Bristol Channel, coastal marshes have been overwhelmed by the sea and blanketed in estuarine clays, only to be exposed and recolonized by reed beds and dryland forests when the waters receded again. Several repetitions of the cycle have buried early sites under many layers of clays, silts and peat, waterlogged but squashed by the weight of deposits over them.

Many coastal sites have been discovered through storm erosion, exceptionally low tides or a combination of these two events. Ozette, a particularly well-preserved settlement on the Northwest coast of the United States, buried under a landslide, was being eroded by successive storms and pilfered by treasure-hunters when archaeologists were invited to excavate as neither process could be halted. Storm action and low tides have led to the discovery of trackways on the Welsh coast of the Bristol Channel, and even to the sighting of Mesolithic footprints, fossilized in the mud and protected for several thousand years by overlying deposits which are only now being washed away. Wave action can also wash the sediments off a submerged site, revealing parts of a structure or a group of artifacts to divers. Many submerged Mesolithic settlements off the south coast of Denmark have been found in this way, including Tybrind Vig.

On reclaimed land, the settlements of ancient coastal dwellers have been revealed by drainage, either through the exposure of features and finds in the side of a ditch, or through planned archaeological survey ahead of ditching and desiccation. The work of the Assendelver Polders project in the Netherlands has shown just how much information can be retrieved in this way, and there are many similarities with survey in drained freshwater wetlands. And in both fresh and saltwater conditions there are instances of ancient settlements being grubbed up as fertilizer. This is what happened to Key Marco on the Gulf Coast of Florida in the 19th century, dug initially as fertilizer for an orange grove and only later by Cushing for its archaeological potential.

America

The coasts of the New World offer great stretches of marsh and lagoon and numerous estuaries where archaeological potential must be high but little investigation has yet taken place. Work has recently been undertaken in Belize to

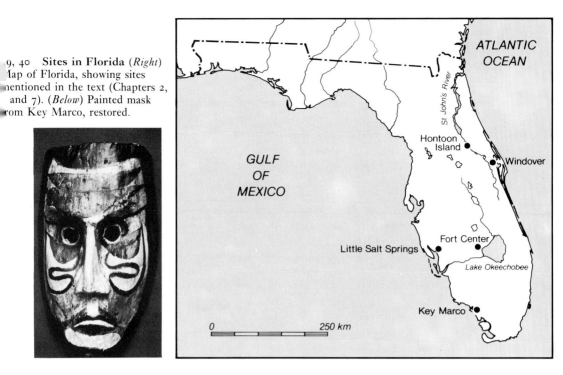

ATLANTIC OCEAN

St John's River

GULF OF MEXICO

Hontoon Island

Windover

Little Salt Springs

Fort Center

Lake Okeechobee

Key Marco

0   250 km

demonstrate such a potential, on an ancient Maya site. This occupied most of a small low mangrove island, Wild Cane Cay, near the mouth of the Deep River in southern Belize. 'Maya' conjures up visions of stone and elaborate inland complexes but here, in the mangrove swamps, organic preservation was good, and direct evidence was found for the foods used by the Maya some 1,000 years ago. Maize cobs, and palm nuts and other wild fruits were identified, and bones from many different species of fish were recovered. Clearly, much could be learnt of the subsistence of the coastal Maya by further work in this zone.

Many years ago now, Cushing revealed the wealth of evidence preserved at another coastal site, that of Key Marco on the Gulf Coast of Florida (*ill. 40*). The story of Cushing's expedition has already been told (Chapter 2); here we shall concentrate on what is known of the site. The prehistoric Indians of Key Marco occupied the tip of a low flat island on the Gulf of Mexico, and seem to have created a system of canals and lagoons protected behind a sea-wall. At the Court of the Pile-Dwellers, the scene of Cushing's excavations, a canal led from sheltered inland waters into a lagoon or harbour roughly 80 × 100 ft (24 × 30 m), Cushing's 'court'. This was surrounded by a shell bank, and shell jetties or extensions of the bank reached into the harbour, the whole effect being not dissimilar to a modern marina. The Indians' buildings were on the dry banks, and little was preserved. Their debris fell into the water of the Court which gradually silted up and always remained waterlogged. Here, a wealth of material was recovered, almost all of it now dated to AD 750–1513, before any contact with European explorers.

Subsistence was water-based, and canoes were probably the means of access to the varied wetland environments in the vicinity of the site. There were plentiful fish, waterfowl and shellfish to be had for food. Little use was made of ceramics and hard stone tools in the material culture from Key Marco. Shell, sharks' teeth and coral supplemented wood and other plants for making artifacts.

Cushing found over 3,000 artifacts, of which 1,000 were taken away in reasonable condition, many having been recorded by photograph and watercolour. There were fish nets with floats, pounders and wooden vessels and many other everyday items. Less domestic in nature were the extraordinary pieces of painted and carved wood. These included, as we have seen, a wooden board with a kingfisher-like bird painted on it (*ill. 33*), another carved and incised with a leaping dolphin (*ill. 31*), the side of a box decorated with a dragon-like creature. A number of carved and painted masks have human or animal features (Chapter 2). The human masks were sometimes painted with geometric designs, sometimes given exaggerated noses or shell-inlay eyes and one had a twisted asymmetry reminiscent of Indian masks from further north (*ill. 31*, *ill. 39*). Animal masks and figureheads include a wolf-like creature, a painted deer's head with separate flaring ears, and a pelican. One human figurine was found, and a delicate small carving of a kneeling feline which Cushing described as a 'man-like being in the guise of a panther'.

Many of the representations, whether painted, incised or three-dimensional carvings, show a mixture of human and animal traits and it is likely that they pertain to the myths and ceremonies of the Key Marco inhabitants. The great number of such objects recovered from the court are suggestive of a ceremonial centre rather than an ordinary village. But a similar wealth of wooden representations has been recovered from other North American wet sites, most notably the coastal site of Ozette (see below). Thus it may be that many villages had such wealth, which has only been preserved in waterlogged conditions. Alternatively, or in addition, the wealth of wetland subsistence resources may have favoured the development of art, as is evident on the Northwest coast of America. A similar situation has been found by wetland archaeologists at diverse sites around the world, and the nature of wetland affluence will be considered again later.

An early and interesting North American site currently under investigation lies near the mouth of the Hoko River, on the coast of Washington State (*ill. 41*). Two phases of occupation on the shore led to accumulation of debris in the river, the first from about 3,000 to 2,500 years ago and the second from about 900 to 100 years ago. People came here to fish, and the Hoko River is known for a strong late summer and autumn salmon run. Several species of fish were recovered, not just salmon. Bentwood fishhooks with spruce-root or cedar-root lines were fairly common, made in several distinct types. Experimental fishing in Seattle aquarium has determined that the different types of hook were good for catching different species of fish. Fish-blood has been identified on some of the stone blades from the site, and analysis of the bones suggests that the catch was being processed to preserve it for consumption elsewhere.

Ninety per cent of the artifacts from the Hoko River site were made of wood and plant fibre. Skirts of shredded cedar bark were preserved, and large baskets for collecting shellfish, along with little baskets that may have been intended to hold a bentwood fishhook. Basketry hats sometimes had a topknot or knob, similar to the hats worn by nobles of the region in recent times. The wooden artifacts include a carved piece, another instance of art being preserved thanks to waterlogging (*ill. 42*).

Ozette, along the coast from Hoko River, is a more recent settlement. It came to an end about AD 1750 when the village was buried by a landslide. Just over 200

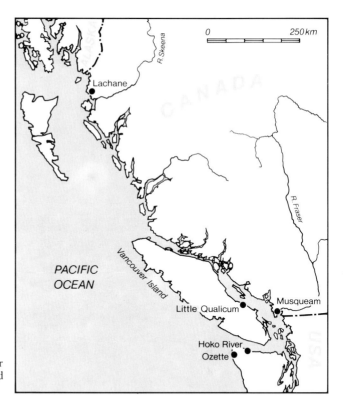

41–43 **Finds from the Northwest Coast** (*Right*) Map of the Pacific coast of North America, showing sites mentioned in the text. (*Centre right*) Mat creaser from Hoko River, about 3,000 years old, used to prepare reeds for matting, with male and female kingfisher designs. Length *c.* 25 cm. (*Below*) Cedarwood carving of a whale dorsal fin from Ozette, Washington State. The object is inlaid with sea-otter molars and canines, and painted red and black. Length about 1 m.

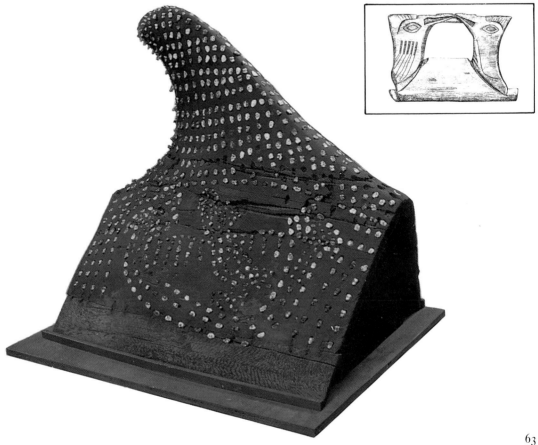

years later heavy seas were eroding the protective layers of mud and baring the remains to scavengers and other destructive agencies. The descendants of the Ozette people, whose oral tradition had kept alive memory of the disaster, asked for the site to be properly excavated in order to save it from looting and to protect the bones of their ancestors.

The site was large and complex, and conditions of preservation were excellent. Four houses were excavated by Richard Daugherty. The many bones, shells and seeds indicated that subsistence had been based on water resources, as at Hoko River, and the village had been well placed for whale-hunting. Again as at Hoko, material culture was based on wood and plant fibres, and several hundred thousand items were recovered including many fragile baskets. Items relating to the water and fishing included paddles and fragments of canoes, nets and fishhooks, harpoons and harpoon sheaths. One whale harpoon head had a mussel-shell blade, antler barbs and string binding and it was protected by a cedar bark sheath.

Many of the wooden objects were decorated, some simple like a club with an owlhead handle, and others elaborate. Wooden bowls might have handles carved into human or animal heads, or the figure could be the bowl, as with a human figure carved so that head and legs made handles and the hollowed-out body a dish. Box-fronts and planks were decorated with incised animal motifs and perhaps inlaid with teeth. A three-dimensional cedarwood carving of the dorsal fin of a whale, standing about 1 m high, was inlaid with over 700 white sea-otter teeth and painted red and black, part of the design being a thunderbird holding a double-headed serpent in its claws (*ill. 43*). The art preserved at Ozette is an important demonstration of the Indian traditions and skills that existed shortly before European contact.

North along the coast, moving into British Columbia, many more wet sites are known, some as old as Hoko River. One such is Musqueam Northeast in Vancouver where many basketry artifacts were found. On the east coast of Vancouver island, 150 km north of Victoria, the Little Qualicum site lies at the mouth of the river of that name. As with Hoko River, there is evidence of occupation on the shore and well-preserved midden material in the intertidal zone in front of it, all dating to about 1,000 years ago. Once again, much of the material culture is organic and much of it relates to fishing, including a heavy stone bound with cedar-branch rope and used as an anchor and a 1.5-m length of lattice-work from a fish-weir. Many salmon and other fish bones testify to what was caught.

Further north still at Lachane, Prince Rupert Harbour, the waterlogged midden of a coastal settlement dating from 2,500 to 1,600 years ago has been investigated. This site has yielded little fishing evidence, and no bone, but a good range of domestic artifacts demonstrates the woodworking skills of the inhabitants and many wooden wedges were found, of the sort used to split wood. There were baskets, wooden bowls, bentwood boxes and a cedarwood handle for a box or bowl lid, carved in stylized animal form.

From Lachane to Key Marco, the coastal wet sites of North America demonstrate a two-fold value for the archaeologist. Waterlogging has preserved categories of evidence infrequently encountered on dryland sites, and that evidence suggests a secure economic base founded on the exploitation of abundant coastal and estuarine resources. Perhaps because of this security, or perhaps only because conditions are right for preservation, many of the sites have yielded decorated and carved wood. Comparisons with northern Europe suggest a similar abundance of resources for the coast dwellers of the Late Mesolithic, but to date only in one rare European case has decorated wood been retrieved.

Late Mesolithic coastal sites of northern Europe

As the sea rose at the end of the last Ice Age, and coastal zones were shifted inland, saltwaters encroached on the North Sea plain, turning hills into islands and in due course submerging them, overwhelming all evidence of human settlement whether on low headlands or old coastlines (*ill. 45*). Some measure of the magnitude of sea rise is given by finds dredged up from the present sea floor, such as pick- and axe-heads of aurochs bone retrieved from the Brown Bank, mid-way between Lowestoft in England and The Hague in the Netherlands; these finds came from an old land surface now 35 to 45 m under water, and they are of Early Mesolithic date. They were discovered by chance, as were similar finds from Dogger Bank, and Leman and Ower. There is little likelihood at present of systematic search for early sites, although there is every chance that much well-preserved evidence does exist deep under the North Sea.

The picture for the Later Mesolithic is rather different. In Britain and in Scandinavia the coastal zone of the period from about 6000 to about 3800 BC is either under only a few metres of water or, in the north, raised a few metres above and inland of the present sea-level. Until quite recently, most of our knowledge of the period came from raised sites, such as the shell midden at Ertebølle in North Jutland. Known in the 19th century, Ertebølle became the type site for the Late Mesolithic of South Scandinavia. From it and other raised sites a limited picture could be drawn of the economy of coastal dwellers in the centuries immediately before agriculture was introduced, when the lands to the south were already settled by farmers whose way of life had spread up the Danube from the Mediterranean.

It was not until sub-aqua clubs began to flourish, after the Second World War, that the full archaeological potential of submerged sites was realized. Amateur divers have been responsible for many discoveries, especially off the south coast of the island of Fyn (*ill. 46*), and since the mid-1970s they have worked with archaeologists to build up a more systematic picture of ancient coastlines and the density of prehistoric settlement. As knowledge increases, it becomes possible to predict the locations favoured by Ertebølle fishermen, and to direct underwater survey to likely areas. The discoveries made in this way have added greatly to the picture of Ertebølle subsistence and settlement. Before turning to the evidence itself, one further point should be noted: at any given period in the Mesolithic, coastal settlements would all have been at much the same level, close to the then sea-level. Today, wave-action tends to disturb sediments underwater at a particular level, and this is where sites are most likely to be found. It is therefore probable that most finds will belong to the same fairly limited time-span, and finds of other periods which are buried in undisturbed sediments are less likely to be found.

Many discoveries have been made off the southern coast of Fyn and its associated small islands, such as the sites of Skjoldnaes and Dejrø. From

44   Head of fish-spear or leister (original, top, reconstruction, above) from Skjoldnaes, Denmark, with hazel shaft, hawthorn barbs, and bound with plant fibre string. The original length of the barbs was 40 cm.

45–47 **Mesolithic Denmark**
(*Left*) Map of the changing
North Sea in the Mesolithic
period. (*Below*) Map of
Ertebølle sites in Denmark with
inset map of southern Fyn. The
tilting of the land has raised
some sites, and submerged
others. (*Opposite*) The bay of
Tybrind Vig, Fyn, showing
Mesolithic and present
coastlines, and the former
lagoon with the site at its
mouth.

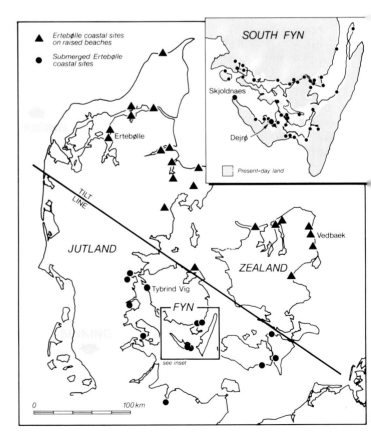

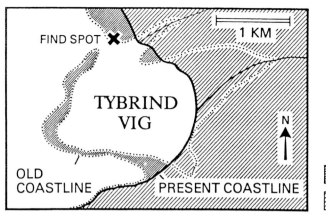

Skjoldnaes, a wooden fish-spear or leister has been recovered (*ill. 44*). It was made by lashing two barbs, each originally about 40 cm long, to a shaft. The barbs were made from hawthorn, the shaft from hazelwood, and the careful lashing was done with string made from plant fibres, probably willow or nettle-fibre. Many single barbs come from Dejrø, made from hawthorn, dogwood, hazel and rowan, all shrubby species. Dogwood derives its name from 'dagwood', the hard horny wood good for skewers or 'daggers', and hawthorn too is sharp and tough. The function of these single barbs might be difficult to determine without the near-complete leister head from Skjoldnaes to show what the finished composite artifact was like.

One site, Tybrind Vig, was discovered by an amateur diver, Hans Dal, in 1978 off the west coast of Fyn, and it has since been excavated. The wealth of evidence recovered from this site has fully compensated for the difficulties and the expense of underwater work in the cold sea waters. Work 'in the field' by the divers continued until 1987. Several preliminary publications by Søren Andersen have already appeared and it is possible to describe the site in some detail.

'Vig' means cove or bay, a sheltered spot, and when people lived at Tybrind Vig and at other sites around the bay in the Late Mesolithic it was even more protected than today, a lagoon of calm water about 1.5 × 3 km across, sheltered by a spit of land from the sea (*ill. 47*). Two freshwater streams flowed in and with probably only one narrow outlet to the sea, the water in the lagoon was not very salty. Reeds grew along the shore, behind them was shrubby growth of hazel, birch and elder leading up to an oak woodland where the occasional lime, elm or pine tree could be found. The settlement was just above the reeds on the north side of the opening to the sea. Here, people fished in the shallow waters or set off by boat for other places, and they threw out the rubbish from house and hearth. The debris of all this activity accumulated underwater amongst the reeds. When the sea level rose and the inhabitants moved away, material which had accumulated in the reed bed was protected by sediments although the settlement itself, on slightly higher ground, appears to have been eroded away. The excellent preservation of wood and other fragile plant materials indicates that Tybrind Vig has been continuously waterlogged since the time of occupation, which was from about 5500 to about 4000 BC.

The excavated evidence included a cobbled area which may have been a slipway, and vertical hazel sticks in rows as if for fish traps. Many of the artifacts were connected with fishing, including two fine canoes made from the trunks of lime trees. One of these was near-complete, about 9.5 m long and 65 cm wide, with sides at least 30 cm high and a fitted sternboard. A hearth of clay and sand had been made near the stern, to give light for night fishing perhaps, or to cook the catch and to warm the fishermen. The other canoe was less well-preserved; it appears to have been much the same, only a bit bigger. Ashwood was used for the paddles, which had heart-shaped blades and relatively short straight handles. Three paddles stand out from the collection, for their blades were decorated with a pattern cut into the light ashwood and filled with a brown colour. Enough survives on one blade to show a penchant for bold and symmetrical curvilinear patterns, infilled with lines of dots (*ill. 48*). Another blade has a light, linear pattern. Other forms of art and decoration are not unknown but scarce at this time, and the Tybrind Vig wooden paddles show us something quite new in the inventory of Ertebølle material culture. Fine basketry, netting, coarse textiles, rope and string have also been recovered and conserved; much use was made of willow bast and twigs for these, and their condition of preservation is good enough for details of the plaited ropes and not-quite-knitted textiles to be examined (*ill. 49*).

To return to fishing, equipment for catching the fish was varied. A trap of the lobster-pot type was woven out of split alder and viburnum twigs, and weighted down on the seabed with a stone. Fish nets may have been used, but only one wooden float was found. Leisters, in shape like those from Skjoldnaes, had prongs or barbs of hazel wood and some may have had a central bone point. Fishhooks were carved out of red-deer ribs and one had a fragment of line still attached, tied with what looks like a clove-hitch. The knot is at the front, and experimental fishing has shown that this helps the hook to stick firmly in the fish's jaw when it bites. The line is not animal gut but plant fibre, probably willow. A wooden hammer may have been used to despatch the fish once hooked and landed.

With boats, hook and line, traps, leisters and perhaps nets, the fishermen were set up to catch a range of species. Many fish bones have been identified from the site, including cod, herring and mackerel, salmon and eel, plaice or flounder and dab, and several small species that were not necessarily for consumption, such as stickleback, Black Goby and Broadnosed Pipefish. That people did eat fish is clear from two other sources of evidence. Pottery encrusted with burnt food was found and amidst the charred remains were bits of fishbone and scales, probably from cod, mixed up with grasses or herbs. Analysis of the C-13 content of the burnt food shows that it derived mainly from land sources, despite the bits of cod (a mainly marine source would have given a higher C-13 content). However, analysis of the skeleton of a young woman buried at Tybrind Vig shows a high level of C-13, indicating that she ate mostly seafood and her diet can only occasionally have included stews such as that burnt onto the pot.

Seafood includes mammals, birds and molluscs; seal, dolphin and whale were hunted, a few sea-birds such as pelican and guillemot were taken, and oysters, mussels, clams and winkles were collected. A few duck, goose and swan bones suggest some use of migrating waterfowl, but less perhaps than one might expect given the reed-fringed lagoon. Many bones of land-mammals have been

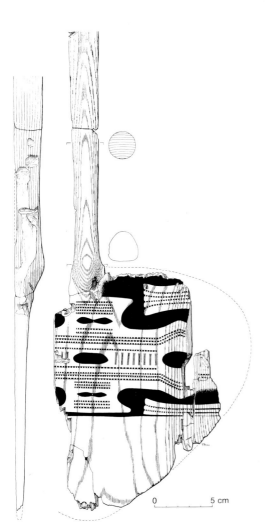

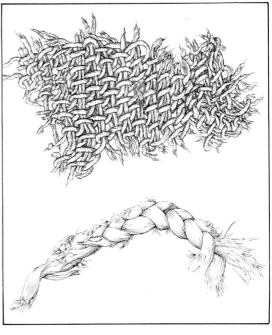

48, 49 **Artifacts from Tybrind Vig** (*Left*) One of the decorated paddles. (*Above*) Plant fibre textile and plaited fibre rope 8 cm long.

identified, some hunted to eat, like pig, deer and aurochs, and others such as fox, wildcat, otter and pine marten taken for their fur. The evidence for this distinction comes partly in the form of different arrowheads: sharp flint to wound and kill meat animals, in contrast to blunt wooden bolts to stun the furbearers without damage to their pelts. Moreover, the bones of the meat animals were found broken and scattered, indicating butchery, whereas bones of pine marten and other fur-bearers were found articulated, showing the whole carcass had been thrown out. Cut-marks on the skull indicate that the carcasses were skinned first.

Were the Tybrind Vig inhabitants permanent coastal dwellers? The question of whether or not they lived by the sea all year, or only seasonally, can now begin to be answered. We have seen that the young woman lived predominantly off a marine diet. Contemporary human and dog skeletons from inland settlements reveal a terrestrial diet. Only a very few bones have been analyzed in this way, but the results so far are consistent with a picture of distinct groups of coastal and

child

inland people. Certainly, Tybrind Vig was well-placed for people to find ample food most of the year, and the recovered evidence shows summer, autumn and winter presence at least. But this need not mean every summer, autumn and winter for 1,500 years, although that is not impossible. Sporadic visits at all seasons of the year or year-round settlement for a few years at a time should be considered, and perhaps there were always a few people around even if the bulk of the inhabitants shifted elsewhere from time to time. Any statement about the nature of occupation at Tybrind Vig must be speculative for the moment, but a brief look at other coastal sites may help to put it in context.

There are at least three other major Ertebølle sites in locations similar to that of Tybrind Vig: Ertebølle itself in North Jutland, Vedbaek on the east coast of Zealand and Skateholm on the south coast of Scania. None has the fascinating wealth of wooden artifacts found at Tybrind Vig, since all have risen in relation to sea level since the time of occupation, but all add to our knowledge of coastal Ertebølle settlement. In each case a sheltered bay or lagoon was the setting for several settlements, although generally only one site has been excavated and analyzed in detail as at Tybrind Vig. At Vedbaek and Skateholm, freshwater streams fed the lagoon. At Ertebølle, a small spring rose near the settlement and a large freshwater lake lay no more than 3 km to the south-east. Recent work at Ertebølle has shown that a surprising number of freshwater fish were caught and brought back to site, as well as the expected cod and plaice and herring. The same picture emerges from the Skateholm evidence, where two sites have been examined; people here were also keen fowlers, catching many species of duck and other waterfowl – only one quarter of the thirty-odd birds identified were land-based species. Mammals, as one might expect, were more often terrestrial, but all the sites show an interest in seal and porpoise, while otter and beaver represent freshwater habitats. Whether salt or fresh, watery environments were important sources of food, and may have enabled year-long settlement along the shores of bay or lagoon.

The woman buried at Tybrind Vig had a new-born baby with her. At Vedbaek and at Skateholm cemeteries have been found associated with the settlements, and the Tybrind Vig burial falls within the range of methods and types of burial found at these two sites (ill. 50). At Vedbaek, published by Albrethsen and Brinch Petersen, over 20 graves were identified and there were probably more. Skeletons were often well preserved and could be identified as those of old men and women, or young women with babies, or infants. One or two stand out for the light they appear to shed on the living. In Grave 8 at Vedbaek lay the skeleton of a young woman, about 18 years old. Perforated teeth and snail shells around her head and below her pelvis had probably been sewn as decoration on deerskin clothing, which had long since decayed. Beside her lay a baby, an 8–9 month foetus perhaps born prematurely. It lay on a swan's wing, with a flint blade by its pelvis. Red ochre was found around both skeletons. Grave 19 (ill. 50) contained 3 skeletons: 2 adults and an infant. Neither adult could be sexed, but the one on the right was 35–40 years old and had half a lower jaw of a pine marten, a few perforated animal teeth and rows of red deer teeth on its chest, items reminiscent of the ornaments found in other definitely female graves. This individual had a flint blade below its jaw, and perhaps had its throat cut. The second adult was younger, 25–30 years old, and had definitely been killed, for a bone point was lodged in its neck. The infant, about one year old, lay

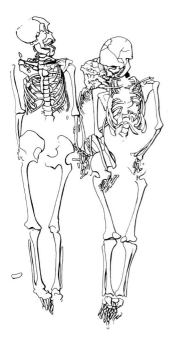

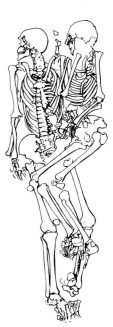

50 **Burials from Ertebølle sites**
(*Far left*) Burial of woman with baby
from Tybrind Vig. (*Left*) Triple burial
of two adults and an infant from
Vedbaek Grave 19. (*Right*) Double
burial of old man and young woman
from Skateholm I Grave 14.

between the two adults. The impression is of a family burial, though little firm
evidence exists for such an interpretation.

At Skateholm, recently excavated by Lars Larsson, there were two, if not
three, Late Mesolithic settlements and associated cemeteries. Skateholm I and
II were on adjacent small islands, the probable Skateholm III on a promontory
250 m to the west. Occupation began slightly later than at Tybrind Vig, and
lasted some 500 years, during which time there was a shift from Skateholm II to
Skateholm I. The burials excavated are more numerous and more diverse than
those from Vedbaek, though an overall similarity is clear. Of the 16 graves
identified at Skateholm II, 11 were fully investigated. Some contained the
skeletons of adults lying flat on their backs, and a few grave goods. In Grave IV
for example, a man had been buried in a wood or bark coffin along with 2 stone
axe-heads, a bone harpoon head, 4 blades, assorted other stones and a bone
needle. Grave X was more unusual to our eyes: in it were the skeletons of two
men side by side and facing each other, one lying flat and the other seated with
his legs stretched out in front of him. The seated man had beads made of red
deer, wild boar and elk-teeth around his neck, chest, hips, thighs and lower
limbs, probably sewn on to leather clothing as with the Vedbaek woman. A piece
of worked bone lay on his skull. The other man had a flint blade, a pecked stone, a
boar's tusk, an arrowhead and a single pierced animal tooth. The body in Grave
VIII had a large, decapitated dog at its feet.

The cemetery at Skateholm I reminds us that these people were fishers, for
here a 35–40-year-old woman was buried sitting, her hands in her lap on which
lay the skeleton of a premature baby and about 30 boar's tusks whilst by her right
calf was a concentration of bones from roach, rudd and stickleback. The
fishbones are hardly the most spectacular aspects of this burial, however, and it is
noteworthy that recognizable fishing equipment figures in none of the
Skateholm burials. Fifty-two other graves have been examined at Skateholm I.

Seven were for dogs which were buried lying on their sides with their legs bent, some being strewn with red ochre. People were usually buried flat, or on their sides with legs bent, although one man was buried face down and several were sitting. Grave 14 was a double burial, of a 50-year-old man and a 17–19-year-old woman on her side, legs bent over his thighs (*ill. 50*). Grave 41 also contained 2 skeletons, one an adult, probably male, lying on its side with legs and arms bent, hands at face level; a child's skeleton lay below the adult's arms, in a similar position but facing the adult, and with varied grave goods including 4 pieces of pierced amber, a flint knife and a bone point and 2 pierced bear-teeth. The majority of the burials were of single adults, like the tightly flexed elderly woman in Grave 26 or the cremated man in Grave 11. Grave goods were found mostly with old men or young women, and not with 20–40 year olds of either sex. This strikes a chord with the apparent situation at Vedbaek, where few 20–40 year olds were buried whereas a number of young women were found, as well as old people of either sex, and the old people tended to have distinctive grave goods, especially red deer antlers. Tybrind Vig fits the pattern, insofar as a single grave can be said to do so, with the double burial of a young woman and a new-born baby.

The Ertebølle coastal-dwellers are unusual amongst European hunter-fishers in having recognizable cemeteries and in living what was possibly a relatively settled life. The two factors may well be connected, and linked to the exploitation of particularly rich and varied environments in and around sheltered lagoons. Further affluence may have come from trade of fish, fur and fowl with the farmers who were by now settled in the lands to the south.

Britain

In northern Britain the land mass has risen since the retreat of the ice, and Late Mesolithic shorelines are now above sea-level. Coastal settlements of the period have been left high and dry, just as the site of Ertebølle was in North Jutland. At Morton, on the east coast of Scotland, a midden full of bone and shell provided evidence for the exploitation of sea and shore and estuary. Many species of mollusc, seabird and fish were eaten, along with various land animals. Middens on the island of Oronsay, over on the west coast, show a similar, sea-orientated economy. But neither site is a Tybrind Vig with waterlogged wood, nor has any such site been discovered in southern Britain, where, in theory, the chance of survival should be high thanks to rising sea levels. However, the coasts of south Wales, the Bristol Channel and the south-west may yield well-preserved wet Mesolithic sites one day, for scattered evidence is known. This includes a midden at Westward Ho! off the north Devon coast, and footprints in the mud off the south coast of Wales near Newport, the mud being of Mesolithic age. There are both animal and human prints, walking away from Wales into the Bristol channel. It is probable that there is more evidence, sealed under later deposits and not currently exposed by erosion.

Along the east coast of England, from Hartlepool Bay to the Thames estuary, the archaeological record runs from the Late Mesolithic onwards. There are settlements and other sites, and stray finds, associated with ancient coastal marshes and tidal creeks. The rise in sea level was not always steady, but in general there is evidence for increasing salinity through time, as the salt waters

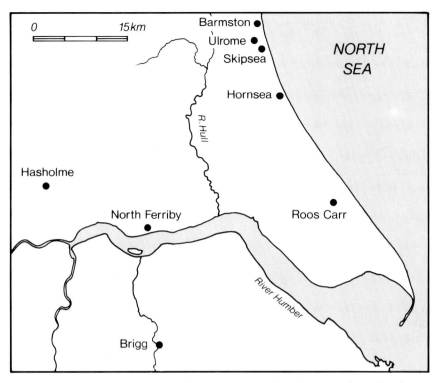

51, 52   Maps of the east coast of England, showing sites mentioned in the
text (*Above*) Humberside and East Yorkshire. (*Below*) Essex.

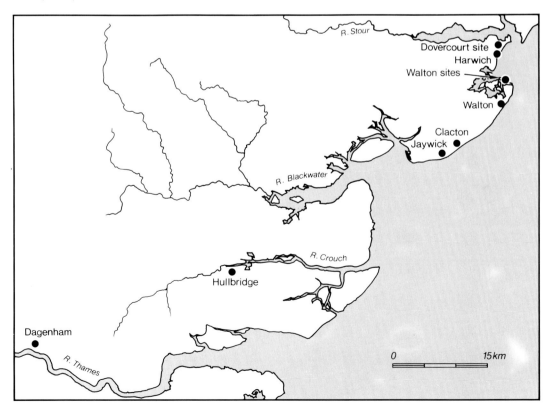

pushed further inland. In Holderness (*ill. 51*), the coastal region north of the Humber, a series of freshwater meres were protected from the sea by land barriers, but their water levels reacted to the changing sea level, and southern Holderness was interfingered with tidal creeks draining into the Humber. The best-known evidence from these wetlands is described in Chapter 6: the Brigg, Ferriby and Hasholme boats and the carved wooden figures from Roos Carr. These all come from probably tidal waters.

Less well known is the prehistoric settlement evidence from Barmston and Ulrome, just north of Skipsea. In the 1880s workmen cleaning drains around Ulrome came across wood, which Boynton, one of the Drainage Commissioners, examined. He identified two settlements, one at West Furze and one at Round Hill. R. A. Smith of the British Museum, who visited the sites and published them in 1911 as 'Lake-Dwellings in Holderness', reported an area of horizontal timbers 50 × 70 ft (*c.*16 × 23 m) at West Furze, and definite rows of vertical piles. There were apparently two distinct phases, the lower one associated with flints and attributed to the Stone Age and the upper one, where a bronze spearhead was found, not unnaturally thought to be Bronze Age. A difference was noted in the woodworking techniques of the two phases. At Round Hill there were fewer piles and less regular arrangements of timber, and much charred wood. Many flints were found, and a polished stone axe, a jet armlet and a macehead with an hourglass perforation. This evidence could represent the remains of a burnt Late Neolithic settlement.

Smith noted three other possible settlements in the region and one of these, Barmston, was examined by Varley in the early 1960s. His report describes a cobbled floor and a quantity of collapsed timber to one side of it, two hearths and what may have been a cooking pit. Varley interpreted birch-bark sheets three layers thick and separated by birch twigs as walling, and the timber suggested to him a rectangular house about 18 ft long and 12 ft wide (6 × 4 m) with a pitched roof and gable ends. The cobbled floor was outside one end of the house. Other worked wood, post-holes and probable cooking pits were noted in the area, enough to suggest a small hamlet. Radiocarbon dates place it around 1300 BC and environmental evidence indicates that the hamlet, if such it was, lay in a marshy hollow surrounded by fenwood. In due course the settlement was overwhelmed by peat, and there is some slight evidence for later, Iron Age activity.

The evidence for settlement from northern Holderness thus spans the later prehistoric period. None of it is very clear, not even that from the most recent investigations by Dave Gilbertson around Skipsea Withow, although his work has underlined the wet, marshy nature of the area. Regrettably, there is virtually no information about subsistence and we cannot tell how far people exploited the great diversity of wetland environments that lay within easy reach of their homes.

In the early 1900s, when Smith was publishing the Holderness sites, Hazzledine Warren began fieldwork along the Essex coast (*ill. 52*). He was joined in the 1930s by Piggott, Clark, Burkitt and both Godwins, a formidable team. Now, half-a-century on, their work is being continued by Murphy and Wilkinson with the Hullbridge Basin survey. The earlier team concentrated on the coast from Harwich to Clacton, whereas the present work focuses on the estuaries between Clacton and the Thames; it will be simplest to consider the two areas separately, although their past histories have much in common.

The finds made by Hazzledine Warren and the Essex Coast Sub-Committee of the Fenland Research Committee, namely his 1930s colleagues, ranged from the Palaeolithic to the Early Bronze Age. They were able to demonstrate that finds of Neolithic and Early Bronze Age date were *in situ* on an old land surface, Hazzledine Warren's 'Lyonnesse' surface. This was subsequently buried by thick layers of peat which formed when the land turned to salt marsh and then by clay as the rising sea submerged the area. The old land surface stayed safely buried for many centuries until tidal action began to expose and erode it, together with associated features and artifacts. Finds were concentrated in three areas, at Clacton, at Walton and at Dovercourt.

At Clacton the evidence stretched along the coast for nearly 2 miles (3.2 km). Early Neolithic pottery and flints were found associated with a 'pit-dwelling' and a cooking-hole. Pottery of the Late Neolithic was recognized and described for the first time by Stuart Piggott, who called it Grooved Ware; it came to be called Rinyo-Clacton ware after this site and one in Scotland but is now once more generally known as Grooved Ware. It was also associated with a 'pit-dwelling' and 23 cooking-holes spread over 150 yards. Another pit-dwelling had abundant remains of wood and bone and sherds from both round-based and Beaker pottery, and a cooking hole with Beaker sherds. Two wooden paddles with knife-like blades were found, one definitely in the occupation layer and therefore probably of Neolithic or Early Bronze Age date. At Dovercourt, pottery and flint of Early Neolithic and Beaker date were recorded.

At Walton, more Early Neolithic and Beaker pottery and flints were found, and a fair amount of evidence for wooden structures. There was a rectangular building with horizontal beams on the ground and the stumps of vertical posts. Nearby a heavy beam with a mortise hole at one end was pegged down, perhaps the door sill of another house, and remains of interlaced small boughs must surely have been hurdle-work, used either for house walls or for pathways on a wet surface. A small dugout canoe was apparently exposed and carried away on the tide before any details were recorded, a vivid illustration of the problems of survey in an intertidal zone. Hazzledine Warren called it 'snatch and grab' archaeology, and reckoned the difficulties were well-compensated for by the undisturbed nature of the sites and the preservation of unexpected evidence such as burnt food in a cooking-pot.

Hazzledine Warren noted another type of feature on the Clacton foreshore, parallel straight trenches about 100 yards apart, 3 ft deep and 6 ft wide (1 × 2 m) covered by the peat which sealed the old land surface. He found occasional sherds in the trenches, none later than Beaker in date. In one area, two sets were noted at right angles to each other. Discussion with C. W. Phillips led to comparison with the rectangular enclosures revealed by aerial photography in the Upper Thames and Welland valleys, enclosures which Leeds had dated to the Neolithic or Early Bronze Age. Between them, in the 1930s, these archaeologists had established the antiquity of regular field systems, but it was to be 40 years or so before the archaeological world in general recognized them.

The Hullbridge survey is still in progress, and it is too soon to give a detailed account of the prehistory of the area from Clacton round to the Thames estuary. There is varied evidence for settlement ranging from Mesolithic sites on what was then dry land, through Neolithic sites on the banks of tidal streams and rivers to marshy, estuarine Bronze Age sites. One of the Bronze Age sites was a causeway or jetty associated with an oyster bed, and a second was a salt-making site dated to about 1300 BC. A third site produced evidence for collection of oysters, mussels and cockles. All told, the Bronze Age people appear to have been true coastal dwellers, using marshland, creek and estuary for food and for salt production. Later, in the Late Iron Age and Romano-British period, salt production seems to have been a major industry but settlement itself was located inland. Increasing specialization in the use of coastal resources is a phenomenon which can also be seen in the evidence from the Netherlands and north Germany, which we shall turn to next.

North European coastal Neolithic

The inhabitants of much of the Low Countries or Netherlands were, until quite recently, wetlanders *par excellence*. Since the Middle Ages they have attempted to protect land from sea, with some success, although the sea has always been liable to reclaim its territory and did so with a vengeance in the disastrous floods of 1953. The wetlands of the hinterland have, not surprisingly, a different history of settlement and land-use from that of the slightly higher and drier parts of the country (although they too have their peatbogs, see Chapter 6), and the history of preservation, discovery and archaeological investigation has also differed. In the coastal regions, considerable research has been carried out in recent decades, partly to understand better the vagaries of sea-level change in order to protect against it, and partly to recover and record archaeological and palaeo-environmental evidence before it became desiccated and disappeared in the wake of increasingly effective drainage schemes.

The marshes, estuaries and tidal creeks of the coastal Netherlands (*ill. 53*) were latecomers to farming. The loess soils of the upland were colonized at an early stage, by 5000 BC, while the wetland areas remained for another 2,000 years or so the province of people who, in the words of Leendert Louwe Kooijmans, were 'semi-agrarian' at most, and who had much in common with the Late Mesolithic peoples of southern Scandinavia and north Germany.

Their world was one of water, vegetated water, broken by the sinuous lines of the raised banks that followed rivers and creeks. Tidal influence reached far inland, causing freshwater creeks to rise and fall by as much as a metre. The banks or levees that bounded the watercourses were covered with alder, and oak and other deciduous trees on the drier parts. Behind them was more water, the back swamp, where reeds and other marsh vegetation might grow. Occasionally, a relic sand dune stood out, a rare island of sandy dry soils. Inland were great peatbogs cut by creeks and rivers; seawards lay salt marshes and a narrow belt of coastal sand dunes. The systems of creeks, levees and backwaters underwent many changes as the sea level fluctuated and wet phases were separated by phases of brushwood growth and peat formation. Archaeological evidence for human occupation of the area would seem to be associated with intermediate wet phases. This may simply be when the evidence had a chance of being preserved, but it may also be a true reflection of when people were attracted by the resources of the area.

'Semi-agrarian' settlement is apparent at two recently excavated sites, Hazendonk and Swifterbant. At Swifterbant, a complex of river dunes and old creek levees was occupied, a number of relatively small occupation areas being

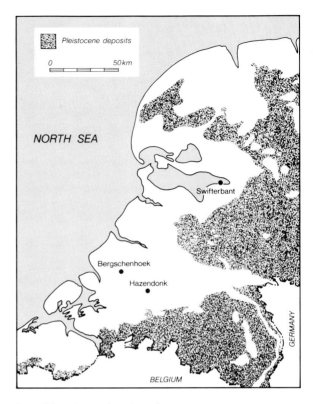

53 Map of the Netherlands to show
coastal Neolithic sites mentioned in the
text. The Pleistocene deposits represent
dry land, with the sites in the coastal
wetlands.

settled for a generation or so at a time. Bundles of brushwood and reeds were
used to raise the ground surface, and thin stakes and posts suggest that light
shelters were built. Clay hearths were made, in true wetland tradition, and
renewed on the same spot over the years. Fish, fur and fowl are well represented
in the bone refuse, indicating that wild resources were important. Amongst the
species taken were land animals such as deer, aurochs and brown bear, the elk
which likes water and dives to graze bottom-growing lake vegetation, and otter
and beaver which are both aquatic. Cormorant, swan, crane, duck and white-
tailed sea eagle along with fish such as sturgeon, salmon, mullet and catfish,
underline the wealth of water resources available, and a number of these species
are at home in coastal, brackish and freshwater conditions. Many wild plants
were collected. The 'agrarian' side of the economy is represented by bones of
domestic cattle and pig, and charred grain and chaff from barley and wheat.
Because all parts of the animals' skeleton were found, and because chaff was
present on the site, it seems at first sight that the inhabitants were themselves
farming. However, the presence of stone axes, and of pottery not unlike that of
the Danish Ertebølle groups, shows contact did take place with other peoples.
There was very little land at Swifterbant suitable for cultivation, and possibly
the levees and dunes were too wet in winter for any sort of occupation, so maybe
the inhabitants moved elsewhere for a season and traded for meat on the hoof and
unthreshed cereals. Both types of food would keep well this way.

Hazendonk (*ill. 54*) was a small sand dune, about 1.2 hectares or 3 acres in
extent when it was settled a century or so before 4000 BC. The inhabitants did not
clear all the forest on the dune, so there can have been little room for fields, and
apparently little or no dryland nearby which could have been used to grow crops.
Here too the cereals which were found may have been imported, along with

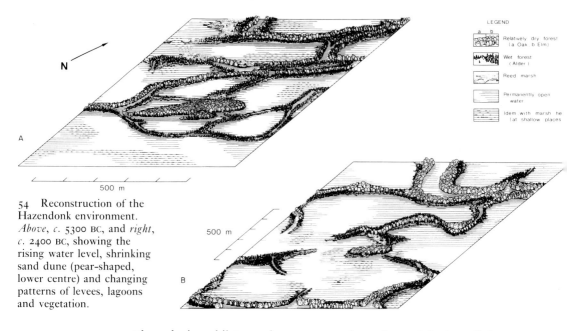

LEGEND

a	b	
		Relatively dry forest (a Oak b Elm)
		Wet forest (Alder)
		Reed marsh
		Permanently open water
		Idem with marsh he [at shallow places

500 m

54 Reconstruction of the Hazendonk environment. *Above*, *c.* 5300 BC, and *right*, *c.* 2400 BC, showing the rising water level, shrinking sand dune (pear-shaped, lower centre) and changing patterns of levees, lagoons and vegetation.

500 m

cattle and pig, whilst people concentrated on the exploitation of the water resources all around them. A single household could have farmed the dune, with a cleared patch for crops, another patch for grazing, an area of forest for browze and pannage and fuel, and ample vegetation on the levees to help feed the cattle. The spread of settlement refuse on the dune suggests, however, that more than one household lived there, in which case cultivation of more than a kitchen garden becomes unlikely. In time, local water-levels rose and the sand dune decreased considerably in size, making local cultivation ever more unlikely an option for the successive Neolithic inhabitants of Hazendonk.

At a third site of this Early Neolithic period, Bergschenhoek, farming does not even enter into the question, for Bergschenhoek was a tiny floating island of peat, most of which was taken up with a 3 × 4 m living platform. The platform consisted of reeds, boards and small trees, and in the centre was a hearth which had been refurbished eleven times. The evidence points to short winter visits to the site for about a decade, and the location of the island near the shore of a reed-fringed lake was apparently ideal for fishing and fowling and hunting aquatic mammals, many of which would live in brackish and fresh waters. Grey seal and otter were taken, perhaps for their skins; catfish, eel, perch, carp, roach, bream and tench were caught, no doubt to eat. Three beautifully preserved fish traps were found on the site, woven out of slender dogwood stems (*ill. 55*). Cut-off dogwood root systems indicated that the traps were made on the site. The waterfowl included winter migrants such as Bewick's swan, goosander, goldeneye and widgeon, and eider duck which would only have come to such a location in very severe winters, hence the interpretation of the site as a winter camp. Pottery similar to that from Hazendonk was found, and a fragment of a polished stone axe, making contact with Neolithic peoples likely, if the Bergschenhoek inhabitants were not themselves farmers having a winter break in the marshes.

A thousand or more years later, at the close of the Neolithic, pottery styles and stone tools had changed, and the marsh dwellers were making and using artifacts which prehistorians have termed Vlaardingen. Settlement and economy were

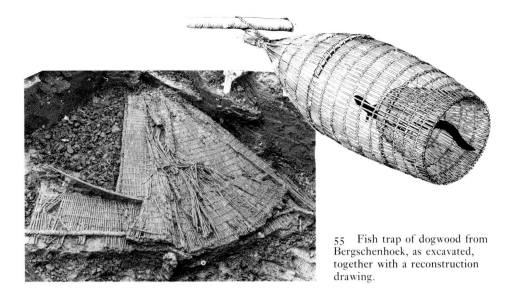

55   Fish trap of dogwood from Bergschenhoek, as excavated, together with a reconstruction drawing.

much as before, and underline how strongly the environment of estuarine marshes governed the possibilities for human settlement and subsistence. Early Neolithic sites like Swifterbant and Hazendonk have Vlaardingen occupation too, for dry land was scarce and used for settlement whenever water levels were low enough. Evidence for cultivation is slight, for wild foods ample, and once again the questions are raised of traded versus home-grown cereals and seasonal versus year-round occupation for the sites on river dunes and levees between creek and backswamp. In this environment, little had changed. But in the salt marshes and amongst the coastal dunes and on the river clays and peats inland, Vlaardingen settlements were to be found, with an established farming economy, or at least good evidence for domestic animals. These were the pioneers of wetland farming in the region, where attempts to control the landscape were to lead, over the following centuries, to increasing specialization of both environment and economy. In the process, the rich and varied wetlands were to disappear.

Later prehistory

As in earlier periods, the sea-level fluctuations of the first millennium BC and the early centuries AD had a direct effect on the settlement and exploitation of coastal marshes, estuaries and inter-tidal regions. Several regions of the Netherlands and north Germany have been intensively studied for this period; results from at least one of them, the Assendelver Polders which lie about halfway between Amsterdam and the sea, illustrate the fluidity of a landscape where any one spot might undergo a succession of diverse wetland environments through the centuries, and at any one time most of these environments could be found somewhere within the region.

The Assendelver Polders Project has shown that as sea-levels fell relative to land in the 9th century BC, people moved in to the emerging marshes, at first probably to gather wild foods but increasingly to find summer grazing for their animals. By 800 BC they were settling on the driest land available, often the levees

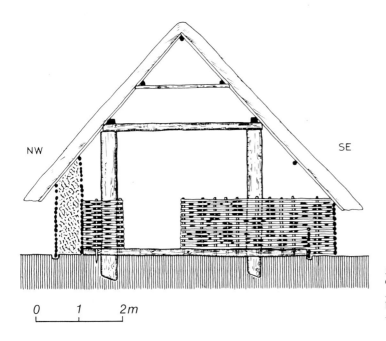

NW

SE

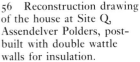

56 Reconstruction drawing
of the house at Site Q,
Assendelver Polders, post-
built with double wattle
walls for insulation.

0   1   2m

of tidal creeks. To the east of them at this time were peatbogs, to the west salt marsh and tidal flats with sand dunes beyond. One settlement of this period which has been excavated, Site Q, consists of a single building, a little over 18 m long and 6 m wide, set on a relatively dry hillock of peat (*ill. 56*). One end of the building was partitioned off for people, with a sleeping area at the far end. The remaining two thirds was divided into stalls, a row down either wall, with a centre aisle and drain; there was room for about 14 cattle and the same number of sheep or goats. Some interesting differences were noted in the woods used in building: oak posts and willow and alder wattle walls for people, ash posts and alder, ash and birch wattle for their animals. Perhaps the idea was to keep the cows from nibbling willow bark, which is not good for their milk.

Much animal dung was preserved, containing identifiable plant remains. These enabled the eating habits of the animals to be reconstructed to a certain extent, and moreover showed that goats rather than sheep were present since bog myrtle was identified, a pungent shrub which sheep will not eat. The goats seem to have been pastured on the fairly dry peat bog, whilst the cattle were grazing a range of freshwater and brackish marshy areas and damp grasslands. It is probable that small areas of land were suitable for cultivation, and that gold-of-pleasure (*camelina sativa*) was grown, a crop with seeds rich in edible oil. Barley and other cereals are more likely to have been imported. Given the restrictions on arable farming in such an environment, and the slight evidence for the exploitation of wild resources, domestic animals must always have been the mainstay of subsistence. The settlement was short-lived, occupied only for one or two generations before rising water-levels drove the inhabitants away.

The increased wetness was general, and several centuries were to pass before people once more settled the region. They did so at a time when much of the coastal and estuarine marshland of the Netherlands and North Germany was occupied intensively for the first time. Water was never far off, as Pliny's evocative description of the setting makes clear (Chapter 2); low platforms or mounds of turf were made to raise houses and other farm buildings above the

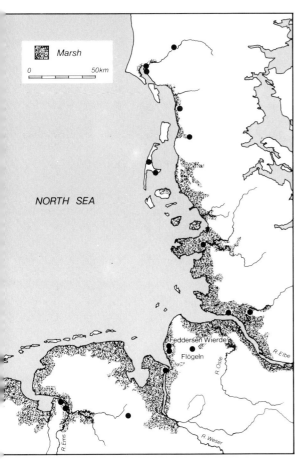

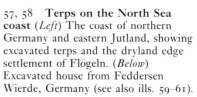

57, 58 **Terps on the North Sea coast** (*Left*) The coast of northern Germany and eastern Jutland, showing excavated terps and the dryland edge settlement of Flögeln. (*Below*) Excavated house from Feddersen Wierde, Germany (see also ills. 59–61).

Marsh

0   50km

NORTH SEA

Feddersen Wierde
Flögeln

R. Ems
R. Oste
R. Elbe
R. Weser

floodwaters. These mounds are known as 'wierde', 'wurt' and 'terp'; archaeologists speak of the settlements as 'terps' or 'terpen' and one of the best known is Ezinge, investigated by Van Giffen several decades ago (Chapter 2).

Feddersen Wierde was selected in the mid-1950s as a terp where conditions of preservation appeared good, and excavation from 1955 to 1963 showed that this was indeed the case (*ill. 57, ill. 58*). Ample evidence was found to reconstruct the history of the settlement in the flat salt marshes north of Bremerhaven and the Weser estuary, an area where the Iron Age terps were to be found 1–2 km apart. The site lay on an elevated levee and adjacent clay deposits which formed an island of about 6 hectares in extent, lying between two creeks. In the 1st century BC 5 farmsteads were built on the island, each consisting of a long building and a small square building and all orientated in the same direction (*ill. 59*). In time this settlement layout expanded to 11 farmsteads. In the 1st and 2nd centuries AD a change came with rising water-levels. Each farmstead was raised on its own terp, surrounded by a fence and ditch, and the 15 farmsteads of the village were arranged radially around a central open area. Roads and paths led out from the centre, past the farmsteads and down into the marshes. By the 3rd century AD the individual terps had been merged into one large raised area, with only slight divisions between the individual farms. There were at this stage some 39 buildings, and one cluster stands out as a possible chief's house with craft workshops nearby. After this, the settlement shrank, houses became smaller, and as the rising sea-level rendered fields and pasture useless Feddersen Wierde was abandoned, some time in the 5th century AD.

The long buildings housed people and animals, and the smaller square buildings were probably granaries or some other form of store. By the time buildings radiated around the central area, longhouses of varying size and perhaps of variable function were being built (*ill. 60*). The basic design was very similar to that of the Assendelver Site Q building, namely a long rectangular structure divided into a short domestic end and a longer byre or stable end with stalls and drains. There was a fireplace in the middle of the domestic quarters and possible sleeping areas; at the top end of the stable part was a wide transverse passage with doors to the outside and some suggestion that this was a working area. The stall-aisle opened off the transverse passage, and a large house might have seven or eight stalls down each wall. Sometimes there were two larger pens at the end, for keeping horses or several small sheep and goats, whereas the stalls were probably for cattle, tethered individually or in pairs. To give an idea of overall dimensions, the domestic end might be 9 × 6 m, the working area 3 × 6 m and the byre 12 × 6 m, a relatively generous provision of housing for man and beast. Small houses had not dissimilar domestic areas to the big long houses, but much curtailed byres, perhaps with only two or three stalls set against the end wall, opening directly onto the cross passage. Wattlework was used extensively for walls and partitions, a reminder that all the heavier building wood had to be imported.

The possible chief's house was long and without any transverse walls or stalls or drains, but seemed to have been lived in. A second similar building with little occupation evidence was thought to be a meeting house. Craftsmen's houses or workshops were nearby, for example a blacksmith's, along with one or two ordinary farms to make a viable economic unit. Imports, including Roman objects, reinforce the idea of chief or headman's house and dependencies.

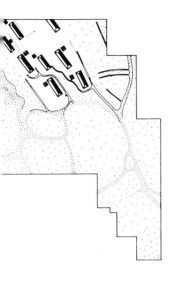

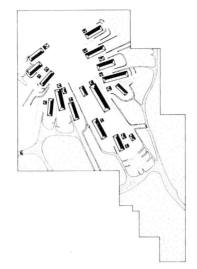

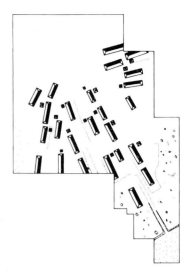

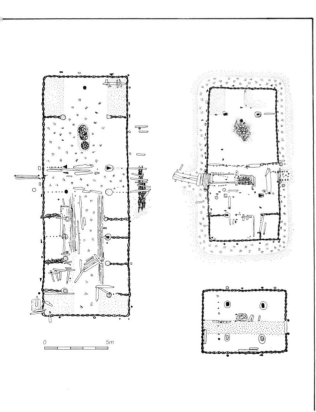

59–61   The terp of Feddersen Wierde
(*Above*) The development of the
settlement from the 1st century BC to the
5th century AD. (*Left*) Three different
structures at the site. Far left, house with
living area, cross passage and long stalled
end. Near left, house with living area,
cross passage and short stall end. Lower
left, smaller structure without stalls.
(*Below*) Heap of half-finished lathe-turned
wooden bowls from a workshop at the
site.

Various crafts were practised by the inhabitants, who worked in bone, horn and antler, clay, bronze, iron, wool and wood. The discovery of a heap of half-finished wooden bowls (*ill. 61*) and evidence for a local wheel-wright may seem odd, given the shortage of wood growing naturally in the vicinity, but if timber was imported for buildings then no doubt the quantities needed for making artifacts could easily be brought in as well.

Animal bones were preserved in the terp, and of 70,000 recovered in the excavation, 60,000 were identified. Cattle accounted for half the animals, sheep or goats for a quarter and horse and pig for the remainder along with a few dogs. Three-quarters of the cows lived long enough to give milk, but 40 per cent of the horses were killed as foals, presumably for meat. Sheep were kept to a good age, and provided wool. Based on the number of stalls in the village in any one phase, the size of the winter herd can be estimated. In the 1st century BC there was byre-space for 100 animals, and by the 3rd century AD 450 animals could be sheltered, whereas a century later, with shrinking fields and pastures, the byre-space had been cut back to 240 animals. Less than 1 per cent of the identified bones came from wild animals.

What seemed to be kitchen gardens, or vegetable plots, were found on the terp, and some evidence for ploughed fields, although these were never extensive. About half the crop was cereals, barley and oats, a quarter beans and a quarter oil-yielding flax and gold-of-pleasure. There is no suggestion that wild plants were important to subsistence.

Feddersen Wierde and contemporary terps can be seen as highly specialized adaptations to the wide expanse of coastal marshland, exploiting the land primarily through grazing and surviving through the exchange of surplus animal products such as butter and cheese, woollens and hides, for necessities such as building timber and luxuries such as Roman pottery. There are one or two points to note here. The first emerges by comparison with contemporary Iron Age inland settlements such as Flögeln, a village on a large sandy island surrounded by peatbogs. Houses were similar to but longer than those from the terps, and included byres for domestic animals, from which it would seem that the inland villages had no need to trade for meat and milk and the like. They did, on the other hand, export timber and iron ore and millstones to the terps, so how did the latter manage to acquire these? In general, the terps close to the sea kept more sheep than their contemporaries elsewhere, profiting perhaps from salt marsh pastures free of liver fluke and known for tender, tasty lamb. But cattle were more important to the terp economies, judging by byre space and the identified bones from Feddersen Wierde. If there was no market for their surplus in the inland hamlets and villages, it was perhaps to the Roman world that people exported. The Roman army was not that far away, and is well-known to have been a great consumer of food and leather and woollens. It may even be that the rise and fall of the terps was governed by Roman military needs as well as by the fluctuations of the sea. As a final comment, terp life was probably a good life, for the density of settlement was more than twice that known from the sandy inland soils.

In this brief survey of the coastal settlements of the Netherlands and North Germany, much has had to be omitted. Contrasts between early and late sites are partly false, ignoring the developments and reversals of intermediate stages. Yet a general trend can be observed in the way people exploited the coastal marshes through the centuries from the Early Neolithic to the Late Iron Age. Initially, an enormous variety of wild foods was taken, virtually every sort of plant and beast that was present in salt, brackish and fresh waters. Gradually farming crept in, at first with traded crops and animals and then with small-scale cultivation alongside the use of wild resources. In due course self-sufficient farming communities emerged, importing no food and taking little or nothing from the wild. The last centuries of prehistory saw specialization in one aspect of farming, stock-keeping, together with a little arable cultivation. Heavy grazing probably reduced the ecological diversity of the coastal zones and in particular hindered forest regeneration in the wake of the retreating seas. By farming, people were creating a landscape where dependence on wild foods was no longer possible even if desired; the lack of evidence for fishing in environments where there were surely still fish in quantity, suggests the farmers were happy to rely on their stock. Given that the sea, each time that it encroached on the land and then retreated, presented people with a fresh marshland environment, varying in its detail but broadly similar through time taking the region as a whole, the changing exploitation of the area was probably influenced more by people's cultural perceptions, and by the effects of their actions on the environment, than by purely environmental constraints and opportunities.

4 · Pioneers of the inland waters

THE RETREATING ICE-SHEETS of the last glacial period had an enormous influence on sea-level and coastlines, and in their wake they left many inland bodies of water. A geologist or geographer would define numerous different forms, and for our present purpose, it is necessary to distinguish at least two different freshwater environments. The first consists of large, deep and permanent lakes whose outline today may not be very different from that of the early postglacial period. Sedimentary studies indicate that water levels have fluctuated over the centuries, sometimes higher and sometimes lower than the present, without there being any consensus of opinion on the reasons for the fluctuations. The expanse of water is large enough to have a small ameliorating effect on the regional climate, which could encourage settlement. Marginal zones, wetlands between the water and the dryland, may be quite narrow, perhaps no more than the zone covered by seasonal fluctuations in lake level. In some cases, local topography allows for a wider wetland margin, and its maximum extent may well be found around the outlet of the lake. The second form of inland freshwater lake is shallow, and probably much smaller in extent today than when it formed as the ice sheets retreated. The separation of land and water is not as clear cut as with the deep lakes, and there may well be a wide wetland margin which extends onto dryland in flood-times and which over the centuries colonizes the water until, in some cases, what was once a lake is completely filled with sediments, peat and vegetation.

People living on or near the lakes and marshes had access to both dryland and wetland resources. The diversity of species varied from place to place, but one or two general points should be noted. In marshy zones, reeds and rushes provided material for thatch, matting and baskets, and willow was an ideal source of twigs for basketwork. The carr woodlands which colonized nutrient-rich marshes as they dried a little would have been home to nettles, another source of fibre (for textiles, not dietary!). Wetlands may therefore have been regarded as good sources of plant materials for making things.

In terms of edible plants the wetlands themselves were no more attractive than many a dryland environment, except perhaps where the water chestnut, *Trapa natans*, flourished. Shelled, pounded and cooked, the water chestnut could provide an equivalent to flour for people who did not grow cereals and a supplement for those who did, such as the Neolithic inhabitants of Robenhausen and Laibach Moor (Chapter 1).

Edible and useful animals were many. In the early centuries of the postglacial period, temperatures rose rapidly but it took a while for freshwater fish to colonize the newly-available lakes, simply because their routes were restricted. During glaciation, pike survived further north than other species, and they clearly flourished as the waters warmed up, although one wonders what there was at first for these carnivorous fish to eat. Each other maybe, since they are cannibal. Waters linked to the Rhone and the Danube, and hence to southern and warmer regions, acquired populations of other freshwater species of fish with relative ease. Isolated lakes and those linked to rivers draining into northern waters, like the Rhine and Scandinavian and British rivers, may have had an impoverished fish fauna for several millennia, just greedy pike waiting to gobble any new arrival, and the anadromous eel, sea trout and salmon which migrate between fresh and salt waters. All these, fortunately, are good fish to eat.

Edible reptiles and amphibians were available, including the European Pond Tortoise which was found well to the north during the climatic optimum of the Atlantic period (c.6000–3000 BC depending on location). Numerous frog-leg bones fron Clairvaux in eastern France suggest that some gastronomic preferences were established as early as the Neolithic.

As for waterfowl, they could spread quickly northwards, stimulated perhaps by the seasonal migration patterns of many species. Some species occur locally all year round, others appear briefly in vast numbers as they move from north to south, others settle for a season to breed or feed. Shallow lakes with well-vegetated margins and large expanses of wet marshy ground would have seen the most birds. All sorts and sizes feature in the archaeological record, from crane, swan and goose to a multitude of small duck.

Mammals may not move as quickly as birds, and only a few species are truly aquatic, but they too were soon present in abundance in and around wetlands. The largest was the elk, a denizen of light woodland cover and marshland, fond of water, a good swimmer, grazing on aquatic vegetation. Aurochs (wild cattle) and red deer, would also venture into water, and were attracted by marshland grazing, although not quite as at home in the wet as the elk. Wild pig may have been particularly common in the warmer marshland regions. All these mammals were hunted for their meat, and for their various antlers, horns, tusks, teeth, bone, hair and skin which were put to good use by the people who caught them. Amongst smaller wetland mammals, beaver and otter were hunted, both having fine pelts, and the beaver a tasty tail, as well as sharp incisor teeth which made a useful tool. The vegetarian beaver colonized northern latitudes before the otter, which eats fish and which moved into northern freshwaters only when its food supply had arrived.

The attraction of freshwater wetlands is evident in the antiquity of the archaeological record for human settlement in lake margins and in marshland. Olduvai Gorge, that most famous of early sites in Africa, was not a gorge but a lake margin when the Australopithecines and *Homo habilis* lived there over 1 million years ago and foraged and perhaps fished the lake waters. In Europe, early sites at Bilzingsleben in East Germany and Hoxne in England were both in or near wetlands inhabited by the ancestors of modern people. At Hoxne, the group who lived along the lakeshore may have been fishing, and perhaps had nets or some sort of trap in the water to catch the prey. Later, during the last glaciation, some of the most spectacular Upper Palaeolithic sites are to be found on the rivers of southwestern France. Admittedly not waterlogged sites, the caves of the Dordogne and the Vézère nevertheless demonstrate an interest in the exploitation of water resources, and part of the wealth of Upper Palaeolithic cave art may stem from the secure food supply that was available in the rivers. Salmon and allied species were present in these more southern latitudes.

At High Furlong in Lancashire the skeleton of an elk was found embedded in Late Glacial peaty muds; two barbed bone points were associated with the skeleton, there were a number of lesions on the bones, and the condition of the antlers indicated that the animal had died in winter. It has been suggested that the elk was hunted one winter during a warm interstadial period at the end of the last ice age. The animal escaped, although with a bone point lodged in its left lower hind leg. A few weeks later, judging by the degree of healing, the elk was again attacked by hunters who wounded it around the chest and front legs, but the animal once more eluded them and escaped either by deliberately diving into a lake or running out over the winter ice which gave way. Elk are strong swimmers, but the crippled animal was too weak and it drowned. Its body decayed but the skeleton lay protected and preserved in the lake sediments for thousands of years. In time, the sediments dried out or were drained, the lake disappeared, and the dryland was cultivated and then taken for housing. In 1970, excavations for house foundations led to the discovery of the skeleton.

The economic wealth of fens and swamps would appear to have been exploited by early peoples in all continents. Kuk Swamp in Papua New Guinea is a valley-floor wetland where plant domestication and swamp cultivation is attested some 9,000 years ago, evidence for some of the earliest such horticulture in the world. The site also revealed successive phases of more elaborate systems of agriculture, and these involved the first efforts at wetland drainage. Other work in the region has concentrated on fringe grasslands at Ruti where prehistoric stone tools provided a hint of ancient activity. Excavation revealed a complex of low mounds, basins and ditches which probably date to 5,000–6,000 years ago: the swamp was partly drained by primitive channels in order to introduce a cultivation system for banana and taro. This and other sites in the Ruti swamp preserve environmental indicators that suggest upland settlement and cultivation of yam, sugar cane and greens, and thus the swamp-margin occupations reflect a combination of both dry- and wetland interests that provided harvest from three sources: the cultivated upland, the drained wetland, and the untamed swamp with its myriad wildlife.

Prehistoric settlement along the coasts of Japan has only recently come under major investigation, and sites are known both from the Jomon Period and the Yayoi Period. One of the earliest is the Kamo settlement, on Honshu, where hunter-gatherers occupied the edge of a low swampy inlet surrounded by low hills. This provided a wide range of environments, and deer, boar, otter, dolphin and fish show the variety of habitats exploited. Nuts, seeds and fruits of many plants suggest that the gatherers were active. Over time, the debris of 4000–2500 BC accumulated in the marsh and was gradually covered by clays infilling the basin. Preservation of organic material was good, including resins painted on pottery, and wooden artifacts. A logboat, hollowed out of *Apananthe*, six paddles and fragments of bows and other implements provide an unusual look at Early Jomon artifacts, comparable with the near-contemporary material from Tybrind Vig in Denmark.

From the Yayoi Period, 500 BC–AD 1000, a number of waterlogged sites have now been identified. By this time, rice paddy-field cultivation was well established, and settlements tended to lie on slightly raised terraces or mounded areas, like terps, overlooking the wetter fields. A site first occupied in the Early Yayoi Period is Ama, on Honshu, where a mounded settlement was established well out on a floodplain. Around the settlement, two canals were dug to drain the occupied area, and the paddy-fields lay on lower ground beyond. Wooden spades, hoes, handles and domestic utensils were recovered in the excavations. At Ankokuji, on Kyushu, a Late Yayoi Period settlement was located on an old delta of the Tabuka River, with ditches cut for drainage, and rice fields established in a stream bed. Lines of wooden stakes mark ancient trackways through the wet fields. The houses were probably true pile-dwellings, raised above the wet ground by poles holding house platforms. Various logs and planks collapsed into the peats and muds may represent these structures. As well as pottery and stone grinders, wooden artifacts were preserved, including mallets, spades and ploughshares, cups and spoons, and mortice-and-tenoned frames of unknown use, possibly looms or stretching frames. The fruits and seeds of peach, persimmon, walnut, chestnut and acorn indicate a wide exploitation of the environment.

The most significant of these Yayoi settlements is Toro, near Shizuoka, where a multi-disciplinary project has succeeded in recovering remarkable evidence of settlement and economy. The site lies on a levee in the delta of the Abe River, overlooking a low swampy area where rice fields were prepared; the plots were embanked and were about 30 m wide and 30–60 m long. The banks were held in place by thousands of stakes. The houses of the settlement were built of posts and mud, or had walls of vertical planks, with thatched roofs. Inside the walls were low benches held in place by vertical boards and stakes. Small three-piece tables only 30 cm high were probably like individual 'TV-dinner' tables. The rice cultivators also hunted, for deer, raccoon and boar, and they caught many varieties of fish, gathered molluscs, and pastured cattle on drier land away from the wet marsh. Gourds, melons and peach were grown and harvested. The implements used for this variety of activities were well preserved by the muds and silts, and they include a wide range of wooden artifacts of oak, camphor and other species. Among the wooden objects are carved bowls, trenchers, spoons and ladles for use within the houses. Spades, rakes, hoes and picks were used in the paddy-fields, by people wearing flat wooden clogs, like square snowshoes. Wooden swords and scabbards may have been ceremonial, or could have been beaters for some industrial process. Bamboo traps and baskets, and woven mats, are rare glimpses of artistic traditions of the Yayoi people, as are fragments of woven cloth, probably woven as a major industry to judge by the long wooden bolts used to roll up the products of the loom. Only a logboat and fish bones point to the harvest from the adjacent waters, but water transport is also attested in the Yayoi Period by other finds, such as the cargo of bronze mirrors found in a logboat at Onaka. The remarkably detailed information we have about the Toro site is probably a reflection of its abrupt destruction, by an overwhelming flood which submerged the site under muds and silts, like Ozette.

Far north of Japan, at Ekven on the eastern tip of Siberia, a contemporary burial has recently been discovered in a cemetery of the Old Bering Sea culture (500 BC–AD 500). A woman had been buried in a stone-lined grave with a wooden floor. Her many artifacts of ivory, shell, stone, bone and wood were of types thought to be men's as well as women's possessions. Their number, male and female nature, and the inclusion of drums (evident from the surviving handles) and masks of wood suggest that the woman was an important shaman. One of the wooden masks carved as a bulbous human face lay between the knees of the outstretched body. A complex ritual, perhaps both in life and death, is preserved here through exceptional conditions.

It is not difficult to find evidence of wetland settlement and activity elsewhere in the Pacific basin, but we will not pursue sites here other than to note the discovery of wooden tools of 9,000–10,000 years ago at Wyrie Swamp in South Australia. This was a swamp-side camp where both stone and wooden tools were manufactured during a period of relatively low water, the whole site thereafter sealed by rising waters. The wooden artifacts include a spear, digging sticks, a javelin point and what seem to be boomerangs made of the Drooping Shevak which still grows in the swamp. An earlier site at Lake Bolac in Victoria is an encampment on a soil now forming a lunette in the lake. The site may have been a lake-edge kill or butchery camp where red kangaroo, now to be found only 300 km to the north, was captured. Levee sites in Australia, as elsewhere, were favoured places for settlement, industry and burial and it is believed that some of these contain well-preserved evidence for early activity perhaps dating back to more than 10,000 years ago.

In the New World, evidence for early man is slight, and beset with problems of dating. Thus, although there are a number of sites with a respectable claim to an age of 20,000 years or more, one of the earliest reliably dated settlements is that of Monte Verde in Chile, which was occupied around 13,000 years ago. Here, on wet ground, people built small wooden semi-rectangular huts, and they exploited the plants and animals of the diverse watery, marshy and dry environments within easy reach of their settlement. Monte Verde also has indications of much earlier settlement dated to some 34,000 years ago, although the character of the remains has yet to be defined.

To a certain extent there is a bias in the record: early evidence is preserved in a comprehensible form because of waterlogging. Bias notwithstanding, it is clear that at numerous times and in numerous places, early humans chose to settle beside water, and they were adept at exploiting the range of plant and animal resources available. As we move into the postglacial period, the archaeological record becomes such that we can begin to examine the detail of individual settlements and, in due course, to compare foraging peoples with those who had added farming to their means of subsistence, as in New Guinea.

The archaeology of freshwater settlements is dominated by evidence from the Swiss lakes. There are good historical reasons for this (Chapter 1), perpetuated by the level of funding of Swiss archaeology which is well ahead of other countries. In recent years, work has expanded in the circum-Alpine lakes of Italy, France and southern Germany. Northern Europe also has a wide range of evidence, more scattered in place and time, but conveniently concentrated in those periods which are less well represented around the Alps.

The quantity of evidence for prehistoric settlement in lake and marsh could easily fill several volumes. To reduce it to manageable proportions for the present work, much has had to be left out, and the remainder has been divided chronologically into an earlier (this chapter) and a later (next chapter) section. In the earlier period, Mesolithic evidence comes mainly from northern Europe, whilst the circum-Alpine lakes furnish much information about Neolithic settlements and illustrate a mix of wild and farmed resources similar to that noted for early farming groups in coastal regions.

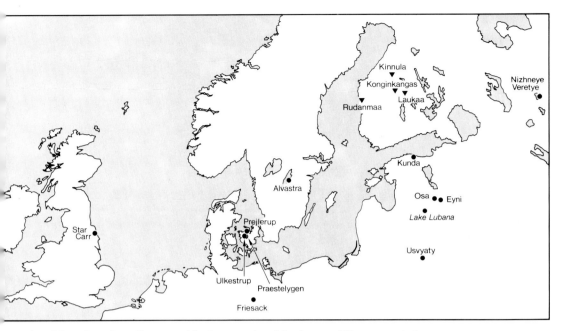

62   Map of northern Europe, with sites mentioned in the text (Chapter 4, circles; Chapter 6, triangles). This map shows the present coastline; for Mesolithic coastlines, see ill. 45.

Freshwater foragers

The many lakes created by retreating ice-sheets have often provided good conditions for the preservation of archaeological and environmental evidence. They are widespread in northern Europe where postglacial foraging economies flourished for several thousand years. The archaeological record for freshwater foragers is therefore particularly rich from this part of the world (*ill. 62*; see also *ill. 45*).

One of the best-known of Mesolithic sites, Star Carr, comes from such an environment. Excavated by Grahame Clark, with environmental work carried out by Harry Godwin, the evidence from Star Carr was soon published and has since undergone many reinterpretations by scholars around the world. The site was on the shore of a freshwater lake in what is now the Vale of Pickering in northern England, and it was occupied early in the Mesolithic, at least 10,000 years ago. The lake was fringed with reeds, and birch and pine grew on the surrounding dry land. As with Tybrind Vig, what was preserved at Star Carr was not the centre of a settlement but its waterside edge, along with the occupation debris which spilled over from the activities carried out there. The shoreline was consolidated with wood, mostly brushwood and small birch trees. Some of the trees were no doubt felled by people using the small flint axe and adze blades found on the site, but recent research has shown that other trees bore beaver toothmarks and had been felled by those industrious animals. It is quite likely that the Star Carr humans took advantage of the wood from a beaver lodge or dam when organizing their own settlement. They may have deliberately chosen a beaver clearing because such places are often full of chopped-up dead wood handy for fuel, and attractive to game such as elk and deer because of the quantity of young shoots which spring up from the stumps of beaver-felled trees.

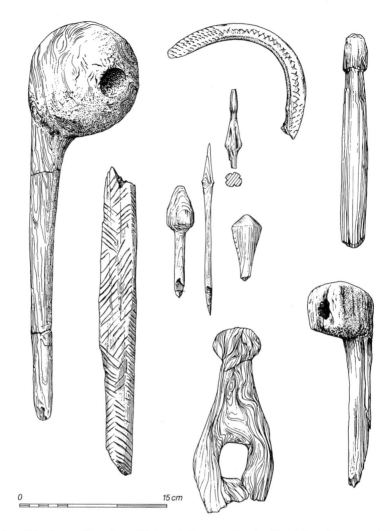

63 Wooden artifacts from Nizhneye Veretye, Russia. Top left and bottom right, hafts for axes and smaller blade tools; top centre and lower left, decorated pieces; top right, end of a bow; centre, various types of arrowheads including two bird bolts and one head grooved for flint inserts; lower centre, handle for small chopper.

The remains of a birchwood paddle suggest that people ventured onto the lake. The best evidence for the exploitation of water resources comes from the bird bones. Most of those identified were from waterfowl, from duck and crane and stork, from Great Crested Grebe and Little Grebe, from Red-throated Diver and Red-breasted Merganser, but perhaps no more than one of each species. Beaver was the only aquatic mammal taken, and the bones recovered came from perhaps seven individuals, most of them young. No fish bones were found, and it has been suggested that few species had yet colonized the lake. In contrast, land mammals are well represented: perhaps 80 red deer, 30 roe deer and 11 elk, 9 aurochs, 5 pigs, and sundry other smaller animals. Even allowing for the over-representation of deer and elk because their antlers were being used to make tools, the excavated evidence suggests that, whilst living by water, people obtained most of their meat from the land.

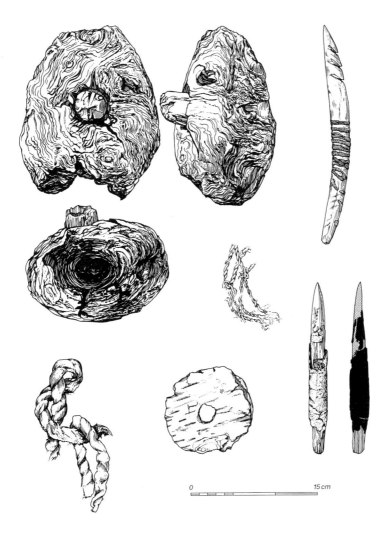

64 Artifacts from Friesack, East Germany. Top left, three views of an alder root axe or adze haft; top right, bone or antler barbed point with binding; lower right, bone point stuck with pitch to wooden shaft; centre, net fragment; lower left, rope; lower centre, birch-bark net float.

A number of well-preserved artifacts were recovered from Star Carr, many of them made from antler and bone, but apart from the paddle there were no recognizable wooden objects. We have to turn to sites from continental northern Europe for wooden finds from the earlier Mesolithic in any quantity. About 300 km north of Moscow, in the Lacha lake basin, lies the site of Nizhneye Veretye. Recent work by Oshibkina has established a Boreal date (roughly 10,000–9,000 years ago), and retrieved a number of interesting wooden artifacts (*ill. 63*). Most were made of pine, either Scots pine (*Pinus sylvestris*) or Siberian pine (*Pinus sibirica*), and some birch, aspen and fir were used. The species reflect the composition of the Boreal forest which colonized northern regions soon after the retreat of the ice.

The Nizhneye Veretye artifacts include the remains of several bows, notched at the ends to hold the bow-string. One possible fragment of a bow is wrapped around with bark as if for a hand grip. Various different types of wooden arrow and arrowhead were found, some blunt-ended to stun birds or fur-bearing animals, some pointed to pierce the quarry, and one slotted for the insertion of small stone barbs. In some cases arrowhead and shaft were made from a single piece of wood, in others a relatively short wooden arrowhead (e.g. 15 cm long) was designed for attachment to a separate shaft, in a manner analogous to the bone and antler points of contemporary and earlier peoples. The bow and arrow were probably first used in Europe in Late Glacial times, and the evidence from Nizhneye Veretye shows that considerable sophistication had developed by an early date.

Axe or adze handles were carved out of a single piece of wood, usually cut from the base of a tree-trunk where the roots splayed out or where there was a burr, so that the bulge of the root or burr provided a solid but resilient lump of wood to hold the blade. A similar choice of material for axe handles was to be made by circum-Alpine peoples several thousand years later (see below, this chapter). One piece of wood with a preserved length of 18 cm had a well-made knob at one end, and about 8 cm up from the knob a rectangular hole had been cut through; it was probably the wooden part of some small hand-held tool. A charred, forked aspen branch may have been no more than leftover fuel but the apparently-worn prongs suggest some other function, perhaps holding food over a fire. Two decorated pieces of wood were found, lightly incised with fairly simple geometric patterns. The artifacts are domestic or for hunting and, as with Star Carr, there is little to suggest the use of water resources despite the lake shore location of the site.

A third Early Mesolithic site to consider here is that of Friesack in East Germany, excavated by Bernard Gramsch. Friesack was a favoured location, occupied off and on over 3,000 years at least, until about 8,000 years ago. Many finds have been made, of flint, bone, antler, wood and fibre (*ill. 64*), and they were well stratified, making it possible to attribute them to particular phases of occupation. Microliths and other worked flint and bone points occurred in all levels. One bone point from early levels still had a bit of its wooden shaft, stuck on with pitch. Among the earliest finds were fragments of Scots pine spears, arrowshafts and a blunt arrowhead, all suggestive of hunting. Fishing is better represented than at Nizhneye Veretye or Star Carr, probably because the location had enabled earlier colonization by freshwater fish. The excavators recovered a mountain-ash paddle and birch-bark net float and pieces of rope perhaps belonging to nets, from early levels. Another paddle and several fragments and pieces of net date a few centuries later. From this period there was also an antler axe with wooden shaft, and an axe handle made from alder root designed for the blade to be held in a large burr or knot of wood as with the Nizhneye Veretye handles of similar date. A wooden tray and a birch-bark container survived in remarkably good condition, along with a possible digging stick and various wooden rods tied up with string. Late finds, dating from about 9,000 to 8,000 years ago, are more enigmatic: a Scots pine stick pointed at both ends, a small rod of alder pierced down the centre.

From the inland waters of Denmark, there is evidence for the houses or shelters built by Early Mesolithic people. At Ulkestrup on Zealand, the remains of rectangular buildings have been found with a floor area about 4 m by 6 m covered with layers of pine-bark which probably insulated the inhabitants from the damp ground below. Hearths were built on the floor, maybe one maybe two. Analysis of the flint-knapping debris from Ulkestrup suggests that there were two work areas inside a hut, hence perhaps two families with a hearth each. There is no good evidence for superstructure from Ulkestrup, nor from other sites where floors are known, such as Svaerdborg and Holmegaard.

Many wooden artifacts have been recovered from early sites in Denmark, a number of them as stray finds. They include paddles, bows, arrowshafts and wooden arrowheads, and axe handles, in other words a range not dissimilar to that described above. One context of discovery is intriguing. In northwest Zealand, at Prejlerup, the skeleton of a very old aurochs bull was found, the animal having drowned, like the High Furlong elk, in a shallow lake which subsequently filled with peat. At least nine arrows had been shot into its left haunch, for the flint barbs were still there along with the remains of one fir shaft. About 8,500 years ago someone's quarry got away.

Although the great majority of Early Mesolithic sites from northern Europe are from water's edge locations, there is relatively little evidence for the exploitation of water resources for food. We have seen that it took time for freshwater fish to migrate north after the retreat of the ice sheets and there may indeed have been few or none at Star Carr when people settled there. Beaver, which eat plant food, were identified from the Star Carr bones but otter, which eat fish, were not and this may be a reflection of the scarcity of fish in northern waters and especially of freshwater fish whose ways and means of colonizing newly available areas were more restricted than for marine species. Of course we should not forget that fishbones and fishscales rarely preserve well, and are often difficult to see in a wet excavation. Hence their absence may be an archaeological phenomenon rather than an actual one. Nets from quite early levels at Friesack and bone fishhooks from various sites of similar date do exist, and from Kunda in Estonia comes proof of fishing in the shape of two pike skeletons, one with a barbed bone point in its skull and the other with a similar point in its back. In the course of the next 2,000–3,000 years fishing was to expand and fishing equipment to develop, as the species and numbers of freshwater fish in temperate and northern Europe increased. By the Late Mesolithic, their diversity is reflected in the species identified, oddly enough, mainly from coastal Ertebølle sites (Chapter 3). Pike were still popular inland and at Praestelyngen around 4200 BC 75 per cent of the 5,000 fish bones identified were from pike, representing at least 250 fish. Analysis of the vertebrae indicates they were caught in early summer, and the freshwater mussels on the site were collected in summer, all suggestive of the seasonal exploitation of water resources. But at the same time the people at Praestelyngen were hunting red deer, which brought in a lot more food than the pike. It seems unlikely that the inland peoples had access to the abundance of water resources available to their coastal contemporaries, and perhaps for this reason there is strong evidence for the inland sites being occupied only seasonally, whereas the coastal settlements were perhaps inhabited for most of the year.

A rather different picture emerges from the lakeside settlements of late foragers in north-west Russia. Around the basin of Lake Lubana a number of sites have been identified. Those dated between 6,000 and 4,000 years ago are attributed to Neolithic peoples, although there is nothing to suggest that domestic animals were being cared for, nor that crops were cultivated; the inhabitants were foragers rather than farmers, termed Neolithic in this instance because they made and used pottery. At the site of Eini, numerous wooden piles were found, suggesting that substantial wooden structures had been built on the lake shore. Bones from the settlements indicate that a wide range of wild animals were hunted, particularly elk and pig. At Osa pine-marten were common, and at Eini beaver, both perhaps hunted for their fur. Neither site provides evidence for the exploitation of fish or plants, and for this we have to turn to another group of lakeside settlements around the Usvyaty basin some 300 km to the southwest (*ill. 62*).

Evidence for wooden structures comes from Usvyaty itself and from a number of other sites in the region, such as Dyazditza and Serteya. In general, little excavation has taken place at these waterlogged sites, but at Usvyaty sufficient evidence has been recovered to show three main phases of settlement on the lake shore, from shortly after 4000 BC. Diverse mammals were hunted, particularly elk, bear and pig. Numerous bird bones were noted, as well as fish bones which included those of pike, pike-perch (also known as zander), bream and carp. Plant remains included acorns, chestnuts and water chestnuts, all of which are edible if properly prepared. The water chestnut has been described as the forager's potato, and its widespread distribution at this time may have been an important factor in the appearance of fairly substantial and permanent settlements, as at Usvyaty.

The Neolithic lakeside settlements of north-west Russia are comparable with the settlements of the coastal Ertebølle groups in several respects. Occupation was relatively permanent rather than seasonal, hunting took place for meat and for fur, and water resources provided an essential stable food supply, whether fish on the coast or fish and water chestnuts inland. Pottery was made, another indication of a fairly settled group. In both cases, contact with farming groups becomes evident as time passes, with the appearance of small numbers of bones from domestic animals and perhaps some artifacts indicative of trade. But throughout, subsistence was based on wild resources. Water resources were particularly abundant in the late Atlantic period: water chestnut flourished, and diverse species of freshwater fish had reached northern waters and proliferated. This abundance, coupled perhaps with a developing market for fish, fur and fowl in neighbouring farming regions, encouraged and enabled people to become increasingly settled.

Foraging farmers

Whereas in northern Europe one can find Neolithic lakeside dwellers who did not farm, in the circum-Alpine zone (*ill. 66*) the first Neolithic peoples hunted and fished, and collected a great array of wild plants, alongside the exploitation of domestic plants and animals and concurrently, before many centuries had passed, with the working and use of copper tools and ornaments. In other words, where waterlogged sites preserve a diversity of different types of evidence, the traditional schemes of prehistory may well need amendment. In the coastal zone of the Netherlands, a semi-agrarian group has been recognized, of people who lived largely off wild resources but had access to farmers' crops and animals (Chapter 3). Around the freshwater lakes of the circum-Alpine zone, there was another variation, of people whose livelihood depended almost equally on

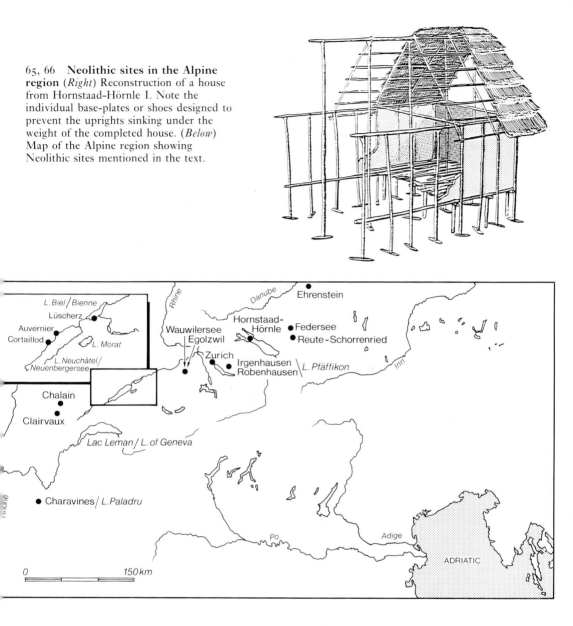

65, 66 **Neolithic sites in the Alpine region** (*Right*) Reconstruction of a house from Hornstaad-Hörnle I. Note the individual base-plates or shoes designed to prevent the uprights sinking under the weight of the completed house. (*Below*) Map of the Alpine region showing Neolithic sites mentioned in the text.

farmed and wild resources and who undoubtedly cultivated their own cereals and raised their own stock. The evidence for these mixed farming and foraging economies has emerged only in the last three decades, beginning with the 1950s excavations at Egolzwil in the Wauwilermoos in northern Switzerland. At the more recently excavated sites, with the benefit of dendrochronology it is becoming evident that the pioneer lakeside farmers not only used many wild resources, but rarely stayed put for long.

The small Wauwilersee, or Wauwil lake, had been a popular resort of later Mesolithic peoples who left many traces around its ancient shoreline. As time passed, the lake shrank, leaving a broad marshy band round the shore (the Wauwilermoos) and towards 4000 BC a village was built in the marshy zone, with three parallel rows of houses and a fence on the landward side. The village, examined by Emil Vogt and colleagues, was called Egolzwil 3, the first of a number of Neolithic settlements in the vicinity of modern Egolzwil. The houses were rectangular, about 8 m by 4 m, and built mainly of ash with some use of oak and other species. The excavators thought the village had been rebuilt at least three times during a continuous occupation of several generations, but as Egolzwil 3 was examined before the great developments of dendrochronology it is unlikely that a precise chronology can be established, and recent excavations (see below) have demonstrated that rebuilding could take place at very short intervals, much less than a generation.

Judging by the quantity of dung the Egolzwil 3 inhabitants kept sheep or goats within their village. These were by far the most common of the domestic animals represented in the bones recovered from the site. Over half the bones came from wild animals, however, mostly from red deer, roe deer and aurochs. Bows and arrows were found, along with bird bolts and fish hooks and net weights and floats, all indicative of the exploitation of wild foods. Sickles and pick- or hoe-like tools, on the other hand, suggest cultivation.

A Neolithic settlement contemporary with Egolzwil 3 and currently under excavation by Helmut Schlichtherle and colleagues is the site of Hornstaad-Hörnle I, on the west arm of the Bodensee (Lake Constance) in south Germany. Two phases of settlement have been recognized here, the first radiocarbon-dated to about 4000 BC. Within the area excavated, which is probably only a small part of the original settlement, many upright posts or piles were found and tree-ring studies have enabled those of the first settlement to be picked out, revealing at least four houses and several other incomplete structures (*ill. 65*). The first settlement burnt down, a disaster for the Neolithic inhabitants no doubt but a bonus for archaeologists because of all the information that was preserved.

Animal remains show a heavy dependence on wild foods. Only about a quarter of the bones identified came from domestic animals, and nearly 90 per cent of these were from cattle, the remainder being mostly pig with a few dogs and goats. The wild animals were dominated by red deer (*c.*60 per cent) with a number of aurochs (*c.*12 per cent) and a few wild pig, beaver, roe deer, hedgehog and birds. A quarter of the bones from wild animals came from fish, almost all pike, together with a few perch and a tench; it seems likely that the pike were speared, harpooned or netted when they came to spawn amongst the vegetation at the water's edge. Pike will spawn over flooded watermeadows, but they do so in early spring which is when the Bodensee water level would have been low and any shoreline meadows dry; the lake rises only as the snows melt in late spring and early summer. Many net weights were found, and fragments of netting, showing one way in which the fish were caught.

Numerous plant remains were recovered, some carbonized and others preserved by waterlogging. Wheat was the main cultivated cereal, with some barley. Flax and opium poppy were grown: they were to be popular crops around the lakes and Godwin (writing of the Fens) notes that flax was a crop of deep, fertile and moist soils and a temperate climate, needing good water supplies to rett the stems if used to make rope and textiles, as it was in the circum-Alpine Neolithic. The opium poppy needs similar growing conditions, and might have been grown as an opiate or sedative or, as flax may also have been, for the high oil content of its seeds. Seeds and fruits of many wild plants were found on the site, the most common being strawberry, raspberry and blackberry, crab-apple, hazelnut, sloe and Chinese Lantern. All of these are still familiar to us except, perhaps, the Chinese Lantern but it was a favourite of the Neolithic lake dwellers and is said to have a high Vitamin C content (to be eaten in small quantities only). A great many other wild plants such as watercress and hedge parsley were consumed, perhaps as flavourings or as medicine. Black bindweed, black nightshade and ground ivy do not sound too appetising, but they may have had their uses.

Together with pollen evidence, the plant remains suggest that small fields were cleared in the deciduous woodland away from the shore, to grow crops. Trees growing on the wet soils around the lake were not cleared, except perhaps very patchily to grow flax and poppies, and there was little or no pasture. The lack of grazing fits with the low percentage of domestic animal bones found, almost all of which were from cattle, the domestic species best adapted to forest browsing. The quantities of wild fruits and nuts collected indicate that the forest canopy was neither dense nor light-excluding, and there must have been vigorous ground vegetation and shrubby layers within reach of the settlement that profited man and beast alike.

One further resource that the people of Hornstaad-Hörnle used was birch-bark. This provided a sticky gum or pitch that was popular across Europe for making tools and weapons, sticking arrowheads onto arrowshafts for example or bone points to a wooden shaft as at Friesack. At Hornstaad-Hörnle and other Neolithic sites in the region an additional use was found, as chewing gum. Oblong lumps with toothmarks in them, all too reminiscent of discarded gobs of modern chewing gum, were found (*ill. 67*). The birch-bark variety is said to be both tasty and medicinal, so perhaps its use should be revived.

Excavations at Hornstaad-Hörnle are still in progress, and it is too soon to catalogue the finds from the site. But preliminary reports make clear the considerable dependence on wild resources, the likely Danubian ancestry of the farming elements present, and the existence of other nearby and contemporary wetland sites with similar material culture. The evidence points to the local development of a settled lakeside way of life which, as at Egolzwil 3, combined elements of foraging with introduced farming. What there was in the lakeside environment to prompt such a development has still to be determined, but whatever it was it favoured a mixed approach to subsistence for some time to come. Many settlements from the centuries to follow depended on a similar mixture of the wild and the cultivated. Archaeological evidence suggests that this was rarely the case for dry land Neolithic peoples who had been long-established in the Danube valley to the north. Thus the lake itself was an important factor, even if the evidence for its direct exploitation is not abundant. At Hornstaad-Hörnle, although their bones are many, the pike represent little food compared with the deer, and aquatics barely figure in the identified totals of edible plants.

67 Neolithic chewing gum. Gobs of birch-bark gum with human tooth imprints, from Hornstaad-Hörnle I.

Elsewhere and at different times, but also along lake shores, other pioneer farmers were to couple their husbandry with foraging. To the west of the Alps, on the shores of Lake Paladru in eastern France, a settlement many years more recent than Egolzwil 3 or Hornstaad-Hörnle I has been excavated by Aimé Bocquet and colleagues, at Charavines (*ill. 71*). Here, around 3300 BC, the first farmers known to have settled on the lake shore built a house, about 5 m × 12 m. Two years later they built another house beside it, two others to either side, and a fence on the landward side of their little hamlet. Five years later the first house

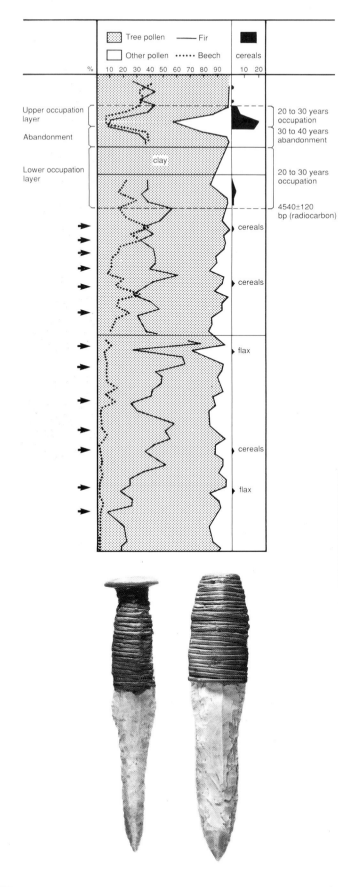

Tree pollen — Fir
Other pollen ····· Beech
cereals

% | 10 20 30 40 50 60 70 80 90 | 10 20

Upper occupation layer
Abandonment

clay

Lower occupation layer

20 to 30 years occupation
30 to 40 years abandonment

20 to 30 years occupation

4540±120 bp (radiocarbon)

cereals

cereals

flax

cereals

flax

68, 69 **Neolithic farming at Charavines** (*Left*) Pollen diagram, with arrowed indicators of early cultivation followed by clearance of trees associated with the two phases of occupation at the site. (*Below*) Artifacts from the site: top, fragment of plant fibre cloth (8 × 7 cm); centre, wooden spoons and ladles (25–30 cm long); bottom, boxwood comb (8 × 7.5 cm); below left, two flint daggers bound with beechwood and fir twig handles (*c.* 20 cm long).

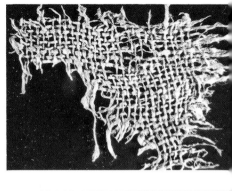

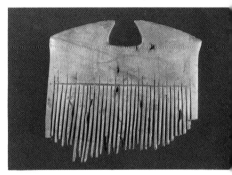

was rebuilt, and rebuilt again nine years on, along with two of the other houses. Within no more than thirty years of the first house going up, the two middle houses burnt down and the settlement was abandoned for a while. Fifty-five years after the first house had gone up, people came again to Charavines to build a new house more or less where the first one had been, and various other buildings. They stayed for two or three decades and then were gone, and the remains of their hamlet were soon submerged by the rising waters of Lake Paladru. A floating tree-ring chronology (see below) from the site enables this detailed history of the settlement to be given, but as the chronology is based on fir not oak it has not been matched to any master chronology, and there are no absolute dates for the site. The approximate date of 3300 BC is based on radiocarbon results.

The two fleeting settlements on the lake shore left their mark on the pollen record, which shows definite episodes of forest clearance contemporary with each settlement (*ill. 68*). The pollen record also indicates several earlier episodes of small-scale clearance and cultivation in the region, before any known lakeside settlement. Fir, which was used for building, and beech, which was a popular fuel, both declined in numbers when people were around, non-tree pollen increased, and pollen from cereals made an appearance. The picture is one of small fields within the forest, probably quite close to the settlement. Cereal grains and chaff from the site indicate that wheat was the most important crop at Charavines, and three different sorts were grown. Barley, peas, poppies and flax were also grown, and perhaps garlic since its pollen occurs during the clearance phases. Bone was not well preserved, but from what could be identified pig seem to have been the most common of the domestic animals, and cattle, sheep and goats were also kept.

The farmers at Charavines made good use of the forest around them, not just for wood to build their houses but also as a source of foods and medicines and raw materials. It is possible that apple, oak and walnut trees were left standing when plots were cleared, because their fruits were popular. Apples were halved and dried, and acorns may have been roasted to make them palatable for humans, or else fed raw to the pigs. Hazelnuts, beechnuts and sloes were found, along with some wild grapes, raspberries, blackberries, strawberries and Chinese Lantern, all presumably collected to eat. Other fruits would have needed cooking to make them safe to eat, for example holly and dogwood berries, and yew berries would have remained poisonous whatever one did to them. Danewort (dwarf elder) berries are also poisonous but can be used to make a dye. Various seeds may have been used as medicines or flavourings, for example marjoram, thyme, wild carrot, plantain, and lime. Seeds of water-lilies and reeds might have been deliberately collected, but could also have washed naturally into the site.

Apart from the wood used for building, where fir and ash were common, many different species were used to make artifacts (*ill. 69*). Boxwood was sought for combs, spoons and pins, holly and viburnum for spindles, maple for axe handles, lime which is easy to carve for bowls and elder with its hollow centre for tubes. Silver fir tops were used to make beaters or whisks, a common artifact of the circum-Alpine Neolithic, and yew was selected for a bow. Beechwood was used to make a handle for a flint dagger blade, stuck on with birch-bark gum and firmly and neatly bound in place with a long stripped fir twig. Other daggers were bound with stripped willow twigs or a root wound over plant-fibre padding. Wood and plant fibres were put to many other uses, including fuel, but whatever the function, little use seems to have been made of oak except for two dugout canoes.

Wild animals were not neglected. Red deer were hunted in quantity, for their antlers and perhaps their skins as well as meat. Wild boar, roe deer, and the occasional bear and aurochs were also taken. Fish bones are few, which is not surprising given the poor conditions for the preservation of bone, but the oak dugout canoes, a beechwood paddle and net weights suggest fishing. Overall, more than half the bones identified from each phase of occupation at Charavines came from wild animals, and given the likely disappearance of fragile fish and bird bones and those of small furry mammals, the original numbers may have been higher still. Although farmers, the Charavines settlers made good use of forest and lake resources, and the balance of their economy is not unlike that suggested for Hornstaad-Hörnle, a millennium earlier and round the other side of the Alps.

Another site set in the wet, with a mixture of farmed and foraged subsistence, is that of Alvastra in southern Sweden (*ill. 62*). Set in a peatbog near the eastern shore of Lake Vättern, some 75 m from dry land, Alvastra is a somewhat enigmatic site. It would seem that a large wooden platform about 1,000 m square was built on the marsh surface, surrounded by slender piles or upright posts, and connected to dry land by a footbridge. Many stone hearths were built on the platform, but neither Frodin who excavated the site early in the century, nor Mats Malmer who recently returned to it, has interpreted the site as a cluster of houses but rather as a single, large open platform. The wood used was mostly young, and not suitable for absolute dates, but radiocarbon places the site around 3000 BC, and internal phasing proved possible. Much of the wood was felled at the start, in winter; 15 to 17 years later there was a fair amount of new wood put in, but then no additions or repairs for 23 years. Finally, 40 to 42 years from the start, a little new wood was added, and that was all. Much of the wood used had begun to grow 40 years before the first building episode, apart from some older apple trees, and some elm which seemed to have grown from a coppiced stool, and suffered a setback in growth 50 years before the first building episode. Thomas Bartholin, who carried out the tree-ring analyses, suggested that there had once been an open area near the peatbog, probably a field with apple trees in it, and coppiced elm which might have provided cattle fodder. The field was abandoned and recolonized by trees, only to be cleared again 40 years later when the platform was built.

The presence of fields fits the Alvastra picture, in that carbonized wheat and barley were found on the site, together with the bones of domestic cattle, sheep or goats and pig. The people who built the platform were therefore probably farmers. They were also hunters and fishermen. They caught pike and other fish, they hunted deer and elk and pig, and numerous furry animals such as bear, badger, pine-marten, beaver and lynx. Little evidence is preserved of their use of wild plants, apart from hazelnuts, apples, lime bast for rope or string and a wooden bowl.

Mats Malmer has argued that Alvastra was occupied seasonally, in summer and autumn, for ceremonies and feasts and perhaps in its later years for the disposal of the dead, since human bones were found in the upper levels. But some of the wood was winter-felled and the pelt of furry animals is at its best in winter, apples would be autumn-culled and wheat and barley harvested in the late summer, so there may have been a year-round presence of people who hunted in the forests, fished the lakes and farmed in nearby fields. Their stay in the area was short-lived, maybe two generations. These first lakeside farmers of southern Sweden were no more permanently attached to the land than their counterparts of the Alpine lakes.

Timber and time, or peripatetic peasants

Where mature oakwood was used for building, and has survived in good condition, it may be possible to use it to provide absolute dates for an archaeological site. In several regions of Europe there are now oak tree-ring chronologies stretching back from the present to 5000 BC or earlier. These have been built up by overlapping patterns of tree-rings from living oaks, standing buildings, ancient structures and still more ancient bog-oaks, until a continuous sequence of variation in ring-width is established, and the precise year of growth of each ring is known. Timbers from an archaeological site can be matched against each other to provide a local chronology, known as a floating chronology, which is then dated by comparison with the master chronology. At this stage, it may be possible to date the growth rings on an individual timber; the final, outer ring, if it is at the sapwood and bark junction, represents the last year of growth, and felling must have occurred when growth ceased. Thus, by careful calculation, ancient timbers can be assigned absolute dates in years BC with very little margin of error. Radiocarbon dates in these circumstances are imprecise and unnecessary.

A new village was built at Hornstaad-Hörnle 1 a few centuries after the first settlement there had been abandoned. Oak was used in the building, and this time the local tree-ring sequences can be matched to the regional master chronology to give absolute dates for the site. Detailed study of the size and the age of the wood has also enabled André Billamboz to reconstruct various aspects of the local forest and its exploitation. Broadly speaking, building took place over a period of 80 years, in five bursts of activity (*ill. 70*).

In 3586 BC the first trees were felled and two houses were built within the excavated area. The oaks used were 80 to 90 years old and 30 to 35 cm in diameter; the trunks were split longitudinally into quarters or more and used to make a framework about 10 m by 5 m. The next main phase of building was from 3570 to 3562 BC, when the first houses were repaired and one or two new buildings were put up. The oaks used were 50 to 60 years old and generally under 30 cm in diameter; the smaller trunks were split only in half, larger ones as before. Bit by bit during these years, one of the first houses had most of its uprights replaced.

After a gap of 21 years, there was a great burst of activity from 3541 to 3531 BC, and new structures can be traced within the excavated area. From the evidence available, the settlement was not so much expanding as filling in. The trunks used were generally 40 years old and 20 cm or less in diameter, and they had begun to grow after the first building phase. In their early years they had grown vigorously, but then the rate slowed, a pattern typical of coppiced growth and it is very likely that the wood used had sprung from the stumps of the oak trees

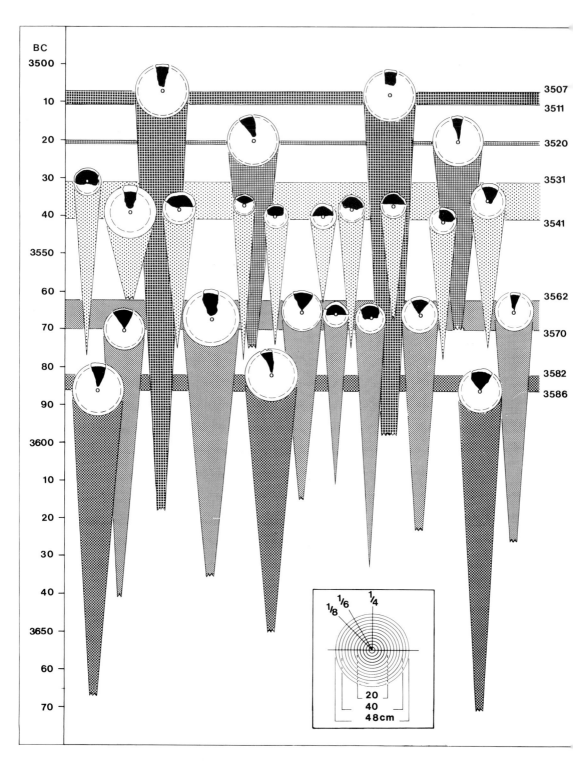

BC
3500
10 — 3507
    3511
20 — 3520
30 — 3531
40 — 3541
3550
60 — 3562
70 — 3570
80 — 3582
    3586
90
3600
10
20
30
40
3650
60
70

1/6 1/4
1/8

20
40
48cm

70   Dendrogram from the south German site of Hornstaad-Hörnle I. Each cone represents the approximate lifespan of an oak tree – based on a known piece of wood discovered at the site – from the inner rings of its earliest years (base of cone) to its year of felling (centre of circle). The circle indicates the diameter of the tree at felling, and the black section shows how the piece was split from the trunk. The horizontal bands pick out the main felling episodes. The dates are calendar years BC.

felled in 3586 BC or soon thereafter. Most of the trunks were simply halved, and the houses were slightly smaller than before, a reflection of the size of the wood used. Within this phase, some structures were rebuilt or extensively repaired, such as the house built in 3540 BC and given a new set of uprights only 4 years later.

From 3522 to 3518, house builders were active again and setting up larger-sized houses once more. Their source of wood was probably the same coppiced oak used in the previous phase. In the interval and with reduced competition, the trunks had reached diameters of 35 cm or so. Finally, in the years 3508 to 3507, trees over a century old were felled, trees of an age and size that one might have thought no longer existed in the vicinity, given the use of coppiced wood in the preceding decades. But in the 3530s they were already older and bigger than the trunks used then.

This pattern of forest exploitation is fascinating, as it emerges from the detailed tree-ring analyses still undergoing refinement. A progression can perhaps be traced from initial settlement in an area of closed, mature forest where large trees were felled as much to make fields as to build houses. Regeneration from the stumps was soon allowed or encouraged, whilst further mature trees were felled. Once the coppiced growth had reached building size, effectively four decades after the first felling, it was used exclusively despite larger wood being around. This suggests it was preferred, understandable given that it is easier to fell a small tree than a big tree with a stone axe, less splitting is needed to prepare the wood for use in a building, and the coppiced pole is effectively a ready-made house post. The return to mature trees might suggest the supplies of well-grown coppiced wood had run out, although the stumps should have regenerated anew. Whatever the case, the Hornstaad-Hörnle piles tell not only of dwellings, but also of eight decades' settlement in a forested landscape, and something of the interaction of people and forest. It is doubtful if such precision could be obtained from a dried-out Neolithic settlement.

Eighty years is not long. Nor is four years much of a life for a house before it is rebuilt. Many of the Early Neolithic settlements preserved in wetlands, where ephemeral occupation levels have been preserved between layers of sterile lake sediments and where detailed tree-ring studies have been possible, are seen to be short-lived. Individual structures within them are barely completed before they are replaced. Egolzwil 5, excavated in the 1960s and published in 1976 by René Wyss and his colleagues, was built mainly of alder, with some birch and only a little oak. As at Charavines, no absolute date could be established, but in this case radiocarbon dating placed the settlement around 3700 BC and combined studies of wood and stratigraphy suggested that the settlement had lasted about 12 years. Initially 7 houses were set in a row, 6 close together and 1 a little to one side, with the lake in front of them and a fence on the landward side. It was discovered that 3 of the 7 were substantially or completely rebuilt within the 6 years of the first phase of the village. Then the second phase started with a complete rebuilding of most of the houses and 2 new ones added, followed by some further renewal. The houses were about 9×3.5 m with three rows of posts each, wattle walls, reed roofing, bark on the ground for flooring and a clay hearth. The hearths were frequently renewed, and set on a layer of twiggy fir branches for insulation and to stop them sinking into the soft ground of the lake shore. About 12 years after the first buildings had gone up, the Egolzwil 5 inhabitants left, taking with them most of their belongings apart from their pots. Wyss suggested that people left because the yields from their fields had fallen; the pollen diagram shows a rise in cereal pollen during the early years of the settlement, followed by quite a marked decline. It should also be noted, however, that the lake level rose shortly after they had left and the period of occupation coincides with a short episode of low water levels.

Egolzwil 5 was about 150 m from the earlier Egolzwil 3, and adjacent to the slightly later Egolzwil 4. Pollen analyses related to Egolzwil 5 shows two episodes of clearance and cultivation before the one associated with the 12 years of occupation, and four after it. Taken together, this evidence suggests a series of occupations separated by periods when the lake shore was abandoned and the forest regenerated, a pattern similar to that found at Charavines. Both are what one would expect of a system of shifting agriculture, where people regularly moved their fields and their settlements around a large territory.

Of the various settlements near Auvernier on Lake Neuchâtel, Auvernier-Port may be selected to illustrate the same phenomenon of repeated short settlements, in this case spread over eight centuries. As with Egolzwil, various adjacent clusters of buildings have been found, and the full settlement history has yet to be established. In the area of Auvernier-Port, tree-ring dating outlines a sequence which could be interpreted as five short occupations in the 250 years from the 3780s to the 3540s, followed by two short occupations either side of 3200 and a further short occupation from 3000 BC.

Whether short-lived settlements and repeated renewals of houses were to be found across temperate Europe in all environments, or whether they were in some way a reflection of the wetland environment is uncertain. Had Auvernier-Port been a dryland site, with postholes but no posts, the archaeological record might have suggested a single long occupation or at most two phases separated by a sterile layer belonging to the 300 years abandonment after the 3540s. So the lakeside pattern could well be typical but invisible in the dryland record. On the other hand, damp conditions could have accelerated the decay of houses, and rising lake levels sometimes forced a move perhaps before it was otherwise needed or desired. Yet the great number of settlements now known around the circum-Alpine lakes, people's habit of returning to old sites, and the wealth of material culture evident in many cases (see below), all combine to suggest that people made a positive choice to live by the water, that it was for them an advantageous place to be, and that rebuildings and frequent moves were an accepted norm. It would be as well, when contemplating the postholes of a dryland site, to remember the armies of posts at Hornstaad-Hörnle and Egolzwil, Charavines and Auvernier and the short spans of human habitation which, thanks to dendrochronology, we now know they represent.

Settling down

There is no simple pattern of settlement evolution around the lakes and in the marshes of the circum-Alpine zone, satisfying though it would be to trace a steady progression from short-lived pioneering hamlets to large permanent villages. Yet it can be argued that there was a general tendency for villages to be occupied for four to ten decades in the later Neolithic, in contrast to the one to two decades of the Early Neolithic farming settlements.

On Lake Neuchâtel and the adjacent small lakes of Bienne and Morat, in the first quarter of the third millennium BC, a number of villages were built whose inhabitants had a common material culture. This is named after one of the settlements of Lake Bienne, Lüscherz. On the shores of Lake Neuchâtel at Auvernier, Lüscherz-type deposits were found at the site of Ruz Chatru, associated with wood dated from 2908 BC onwards. Forty years later (2871 BC) a second settlement appeared a couple of hundred metres along the shore, and twenty years on (2850 BC) a third settlement sprang up another 300 m away. A satellite of the second settlement appeared in 2841 BC, and in 2830 BC a fifth and final settlement was built about 200 m beyond the initial foundation, which was still occupied. In the year 2776 to 2775 BC all of the villages were abandoned, perhaps because of a rise in the lake level.

At this point, the first village had been occupied for 133 years and would apparently have continued but for the natural disaster of rising waters. The success of this phase of lakeside occupation is, however, evident more in the multiplication of sites than in their duration. The increase from one nucleus to five adjacent groups of buildings strung along about a kilometre of lakeshore is indicative of population growth both locally and elsewhere around the lakes, since people expanded an existing focus of settlement instead of moving into vacant areas. During the Lüscherz phase, 16 settlements are known around Lake Neuchâtel, 6 on Lake Morat and 2 on Lake Bienne, with 3 others on the rivers linking the lakes. Several were abandoned in the same year as the Auvernier cluster, suggesting a general rise in water-level in the three interconnected lakes, and incidentally demonstrating the contemporaneity of the settlements. They represent a full landscape, given the technology and resources available. Population increase and lack of free land suitable for farming were probably major factors influencing the longer duration of settlements. Why population should increase is, as usual, another question. Unfortunately, the economic evidence from the Lüscherz group of sites is insufficient to detect any major change in subsistence or methods of farming which could explain the demographic increase. The answer, if it comes at all, is as likely to be given by dendrochronology and more precise interpretation of settlement history, which may one day provide an entry to the informed discussion of prehistoric social organization. For it is the ways people relate to each other, their law and organization and systems of authority, as much as how they feed themselves which affects numbers.

The change to a more sedentary way of life can be traced on other lakes, at Clairvaux for example. Around the small body of water, there had been a series of short occupations from about 3500 BC. In the space of 700 years people had settled on the lakeshore some six to eight times, probably for less than a generation each time. They lived in small hamlets of 6 to 12 houses set in a row along the shore, an arrangement similar to Egolzwil 5. Later in the third millennium BC the settlements lasted longer, and were larger than before. Several hamlets consisting of 4–15 houses, set in rows separated by narrow alleyways, clustered around the northern end of the lake. Clairvaux lake is now only slightly over 1000 m long and 500 m wide, and was larger than this but not by much in the Neolithic, and the hamlets were no further away from each other than those of the Auvernier Lüscherz group. At Clairvaux, as at Auvernier, the phenomenon of small, adjacent and probably contemporary settlements may be

71   Reconstruction drawing of a lakeside Neolithic settlement.

explained by the expansion of an initial settlement at a time when the contemporary landscape and social organization had no space for the foundation of new and independent villages. In the case of Clairvaux, Pierre Pétrequin has demonstrated a general increase in population away from the water as well as around it, some of which he attributes to the arrival of immigrants from the south. He notes the defended character of both dryland villages and those at the water's edge, the latter often set on a peninsula or little knoll linked to the shore by a narrow strip of land or by a footbridge across the intervening marshes. The Clairvaux settlements are not, however, protected by heavy palisades.

The extent to which lakeside and marshy locations were defensive, and selected for that reason just as hilltops might have been, is a question that recurs in the study of wetland settlement. It will crop up in the following chapter, and should be noted here as one possible factor influencing people's choice of site. Another benefit of lakeshore settlement is the milder climate of the lands immediately around the lake compared with those inland. A degree or two difference in temperatures can mean earlier crops, better ripening and a longer growing season, aspects beneficial for both wild and cultivated crops.

Neolithic material culture

The preservation of fragile objects in waterlogged contexts has been apparent at a number of the freshwater settlements discussed in this chapter. The range of organic materials is sometimes so stunning that one tends to ignore commonplace pottery and stone, but the understanding of these well-known categories, prolific on many a dryland site, can also be enhanced by the circumstances of preservation in marshland peats or in soft, wet lake sediments.

We have already come across fish and vegetables in the pottery from Tybrind Vig, to which can be added the honey and dripping identified on Neolithic pottery from a riverside settlement at Runnymede on the Thames, and numerous references in the 19th-century literature to food remains in pottery, alas unidentified. At Charavines and elsewhere it has been possible to sort cooking from storage and eating vessels thanks to the presence of burnt encrustations on the former.

From circum-Alpine sites, another aspect of pottery preservation is apparent, the survival of applied birch-bark decoration on the outside of pots. This is found particularly on small bowls from the earlier of the Neolithic sites in the south-western part of the region (*ill. 75*). The bark was cut out in geometric designs and stuck on with none other than the universal glue of the period, birch-bark pitch.

Flint likewise has a new dimension through the preservation of associated organic matter. The Charavines daggers with their carefully bound handles (*ill. 69*) need only be compared with similar but unhafted flint blades from a dryland site to illustrate the virtues of wetland preservation. Similarly, more mundane flint blades, whose hafting does not often feature in typological discussions, are found on sites around the Alps with a strong wooden or bark backing, again attached with birch-bark pitch (*ill. 73*). The backing was normally slightly longer than the blade, and often had a hole drilled through one end. A Neolithic version of a penknife on a chain, or kitchen knife hung out of the reach of small children? Flint blades could also be hafted to make a sickle, and some interesting differences are apparent in the varied methods of hafting what are basically very similar blades.

Axe and adze handles are abundant and some aspects of their regional and chronological variation can be determined. Reference has already been made to Mesolithic handles from Friesack and from Nizhneye Veretye where wood from the base of a tree stump or root was used to hold the blade. There are few examples, and they are by no means identical, but it would seem that the blade fitted into a socket cut into the projecting end of a mass of wood, with the handle on the other side (*ill. 64*). Early examples of axe handles from the circum-Alpine sites show a similar use of the natural shape at the base of a tree trunk where the roots fan out, but the socket for the blade was cut on the same side as the handle and the mass of shock-absorbing wood curved away above the blade (*ill. 72*). Before long, the stone axe blade was set in an antler sleeve which in turn was set into a socket in a solid wooden handle. A further variant came with the use of handles cut from a tree-trunk with a small side branch which was used to hold the blade, either by lashing it on or by using an antler sleeve as a joining piece. Examples are also found where the branch forms the handle and the trunk an angled prong, perhaps split to hold the blade. Shaft-hole axes, that is axe-blades with a hole drilled through them, had a simple straight handle.

The wood used for axe handles was most commonly ash or maple; beech, oak and some holly handles are known, along with short handles of elm, alder, apple and other species. The preference for resilient ash and maple shows a good understanding of wood, and this was followed through in the use of naturally strong elements of a tree such as stump-root and trunk-branch junctions. Heartwood was not used, probably because it was too rigid. The wood was orientated so that the shock of the blade in use was transmitted transversely to

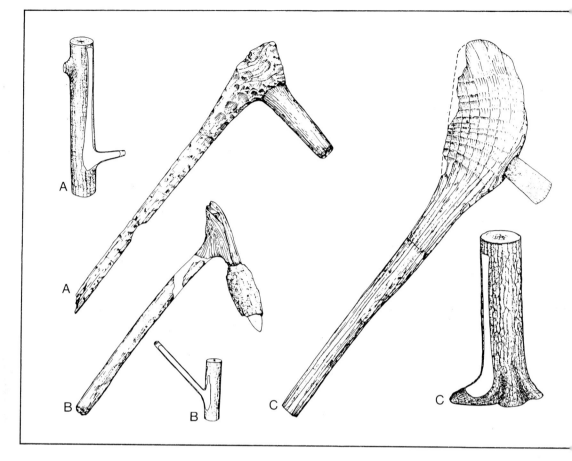

72, 73 Hafted Neolithic tools (*Above*) Axe hafts from south German Neolithic sites with sketches to show where the wood was taken from the tree, utilizing stem-branch angles and root-stem curvature. Length of hafts 30–50 cm. (*Below*) Hafted Neolithic blades of flint from Swiss sites. Lengths 33, 26 and 16 cm (from top).

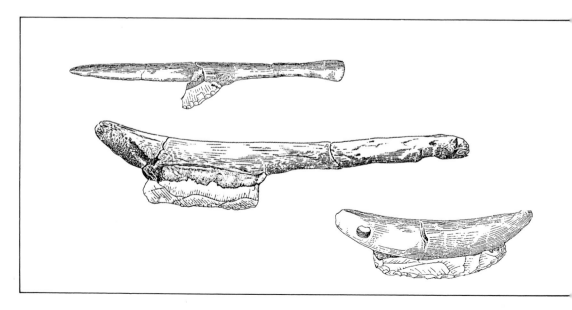

74, 75 Unusual containers of the Neolithic (*Right*) Oak tub and maplewood cup from Reute-Schorrenried. (*Below*) Small clay pot with applied birch-bark decoration, from the Neolithic settlement at Estavayer, Lake Neuchâtel.

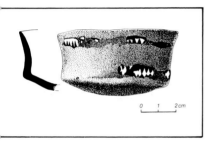

the growth rings and from inside-wood to outside-wood (see *ill. 72*), thus the structure of the tree itself was used to strengthen the most vulnerable part of the handle.

Artifacts made entirely of wood and of bark are numerous, and many are of a personal or domestic nature such as combs, bowls and spoons. Combs were usually made of boxwood or yew, tough dense woods suited to making fine teeth that had some chance of surviving in use. The shape of combs varies from place to place, suggesting that each group of people had their own style. Bowls were carved out of ash and maple wood, either taken from a split trunk or from a burr or bole with twisted grain that meant the bowl was less likely to split as it dried, and which gave a natural swirling pattern to a well-finished vessel (*ill. 74*). Most bowls were small, of a size to hold in the hand. Larger wooden vessels are less common but include a hefty irregular oak tub from Reute-Schorrenreid in southern Germany. Containers were also made out of bark, both shallow trays and deeper containers being made by sewing a band of bark to a circular bark base-plate. Spoons and ladles of wood survive from many sites (*ill. 76*). Ash and maple wood were again favoured species along with boxwood (all the Charavines spoons), birch, willow and poplar. An interesting example from Chalain makes use of a burr of maplewood for the bowl of a ladle, the handle carved from the parent trunk or branch.

76 Wooden ladle from Burgäschisee-Süd. Length 40 cm.

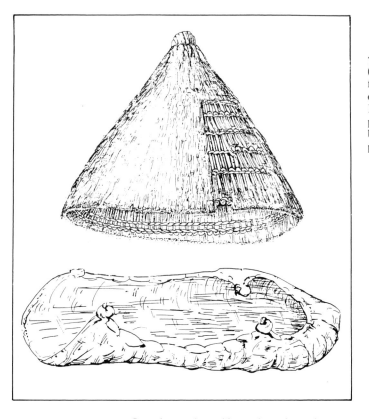

77, 78 **Neolithic clothing**
(*Left*) Straw hat and sandal
from Bodensee. (*Right*) Replica
of patterned textile from
Irgenhausen. The decorative
panels may originally have
been red and yellow. The
panel was *c.* 40 cm wide.

One domestic artifact where ingenious use was made of the natural growth form of a tree was the beater, as found at Charavines. The top of a fir tree was cut off just below the point where a ring of side branches grew out. The stem was stripped, and the branches trimmed to leave short upward curving projections which acted like a beater or whisk when the stem was twirled between the hands. It is an easy artifact to make, as any reader will find who experiments with a redundant Christmas tree, and its manufacture and use continued for many centuries (e.g. Fiavé, *ill. 98*).

Trees provided twigs and fibre for basketry, matting and rope. For the best surviving basketry we have to wait for Bronze Age Auvernier (Chapter 5), but many fragments survive from Neolithic sites, such as the pieces retrieved during early work around Lake Chalain. Containers were made in this way, and trays for threshing and sieving, and also personal objects. Amongst the latter several combs are known, and from Bodensee some fascinating examples of clothing, namely conical basketry hats and woven soles for sandals or shoes (*ill. 77*): ancestral straw hats and espadrilles. To call these basketry is perhaps a bit misleading; they were made from bast fibres taken generally from the underbark of oak or lime which could be processed to give soft, pliable fibres. When woven, the finished product was more pliable than osier work, and perhaps best regarded as a substantial type of cloth. Similar fibres were used to produce rope and string, and fine examples are known from Lakes Chalain and Clairvaux.

Amongst the most delicate of organic survivals are pieces of cloth and spools of thread. Flax was commonly grown, and linen was perhaps the most common type of fine cloth although other plants such as nettle were probably used in its manufacture. Simple over-and-under weave was used, with reinforced selvedges

and perhaps a knotted fringe. The best-known specimens of cloth are from Robenhausen, found in the 19th century (Chapter 1), and the dyed and embroidered piece from nearby Irgenhausen (*ill. 78*), both settlements being on the small Lake Pfäffikon which lies to the east of Zürichsee. The Irgenhausen piece has been reconstructed with vivid yellow and red embroidered geometric designs surrounding two large red triangles and a band of plain yellow and yellow-and-red chequered rectangles. Neolithic settlements around Bodensee, including Hornstaad-Hörnle 1, have yielded fragments of woven cloth decorated with sewn-on beads, and many loose beads. The beads in question are pierced seeds and fruit stones from plants such as Blue Gromwell (*Lithospermum purpurocaeruleum*), Sloe (*Prunus spinosa*), and Yew (*Taxus baccata*). Many wadges of cloth and spools of thread have survived only because they were carbonized, presumably burnt in one of the general conflagrations known to have destroyed a number of settlements. Such is the state of most of the thread from Chalain which was found wound onto spindles or into balls (*ill. 79*).

Cloth and thread and rope, axe handles and bowls and combs must have been in use on dryland sites as well as by the lakes and in the marshes of the circum-Alpine region. They are known only from the latter, even when carbonized, because it is only in undisturbed waterlogged conditions that the wood and plant fibres have survived. Fishing equipment, on the other hand, may well have been restricted to settlements with easy access to water. A number of dugout canoes are known, many of them old finds and undated, but there are examples of definite Neolithic date such as those found within the settlement at Charavines and on sites around Lake Chalain. They were usually made from an oak tree trunk, sometimes from fir. A few paddles are known (Chapter 6).

Having got onto the water, or sitting on the bank, how were the fish caught? The range of artifacts known is basically the same as that recorded from Mesolithic contexts, and not too different from that of recent times: harpoons, hook-and-line and nets, but not, it would seem, the leister (*ill. 80*). Harpoons were made from deer antler, with some variation in their length and the number and regularity of barbs. Fishhooks were made out of bone, antler and boar's tusk. They were several centimetres in length and bent like a modern fishhook, some with a barb and some without. Small slivers of bone pointed at both ends were probably also used for fishing, as gorges.

Nets, as we have already seen, were present from the earliest of Neolithic wetland sites, and were made using several different techniques and with different size of mesh. Examples from Zürichsee sites include a relatively clumsy, thick-stranded net with a 6 cm square mesh, a neatly-knotted medium thick net with 3 × 6 cm diamond mesh, and a very fine, thin net with a 4 cm square mesh. As with the harpoons and fishhooks, the different sizes were intended for different quarry, and it should perhaps not be assumed that all nets were for fishing. Some could have been used in hunting and fowling, especially the heavier examples, and as carrying nets. The evidence which indicates that some were definitely used for fishing comes in the form of weights and floats which would have been attached to opposite edges of a net to keep it hanging vertically in the water. Floats were often cut out of bark, and a hole cut through

79 (*Opposite*) **Textile and cordage from Neolithic Chalain** (*Top*) Thread, probably linen, on a spindle. (*Centre*) Ball of thread, about 11 cm across. (*Below*) Fragment of basketry.

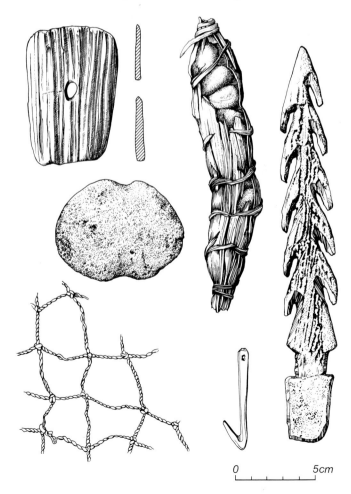

80 (*Right*) Fishing tackle of the Neolithic: float, weights, netting, hook and harpoon-head.

0   5cm

for tying them to the net. Weights could be made from a waisted stone or heavy fired clay, but the most ingenious consisted of a row of pebbles rolled up like a sausage in bark, and firmly tied at both ends. If the bark decayed, who would recognize a few untrimmed pebbles as the remains of an artifact?

This has been necessarily an incomplete survey of the wealth of material culture known from the circum-Alpine lakes, and some aspects such as toys, personal ornaments, wheels, and farming equipment have not been included. It would be easy to fill a whole book with their description. But it is not our present purpose to provide an exhaustive catalogue, rather to demonstrate the wealth of information about material culture that can be preserved in waterlogged sites, and the skills of early craftsmen in working perishable materials. Most of what has been described here could probably have been found in equivalent forms amongst contemporary dryland communities. That nets and cloth, hats and combs and even axe-handles and the contents of a pot rarely enter into dryland archaeology is a reflection of conditions of preservation and the mentality of archaeologists, more than of the original state of affairs.

5 · The lake-dwellers

WATERLOGGED SITES OFTEN YIELD EVIDENCE which upsets traditional archaeological classification, but for the sake of ordering the great body of information available into manageable chunks, some arbitrary divisions have to be made. It is in this light that the chronological starting point for this chapter – 2000 BC – should be regarded, a convenience for the prehistorian and no more. In Europe during the second and early first millennium BC, circum-Alpine evidence continues to dominate the picture of wetland settlements (*ill. 81*). From the first millennium BC onwards a number of important sites appear in northern and north-western Europe. Elsewhere in the world the evidence available for freshwater settlements is sparse and scattered, perhaps reflecting conditions of discovery and excavation more than an original lack of interest in such environments.

Circum-Alpine chronology

A decade ago, it would have seemed obvious to anyone working on the prehistory of the circum-Alpine lakes to draw a line at the end of the Neolithic. Many mid-third millennium sites were known, and a few settlements were occupied at the turn of the millennium in the late Neolithic or Early Bronze Age. There was then a hiatus until about 1100 BC, when Late Bronze Age lakeside villages proliferated. In the early 1980s the results from tree-ring dating gave precision to this picture, well-illustrated by the Zürichsee settlements which clustered around 2750–2650 BC and again around 1120–1010 BC. A lengthy abandonment of the lake shores was postulated, due perhaps to changing climate and lake levels, or to a changing social milieu which no longer favoured wetland living.

Recent work has shown that not all the Alpine lakes were abandoned between the Late Neolithic and the Late Bronze Age. All around the Alps, isolated examples can now be given of second-millennium BC settlements which were occupied between the two great *floruits* so long known from the Swiss lakes. Around the French lakes, for example, a number of Late Neolithic and Early Bronze Age sites have been identified. In Switzerland, on Zürichsee, where second-millennium abandonment once seemed so evident, recent excavations directed by Ulrich Ruoff at Zürich–Mozartstrasse have revealed a series of Early Bronze Age occupations, culminating in a settlement with wooden flooring placed directly on the relatively dry lakeshore and dated to about 1500 BC. In south Germany, Siedlung-Forschner in the Federsee peats and Bodman-Schachen on Bodensee both have several phases of occupation dated by dendrochronology between 1750 and 1500 BC. In the north and west of the circum-Alpine region, therefore, there was some settlement around the lakes and in the marshes in the first half of the second millennium BC, followed by two or three centuries when but little is known.

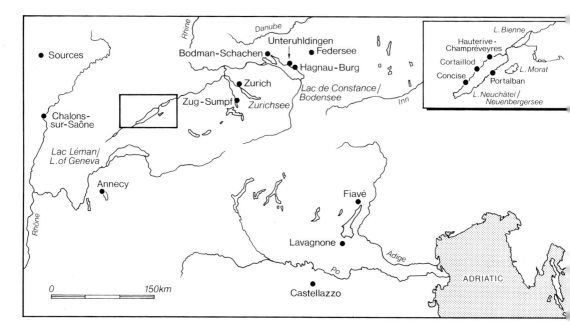

81   Map of the Alpine region, showing later Bronze Age sites mentioned in the text.

In northern Italy, to the north and to the south of lake Garda, two small, peat-filled relic lakes contain the remains of settlements occupied through much of the second millennium BC. The dating is not as precise as for the Swiss or the German settlements, but Lavagnone to the south and Fiavé to the north both have a long series of occupations through the Bronze Age. At Fiavé, excavated by Renato Perini, the best-preserved and most intensively studied period of occupation belongs to the Middle Bronze Age, approximately in the middle of the millennium. Both sites have slight evidence for occupation in the later second millennium BC.

Around Zürichsee, a number of settlements are known which were built between about 1120 and 1000 BC. Lake Neuchâtel had a similar but slightly later and longer burst of activity, from about 1030 to the 770s BC and settlements of the same period are known from Bodensee and Lake Annecy. A rash of sites built between about 1100 and 800 BC can therefore be documented.

The gap in the evidence which still remains may be due to circumstances of preservation and discovery, more than to any real abandonment of the lake shores during any part of the second millennium BC. If the long gap which appeared to exist a decade ago can be now reduced to two to three centuries, perhaps a further decade of discoveries will reveal settlements built during those apparently empty years. One or two points which arise from recent work may justify this confidence. It was noted that at Zürich-Mozartstrasse wooden flooring belonging to about 1500 BC had been laid directly on the relatively dry lakeshore. Such floors are vulnerable to decay, and rarely preserved along the shores of the major lakes. The survival at Mozartstrasse suggests unusual fluctuations in lake levels, which undoubtedly affected not only where people built but also what materials had a chance of being preserved. The situation is well illustrated at the later settlement of Auvernier-Nord on Lake Neuchâtel, where dendrochronology demonstrates a sequence of building from *c*.807 BC to 779 BC, followed by a shift upshore in response to rising water levels. Subsequent events have destroyed the evidence from the higher, later levels and but for the tree-ring evidence for a local shift one might argue for abandonment of the lake edge in 779 BC. Zürich-Mozartstrasse and Auvernier-Nord, in their different ways, remind us that a gap in the archaeological record does not necessarily imply a gap in prehistoric occupation, so much as a change in the circumstances of preservation.

Evidence from Lake Neuchâtel illustrates a further factor which may be distorting the picture. A number of brilliant aerial photographs have been taken which reveal the piles of Late Bronze Age settlements several metres below the clear waters of the lake (*ill. 36*). The present action of the lake waters has eroded the sediments around the piles and leaves them visible. Such erosion tends to take place at a particular altitude, or depth, around the lake. In antiquity, the settlements of any one period tended all to be at the same altitude, their location being closely related to the lake level. Therefore, current erosion will favour the discovery and excavation of settlements from perhaps quite a narrow time span. Likewise modern road construction, the impetus to so much of recent Swiss work, tends to follow a level around the lake shore and so settlements of one particular period are likely to be found, or perhaps the settlements of all those periods when the lake was at a certain level. At Hauterive-Champréveyres, on the outskirts of the town of Neuchâtel, the lake edge of the late Palaeolithic was also that of the Late Bronze Age.

If the lakeshores were occupied more-or-less continuously, then the question of why people chose to live in the wetlands alters. We no longer need to argue that the particular circumstances of the Late Bronze Age, for example, drove them to seek refuge on the water. Instead, and perhaps more plausibly, we can suggest that the lakeshores were attractive to farmers and fishermen throughout the prehistoric period, just as they are now.

The settlements

Wasserburg-Buchau on Federsee, excavated by Reinerth in the 1920s and 1930s, is still the best known of later second-millennium settlements in terms of general layout. Others, such as Auvernier-Nord on Lake Neuchâtel, have been partially excavated and studied in great detail, and a number of settlements are known in general outline from aerial photographs, but only at Wasserburg-Buchau has the complete excavation of an enclosed settlement taken place. The work was carried out long before the development of dendrochronology, and the two main phases which were distinguished cannot be precisely dated.

The settlement (*ill. 82*) was set in the marshy ground bordering the Federsee which was shrinking rapidly and filling with peat and already considerably smaller than in the Neolithic. In the first phase, estimated *c*.1100 BC, a solid palisade of vertical piles set in a band 1–1.5 m thick enclosed an oval area 150 m long. Two gaps in the palisade allowed traffic in and out, one on the landward side and one facing the lake. Within the palisade were 38 small squarish buildings, 3–4 m by 4–5 m, scattered around with areas of open space in the middle of the settlement and between the houses and the palisade. The houses were built like log cabins and the floors were set on horizontal beams directly on the wet marshy ground.

Some while later the village was rebuilt. Larger, rectangular houses up to 15 m long clustered along the lakeside of the enclosed area, leaving a fair amount of open space on the landward side. Some of the houses were joined at right angles to make H and U-shaped buildings, and they were divided internally into rooms. How long this phase lasted we do not know, but it came to an end in a conflagration.

Some 500 m to the south of Wasserburg-Buchau lies Siedlung-Forschner (*ill. 83*). Current investigations by Helmut Schlichtherle suggest that it was of a similar shape and size to its neighbour, with several rows of palisade. Dendrochronology has established felling and building phases from 1760 to 1726 BC and again around 1510 to 1480 BC, two clear phases as suggested for Wasserburg-Buchau, but earlier by several centuries. Settlements which are definitely dated by dendrochronology to around 1000 to 900 BC, such as Unteruhldingen on Bodensee (*ill. 84*), are of a different character from Wasserburg-Buchau and Siedlung-Forschner; in the later sites houses were tightly and tidily packed within a wooden surround which was more fence than palisade. Perhaps Wasserburg-Buchau was built and occupied in the mid-second millennium BC, not towards its end.

The evidence from Lake Neuchâtel for settlement plans of the later Bronze Age is excellent: from the air, through the clear lake waters of a still winter's day, the posts of palisades and houses and alleyways are clearly visible (*ill. 36*), revealing a concept similar to that of Unteruhldingen. Some plans have been checked by underwater survey and excavation, and sampling for dendrochronology allows the sequence of superimposed villages to be established. In many cases, the mass of piles resolves into 2 largely overlapping settlements, as at Concise V where a hamlet encircled by a palisade was followed by an oval enclosure some 140 m long packed with 14 parallel rows of houses perpendicular to the shore. At Chabrey-Montbec 2 overlapping rectangular settlements can be detected, filled with rows of houses perpendicular to the shore.

The adjacent sites of Cortaillod-Est and Cortaillod-les-Esserts have been well studied in recent years. Cortaillod-Est, slightly further offshore now, consisted of 8 rows of houses and a fence or palisade on the shore-side (*ill. 86*). Six rows of 2 to 4 buildings each were set up from 1010 to 1001 BC, with repairs from 996 to 991 BC. The settlement was enlarged between 996 and 989 BC and in 985 BC a fence line was set up on the lakeside. Further repairs can be identified, continuing until 955 BC, with some of the more recent wood coming from the side of the village closest to the shore. Here, at the site of Cortaillod-Plage, the earliest buildings date from 964 BC, indicating a shoreward shift from Cortaillod-Est. Limited study of the adjacent site of Cortaillod-les-Esserts showed a triple, lakeside palisade and building activity between 870 and 850 BC, so this settlement may result from another minor shift within the bay of Cortaillod in response to fluctuating water levels. It is interesting to find that the regimented layout of dense parallel rows of houses within a fence could develop over several decades, as was the case at Cortaillod-Est. If there were only the plans to go by, and no dendrochronology, interpretation in terms of a single short building episode would be likely.

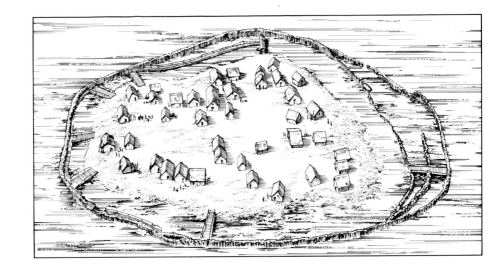

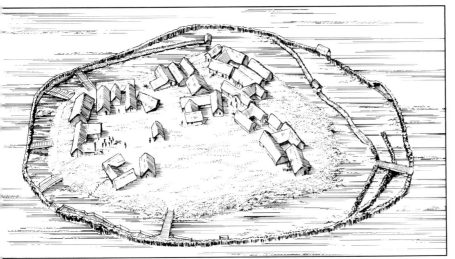

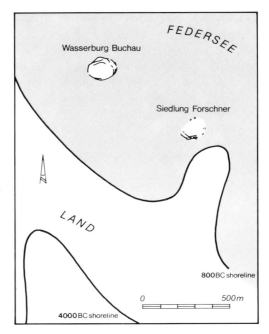

82, 83 **The Federsee** (*Above*) Reconstruction drawings of successive phases of settlement at Wasserburg-Buchau on the Federsee. The upper was the earlier. (*Right*) South-western Federsee shorelines, showing the location of Wasserburg-Buchau and Siedlung-Forschner (founded 1760 BC). Note that the contemporary shore was further away from the villages than the 800 BC shoreline.

FEDERSEE

Wasserburg Buchau

Siedlung Forschner

LAND

800 BC shoreline

4000 BC shoreline

0   500m

84–86 **Unravelling the complexities of Bronze Age settlements** (*Above*)
Reconstruction of Unteruhldingen on the Bodensee, founded in 975 BC. (*Opposite,
above*) Plan of the later Bronze Age settlements at Cortaillod. Cortaillod-les-Esserts
was founded in 870 BC, following Cortaillod-Est, founded in 1010 BC, with an
intermediate phase 964 BC at the poorly-preserved Cortaillod-Plage (not marked),
just on the shore-side of Cortaillod-Est. (*Opposite, below*) The sequence of house-
building at Cortaillod-Est, 1010 BC to 989 BC with a lakeside fence of 985 BC. Note
the orderly layout of the settlement which grew in 21 years from a nucleus of 4
buildings.

Auvernier-Nord is another Late Bronze Age settlement on the shores of Lake
Neuchâtel where recent work has enabled a detailed reconstruction of the
development of part of the village. There were two successive settlements; the
earlier Brena site, about which little is known because of severe erosion, was
followed by the large village of Auvernier-Nord where eighty or so houses were
built behind a palisade 170 m long. The palisade was originally built largely of
silver fir, and later extended using oak; it served principally as a breakwater, to
protect the houses from the storm waves raised by an east wind. Excavations
have concentrated on one third of the village and preliminary results from tree-
ring analyses are available for a part of the excavated area (*ill. 87*). The earliest
buildings date from about 878 BC, the first breakwater to 867–858 BC and the
later breakwater and houses to 854–850 BC. Some of the earlier houses were out
of use when the later buildings went up, so the maximum size of the village at any
one time was probably less than would appear at first sight.

The typical Auvernier-Nord house was slightly smaller than a Cortaillod-Est
house. It had 3 rows of 4 posts, it was about 5 m wide and 7–8 m long, and the
floor was bare trampled earth with a clay hearth supported on hurdlework.
There may have been a roof storage area or loft. The contents reveal something
of the occupants. One, labelled House 20 on the site plan, had probably been
used as a potter's workshop as well as a domestic dwelling. House 11 was full of
bronzes, and pots that were painted or decorated with tin, suggesting a wealthy
owner. The people who lived in House 16 must seem closest to modern
archaeologists, however, for they were collectors and had 5 fossils and 2 polished
stone axes from the by then remote Neolithic period.

Auvernier-Nord was flooded at least twice during its relatively brief history
and after one flood people came in a dugout canoe to retrieve their belongings.

Cortaillod

shore·side

Cortaillod·Est

Cortaillod·les·Esserts

lake·side

0   50m

0   15m

1010 - 1009 BC
1008 - 1007 BC
1005 - 1001 BC
996 - 993 BC
992 - 989 BC
985 BC

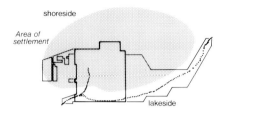

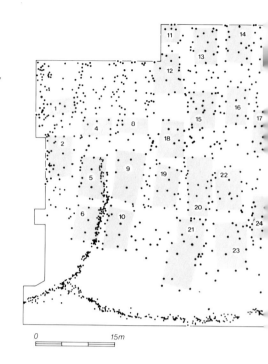

87 **Auvernier-Nord** (*Above*) The known area of the settlement with an indication of the area excavated. (*Right*) Houses built from 878 BC to 850 BC. The numbers identify the houses (see text) but do not indicate the sequence of building.

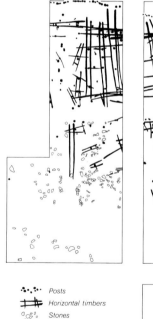

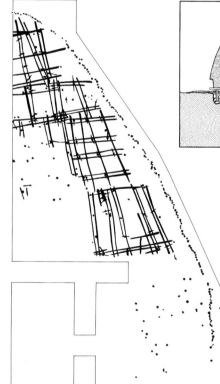

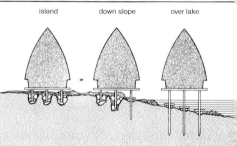

island   down slope   over lake

Posts
Horizontal timbers
Stones

0   5m

88 **The lake-dwellings revived** Fiavé-Carera, Italy (*Left*) Plan of excavated area and main structural evidence. Note the stone concentrated on an island, and timbers in the wet lake sediments. (*Above*) Diagram showing how structures were built contemporaneously on the island itself, on the shore and over the lake.

For some reason now obscure, the canoe got stuck in or under House 4 and there it remained for the archaeologists to excavate nearly 3,000 years later. It may have been a slow steady rise in lake level which prompted the shift of settlement westwards which is indicated by dendrochronology, for there is no sign that Auvernier-Nord came to an end because of flood or fire, nor did it come under attack. People quit their houses with time to spare, and took with them their precious belongings. As at Cortaillod, they moved no distance at all, yet out of the realm of present archaeological knowledge.

The settlements at Fiavé, in the basin of the relic Lake Carera, can be seen to develop throughout the second millennium BC, a period of time roughly equivalent to the Bronze Age south of the Alps. No complete settlement plan is available, to compare with those from the Swiss and German lakes. Much detail has, however, been recovered from the shores of a small island in the lake, enabling a variety of house structures to be reconstructed. Perhaps the most significant result from Fiavé is the demonstration of this variety, which existed both through time and within any one phase in response to diverse topographical conditions.

During the earliest occupation of the island, towards 2000 BC, houses were set with their floors directly on the shores of the island, which had been made up and levelled where necessary. Later, houses were built over the water, true pile-dwellings in Keller's sense. And then there existed a settlement which spread from the island, where house floors rested on the ground, down the shore and out over the lake (*ill. 88*). The posts or piles of the lake houses were anchored on an extensive grid of horizontal beams which prevented the buildings from sinking under their own weight into the soft lake sediments. How the grid was put in place is a matter for conjecture; the good preservation of the associated vertical posts indicates that the basal grid was well below the normal lake level, and as the settlement extended out from the island shore, which sloped deeper and deeper into the lake, so the grid must have been progressively more difficult to construct. Had Fiavé been excavated in the 19th century, the pile-dwelling controversy might never have arisen. Here, well-preserved by the peats, all conceivable types of wetland house co-existed in amicable contemporaneity.

How long was a village occupied?

It is one thing to define felling and building phases through dendrochronology, and to trace repairs, another to determine whether or not occupation was continuous between successive phases of building activity. Some settlements, such as Fiavé throughout the Bronze Age or Zürich-Mozartstrasse during the Early Bronze Age, have long series of superimposed buildings and occupation layers which suggest repeated use of the same site. Elsewhere, quite short occupations seem likely. One neat little site on Lake Annecy, Le Prieuré, belonged probably to the Late Neolithic or earliest Bronze Age. It consisted of a single isolated building, 5 × 5 m and built of oak, hornbeam and maple. This building was kept in repair for 10 years and then rebuilt and enlarged slightly. Within 18 years it had been abandoned.

Larger settlements appear equally shortlived. Siedlung-Forschner, on the shores of Federsee, was built and repaired for 35 years from 1760 BC and then probably abandoned for two and a half centuries before reoccupation. At

Bodman-Schachen on Bodensee, evidence from the lake stratigraphy indicates three separate occupation levels and dendrochronology gives three felling phases, at 1640 BC and at 1600–1589 BC and again at 1501–1499 BC. Without the stratigraphy this might have been interpreted as initial building and subsequent repairs and subsequent extension, then a gap in occupation followed by renewed activity some eight decades later. As it is, Bodman-Schachen was probably occupied for three quite short episodes spread over 150 years; the alternative is to suggest continuous occupation during which two episodes of flooding, severe enough to be marked in the stratigraphy, were followed by repairs and refurbishment of the damaged village.

The later Bodensee settlement of Unteruhldingen-Stollenwiesen also saw three phases of building activity, at 975 BC, 925–913 BC and 858–846 BC. In this case, the phases can be linked with repeated shifts of occupation shorewards, and the settlement could be said to evolve over a century although individual buildings had a much shorter life. A similar sequence was evident for the Neuchâtel settlements of Cortaillod-Est and Auvernier-Nord, described above. At Cortaillod-Est, building started in 1010 BC, the nucleus of the village was up by 1001 BC, soon expansion was complete, and repairs took place until 955 BC. Cortaillod-Est therefore lasted about 55 years, following which a shift shorewards can be documented. Auvernier-Nord lasted nearly three decades before a shift began to more protected waters.

From these examples, it would seem that Bronze Age houses were short-lived. But to argue that settlements were equally short-lived might be misleading. As we have seen, in several cases evidence is preserved to indicate that as one part of a village was abandoned, new houses were put up alongside and perhaps on a slightly different level. Because of the vagaries of preservation and discovery, discussed above, the archaeological record tends to cover just one phase of the evolving settlement. The presence of fences or breakwaters, which appear to delimit a planned, single-event construction of a complete settlement, also masks the development of villages. At Cortaillod-Est dendrochronology has demonstrated the evolution of the settlement, culminating in a shift to Cortaillod-Plage and out of the archaeological record in the 950s BC. Did the settlement endure, to reappear in the record at Cortaillod-les-Esserts in 870 BC?

It is premature to compare the life of houses and settlements in the Bronze Age with those of the Neolithic, since for each period there are still many questions to be answered. But as for the Neolithic, so the Bronze Age wetland evidence demonstrates an abundance of wood, of building, rebuilding, repair and demolition which has left us an inflated impression of the size of settlements and hence of population densities. The posts of Auvernier-Nord reveal that some houses had gone out of use before others were built, and an estimate of 80–100 houses for the known area of settlement cannot be taken as any sort of guide to the number in use at any one time. The answer can only come, if at all, from a complete dendrochronological survey. Meanwhile, the ramparts and postholes of a dryland site, such as the Altes Schloss, Senftenberg, or the Wittnauerhorn, will continue to give an impression of planned, ordered and densely packed settlements full of people. Those who know their wetland evidence will suspect that this was not always the case, and they will scale down their population estimates accordingly.

Subsistence

By the second millennium BC the natural environment of the circum-Alpine region had changed from that of the Neolithic. A slight drop in temperature coupled with the normal progression of forest species meant that beech and pine had replaced much of the mixed oak forest in northern and western regions. As a result, less light penetrated the forest canopy and the shrubby ground layer of vegetation was much reduced. There was no longer the wealth of wild fruits and nuts nor the abundance of forest animals, which had been there for early farmers to exploit. The dark forests were not ubiquitous, and around lake shores in particular tree growth was varied but these were the very places where people cleared away the wild woods and associated flora and fauna, to make fields for their crops. Another development, which has been traced around Zürichsee and doubtless occurred on other lakes as well, was the growth of extensive reed and sedge beds in the marshy zones around the lake shore. This probably encouraged wildfowl, and various species of fish.

Two thousand years of farming, of hunting and gathering, and of culling the forests for building timbers, had had some impact. Something of this has already been seen with the nascent woodland management of Hornstaad-Hörnle and the evolving forests around Charavines. In the later second millennium BC, pollen evidence indicates an expansion of permanent forest clearance, a phenomenon which is noted in many regions of Europe at this time. Around the lakes, it would seem that the farmers were attached to a particular territory to a greater degree than in the Neolithic. Their houses shifted around a settlement, but that settlement was relatively permanent (see above) and so too were the lands which they farmed.

The subsistence patterns of the Late Bronze Age are less well known than those of the Neolithic. Partly this is due to the severe erosion of many of the later sites, and also no doubt to the focus of archaeological studies which has tended to be economic for the Neolithic and artifactual for the Bronze Age. Plant evidence from sites north and west of the Alps is not abundant, although current excavations at Hauterive-Champréveyres look promising. Cultivated plants recovered from Auvernier-Nord include barley, three species of wheat, two species of millet, flax, poppies, beans, peas and lentils. Where known, the range from other sites is similar. Wild plants have been found on a number of sites, and the range is similar to that of the Neolithic, with apples, nuts and various berries, but the quantities would seem to be less than in earlier periods.

Animal bones have been recovered from a number of sites, with over 5,000 fragments from Zürich-Alpenquai and over 9,000 from Cortaillod-Est. At both settlements, 90 per cent of the identified bones were from domestic animals, and a similar ratio is present in a small preliminary sample from Hauterive-Champréveyres, and in the bones from Zug-Sumpf. No wild animals at all were identified from Auvernier-Nord. Hunting was clearly less common than in the Neolithic, and fishing and fowling are equally poorly represented at most sites.

The bones from Cortaillod-Est provide some interesting detail. Nearly half of those identified were from sheep and goats, and just over half of these were killed as adults. Just under a third were cattle bones, from quite small animals most of which (80 per cent) died as adults. A few horn-cores were found which were flattened along one side, perhaps due to pressure from a yoke, and the use of oxen for traction is suggested from other sites such as Zürich-Alpenquai. Pig were less common (7 per cent), and about half died in their second year and half in their third year. All told, the bone evidence suggests domestic animals were kept primarily to provide meat: beef, mutton and pork with a little lamb and veal. Oxen may have been put to work before they were eaten, but milk and wool do not seem to have been of major importance. Dogs were kept, some living to a good age. They were bigger than the dogs of the Neolithic, about 60 cm at the shoulder, and heavy-boned with massive jaws. Guardians of house and herd? Maybe, but at Hauterive-Champréveyres they were also eaten.

Wild animal bones were few but varied. The Cortaillod-Est sample included at least 7 red deer, 5 of them adult, at least 5 roe deer, 4 of them adult, at least 5 wild pig, 3 of them adult, 2 aurochs and one full-grown elk. That represents a feast of meat. In addition one each of the following was identified, often by only one bone or tooth; brown bear, wolf, badger, beaver, wild cat and pine marten. They were probably sought for their fur. Nine bird bones came from 2 domestic geese, 3 species of wild waterfowl and a young buzzard. Only 2 fish bones were recovered, both from a medium-sized pike.

The low numbers of wild mammals and birds can be attributed to two related factors. On the one hand, wild habitats were more distant than in the Neolithic, and the forest composition was less favourable to animals. On the other hand, animal husbandry had become more efficient, partly through the development of pasturelands, and the return of meat for the amount of effort required to feed the animals was probably greater than in the Neolithic. There was both less need and less opportunity to hunt. The paucity of fish bones is probably due to poor preservation, for many fish hooks were found (*ill. 89*). But why so few waterfowl are represented remains an enigma.

South of the Alps, Fiavé has yielded well-preserved plant remains, both cultivated and wild. Those of the Middle Bronze Age have been most thoroughly studied, being preserved by carbonization or waterlogging in the area of the settlement which extended out over Lake Carera and which came to an end by fire. The pollen evidence indicates forest clearance, cereal cultivation and the likely storage of hay within the settlement. Carbonized cereals and chaff include barley, three or four species of wheat, millet and peas. Carrot and chenopodium may also have been grown, or collected from the wild. Diverse fruits and nuts were recovered, some occurring in considerable concentrations which could reflect where they were stored, or where the residues of food-processing were chucked or where there had once been a latrine. The most common fruit identified was the Cornelian cherry, a misleadingly-named plant which is no cherry at all but a type of dogwood with red oval berries. Apples and pears were also present, along with hazelnuts, acorns, grape, fig, and diverse berries. Strawberries were especially popular. All of these may have been eaten, but it is to be hoped that the Fiavé inhabitants were collecting Danewort to make a dye not a poison.

The abundance of wild plants from Fiavé resembles that from Neolithic rather than Bronze Age sites to the north. At present, there is little to compare with Fiavé from other contemporary sites south of the Alps, and no definite reasons can be given for the contrast with the northern sites, but there are one or two interesting indicators. The Fiavé region does not seem to have had a long history of previous settlement, and during the Middle Bronze Age pollen analyses indicate that forest was present in the vicinity of the sites. It was a forest that contained oak as well as beech, and various shrubby species, so wild fruits and nuts may have been abundant within easy reach of home, as they were to the north of the Alps in the Neolithic but not by the later Bronze Age.

Bronze Age material culture

From the circum-Alpine region, inventories of the later Bronze Age settlements are dominated by pots and bronzes, and the record of organic artifacts is in many cases poor. This deficiency, like the absence of fish bones, is probably due to a quirk of preservation which is not yet fully understood. The clues are there that objects of wood, basketry, string and textiles were made and used, and on a few sites the objects themselves are well preserved to prove it. It is likely that the completion and publication of current work at Auvernier-Nord and Hauterive-Champréveyres on Lake Neuchâtel, and Zürich-Mozartstrasse and contemporary sites around the lower end of Zürichsee will redress the balance. At these sites conditions of preservation look promising and they may give us a better idea of the original range of perishable belongings than we have at the moment.

A contrast is evident in the material from eroded Cortaillod-Est and the preliminary results from Auvernier-Nord. The recent extensive underwater excavations of Cortaillod-Est produced two fragments of basketry and one short piece of string, and there was a little worked bone, tooth and antler. Otherwise the artifacts were inorganic, mainly pottery, stone and bronze. Seven hundred bronzes were recovered, predominantly small objects such as pins, rings, needles, beads and buttons and over 100 fishhooks. The presence and the number of these hooks is interesting given that only two pike bones were found. At least 13 different sorts of ordinary fishhook were in use, along with a double-hooked variety. Variation in hook type (*ill. 89*) can be attributed to different methods of attaching the line and different sorts of bait, both factors determined by the habits of the potential quarry. From this it can be assumed that the inhabitants of Cortaillod-Est angled for all sorts of fish even if we can prove only that pike was actually caught.

Auvernier-Nord has already been noted for the association of artifacts with particular houses, a demonstration in itself of the relatively undisturbed state of the site. Late Bronze Age artifacts (*ill. 91, ill. 92*) from the settlement and its surroundings include axehafts of ash, beech and oak, mallets made from ash- and beechwood, and sickle handles with a moulded handgrip, well ahead of any modern plastic design, carved from maplewood or one of the apple family. Cups and bowls were carved of maplewood, lime or alder, all good choices in their different ways. Maplewood was also used to make square boxes, the corners sometimes rounded and the outside perhaps decorated with a geometrical pattern. Box lids were of a variety of species, maple, alder, ash, poplar or one of the conifers, chosen no doubt for their grain and colour.

Supreme amongst the Auvernier artifacts, organic or otherwise, must surely be the baskets. About 150 of these were recovered, and many have now been conserved with great technical skill. Their full study and publication is awaited, but already we can see that if preserved at all, they were in an excellent state. Large containers were woven from hazel rods. For smaller baskets, willow was

89 Bronze fishhooks from Cortaillod-Est. Lengths 4–5 cm.

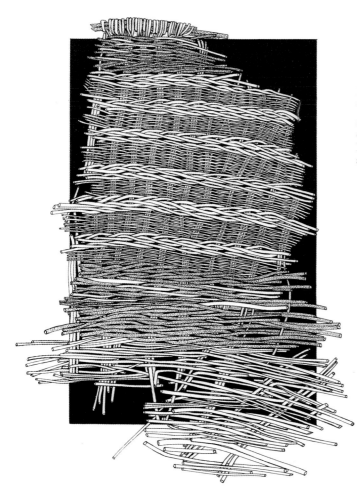

90–92 **Varied materials from the Swiss Bronze Age** (*Left*) Fragment of polychrome basketry from Auvernier-Nord. (*Below*) Handle of wood probably for a sickle, and bent wood box about 13 cm across. (*Bottom*) Small wooden and leather jewel box containing a necklace, from Grosser-Hafner, Zürich. The box is 7.5 cm across.

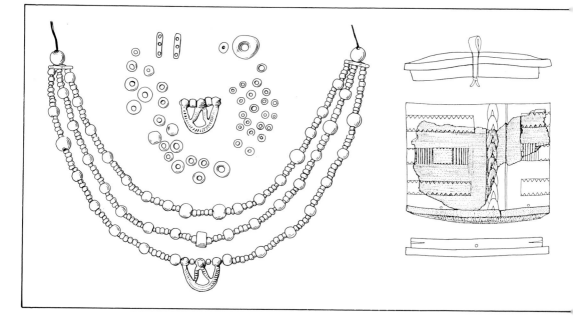

used, and distinct polychrome patterns were achieved using different-coloured rods in diverse weaves (*ill. 90*).

A justly-famous artifact is the small cylindrical wooden box recovered from Grosser-Hafner, Zürich, during the underwater excavation which began in the winter in 1979. It was found in a collapsed state, complete with contents of beads and pendants. Its original state has been reconstructed, as a neat little jewel box about 5.5 cm deep and 7.5 cm in diameter (*ill. 92*). The base and the lid were made of larch, the body of a thin bent sliver of ashwood sewn with a supple larch or fir twig and attached to the base with four minute wooden dowels; horizontal bands of simple incised geometric patterns decorated the body. Inside were several hundred beads strung in three necklaces. They were made of blue glass, golden amber, white mother-of-pearl, and black jet. In the centre was a pendant of pure tin. Lids and bases and beads have been found at other settlements, notably nearby Zürich-Alpenquai, but nothing as evocative as the Grosser-Hafner box.

Fiavé on Lake Carera has yielded numerous organic artifacts, particularly from the Middle Bronze Age levels. Many objects fell from the houses around the perimeter of the settlement into the waters and soft sediments of the lake below. Some were carbonized, others preserved simply by waterlogging. Willow basketry was found, with patterned weave as at Auvernier, and a tightly-woven conical basketry hat, made of flexible viburnum shoots on a framework of split spruce and reed, probably *Phragmites* (*ill. 94*). Small cups with a handle were quite common, eight made of maplewood, with one or two each of silver fir, beech, lime and apple-like wood. One of the maplewood cups had been repaired in antiquity, sewn with flexible spruce where the rim had broken (*ill. 95*). A spruce or silver fir vessel, a narrow cylinder with a separate base, was both sewn together with spruce and mended with it when the container split (*ill. 96*). Beaters, spoons and ladles, spindles and spindle whorls, pins, needles, awls and toggles continue the domestic inventory, all made of wood.

Distinctive hafts for sickles and for axes were recovered, many of them made from beechwood (*ill. 93*). One complete sickle had a beechwood handle, knobbed at the end and curved to hold a flint blade stuck in with pitch (*ill. 95*). Among the other 'outdoor' objects were a bow and several arrows, a maplewood yoke and a beechwood ard (from separate phases of the settlement). Beechwood mallets and beech and oak wedges probably both served for splitting felled trees and reducing wood to the required size for the manufacture of the diverse objects recovered from Fiavé. The presence of some unfinished pieces, cups for example, reinforces the evidence for local manufacture.

This is not the context to discuss the inventories of pots and bronzes from the later Bronze Age sites, except to note that the evidence preserved in peat and lake sediments indicates that both categories of artifact were produced within villages. The Zürich sites of Alpenquai and Wollishofen were both very rich in finished objects, and also in scrap metal, ingots, clay tuyères and numerous stone moulds. Knives, sickles, axes, spearheads and many different types of decorative pin were produced in quantity. At Auvernier-Nord the distribution of industrial debris indicated that pots were fired right in the thick of the tightly-packed wooden houses, not even in the more open space around the perimeter. No wonder settlements caught fire and burnt down.

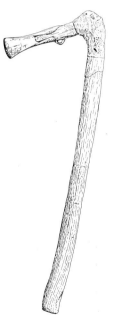

93 Bronze axe in wooden haft from Auvernier-Nord. Length *c.* 55 cm.

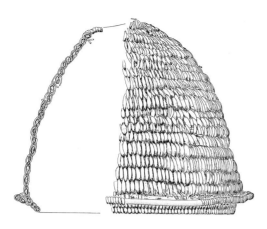

94–96 **Wooden artifacts from the Fiavé
settlement** (*Above left*) Basketry hat, made
from Viburnum, spruce and reed; internal
diameter at rim 21.5 cm. (*Above right*)
Maplewood cup mended with spruce. Diameter
19.5 cm. (*Right*) Sickle made of beechwood, flint
and gum. Length 41 cm. (*Below*) Wooden cups,
a small vessel and an unfinished ladle. The ladle
is 33 cm long.

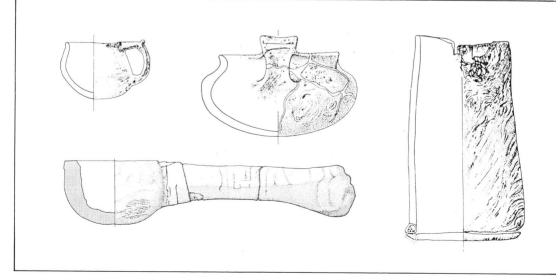

Finally, a fragment from Hagnau-Burg on Bodensee: from a layer dated to 1050 BC, underwater archaeologists have recovered a broken flute. It was made of elderwood, which is naturally hollow, and it was decorated with incised geometric patterns (*ill. 97*). The wood had split longitudinally, and only half the flute survived; the position of one hole was clear. Whether or not there were originally more holes is uncertain, but we should not grumble to have only half a flute, since the survival of musical instruments from prehistory is rare indeed.

Riverside and floodplain

Our knowledge of riverside settlements is sparse compared with that of lake shores and peat moors. The reasons for this have been discussed briefly above, noting that changing river courses, and erosion and deposition, have probably done much to mask or destroy ancient settlements along river banks and in floodplains. Discoveries made recently along the Saône in eastern France and the Thames in England confirm the existence of such settlements and their vulnerability to natural and human destruction. Where river banks are stabilized and waterlogged deposits protected, this is often because of recent and modern settlements. London, for example, overlies medieval and Roman and possibly earlier riverside occupation, and discoveries are dependent on present-day development.

In 1982, underwater survey of the Saône at Chalon located a settlement of Late Bronze Age date, 5 m below the present river surface. The first underwater excavations revealed occupation evidence spread for about 100 m along the ancient river bank in the vicinity of a ford. Several parallel rows of houses were separated from the river by a 2-m wide alleyway and a palisade or breakwater, elements of settlement layout well known from lake shores. Finds included bits of pottery, animal bones, grinding stones, some basketry and worked wood and quantities of grain. Moss, leaves and wood of all sorts suggest a well-protected and continuously waterlogged environment, with unusually good preservation for a riverside settlement. It will be interesting to learn what further work at Le Gué des Piles produces.

A short distance downstream from Chalon, where the Grosne flows into the Saône, dredging in the early 1970s both revealed and destroyed another settlement of Late Bronze Age date, at Ouroux. Rescue excavations between 1979 and 1982 found only 50 m square of the settlement left, which included parts of two buildings but no single complete structure. The occupation lay on river sands and gravels, and there was just one layer of debris with evidence for destruction by fire capped by a clayey layer which probably derived from the walls of collapsed houses. There was much pottery, a little bronze, and well-preserved organic materials including parts of a wooden wheel, basketry and string. The surviving building timbers allowed some dendrochronological analysis which showed the settlement to have been short-lived, in the excavated area at least. The houses burnt down only 13 years after they were first built, having undergone almost continuous repairs in the meantime. Ouroux-sur-Saône, like Le Gué des Piles, shows a number of similarities with contemporary lake and marsh settlements. In this case, the state of preservation suggests that burning houses collapsed into the water where their heavy clay walls settled and sealed the occupation evidence for centuries to come.

97 Elderwood flute from Hagnau-burg, Bodensee. Length 15 cm.

98 Wooden whisk or beater from Fiavé. Length 19 cm.

In a region of France where brandy rather than water springs to mind as the dominant liquid, namely Cognac, the low chalk and limestone hills are cut by rivers which do not immediately look full of archaeological promise. Yet there are areas of marshland, and thick layers of alluvium, and peat in their valleys, where survey by Claude Burnez has identified archaeological sites dating from the Neolithic onwards. The potential of La Palut at St Léger de Pons south of Saintes in the Seugne valley looks considerable. This is a small spring where recent cleaning exposed a dense concentration of early Bronze Age artifacts. Multi-period evidence from deep deposits at Les Orgeries, Courcoury on the south side of the Charente, are also of interest, and it is to be hoped that both of these sites will be excavated before dredging and other river works destroy the evidence.

At Runnymede, on the lower reaches of the Thames but above estuarine London, prehistoric settlement evidence has come to light in bridge building for the M25 motorway. Rescue excavations directed by Stuart Needham of the British Museum have identified two main periods of occupation, one Neolithic and the second Late Bronze Age. Work is still in progress, but already some interesting discoveries have been published. Pottery from the Neolithic levels was well enough preserved for the contents to be analyzed, identifying honey in one pot and in another dripping. The honey is particularly significant, as it provides our earliest evidence for the likely presence of honey bees in Britain.

The Late Bronze Age settlement was probably built on an island in the Thames. Traces of ancient watercourses suggest the island was about 2 hectares in area (4 acres), ample room for a village with a fence or palisade along the water's edge. The dating is based on radiocarbon, not dendrochronology, so precise years of building are not known. So far, four phases have been identified, spread over about three centuries of the Late Bronze Age. The palisade was rebuilt once, each time following a wavy or cusped line; the palisade at Le Gué des Piles was made of posts set in little groups of 3–5, which also created something of a sinuous or wavy line. Although probably contemporary, there is no suggestion of any cultural link between the two sites, but a wavy palisade could be a design response to the flowing waters of a river's edge settlement. Lakeside villages with their smoothly-curved palisades faced storm waves, but not strong currents.

In Italy, numerous floodplain settlements are known in the valley of the Po and its tributaries. These are the *terramare*, literally 'black-earth' sites. They have been known since the 18th century, large flattish mounds made up of layers of clay, sand and ash, speckled with occupation debris and reminiscent in section of a giant chocolate and coffee cassata ice-cream. For long they were carted away for fertilizer, like the crannogs of Ireland and many another archaeological site. In the late 19th century there was a spate of serious investigation (Chapter 2), but modern fieldwork and excavation are only just underway. A classic site, Castellazo di Fontanellato, lies 20 km to the north-west of Parma. Excavated from 1888 to 1896 (*ill. 99*), the settlement was found to cover a trapezoidal area of about 16 hectares or 38 acres, enclosed by a deep water-filled ditch. Inside, a regular layout of streets and houses focused on a central open area. The general impression of a well-planned site is common to the *terramare*, and in a number of cases the surrounding ditch was reinforced with a stout rampart. Whether this was for defence against human enemies or against the deep seasonal floods which

99 Late-19th-century excavations at the *terramare* ('black-earth' site) of Castellazo di Fontanellato, Italy.

covered the plains is unknown, but the influence of water is clear in the use of ditches, in the building up of mounds like *terpen* to live on, and in the preservation of structural timbers and wooden artifacts in the lower layers of the settlements. The *terramare* lay between water and land, seasonally set in a vast expanse of muddy floods, seasonally high and dry. The cultivation of flax indicates humid, organic rich soils, and the long lists of wild plants and animals recovered during the late-19th-century excavations suggest that here, as at Fiavé, the forests of the Bronze Age were as extensive and as prolific as those of the Neolithic had been further north.

In northern and north-western Europe a number of lake and marsh settlements are known of first-millennium BC date. Many are built on artificial islands, or on natural islands enlarged with boulders and brushwood, and their setting is generally thought to have been defensive. Today, the causeways which once linked them to the mainland have often silted over, and the sites stand as peninsulas jutting out into the lake waters or marshy ground. Other settlements are less immediately visible, less prominent perhaps in antiquity and now more deeply buried by subsequent peat formation and the deposition of sediments. A good many of these sites were discovered and examined in the 19th and early 20th centuries (Chapters 1 and 2) ranging from the large settlement at Biskupin in Poland to the village of Glastonbury in southern England to the smallest of Scottish and Irish crannogs with room for no more than a couple of buildings. One important recent discovery is Flag Fen in the East Anglian fens.

The Fens and Flag Fen

The Fenlands of eastern England are the largest area of wetland in the country, and consist of about 400,000 hectares of drained fen peats and silts, centred on the Wash and extending over 50 km south towards Cambridge. The area was recognized for its archaeological and environmental potential by 1930 (Chapter 2), and it has recently been the subject of a major survey and excavation project. The history of the wet Fenland deposits is very complex and cannot be wholly unravelled here, but the area was at times attractive to early communities, and at other times uninhabitable. Much of the Fenland is low and was subject to major flooding from the North Sea on several occasions in the prehistoric past when only the rocky and sandy islands provided shelter. At other times it presented a series of freshwater basins and fen carr with alder and willow flourishing in wide expanses of rich wetland vegetation, rich in animals. Settlement in the past is clearly reflected in this ever-changing sequence of events, which has been elucidated for the 160,000 hectares of the Cambridgeshire fenlands by David Hall (*ill. 100*). Flint scatters mark former Neolithic and Bronze Age occupations on the edge of the fens, where the combination of dryland behind and wetland in front assured early farmers and gatherers a varied set of resources for both seasonal and permanent settlement dependent on proximity to the lagoons in episodes of marine flooding, and on the extent of year-round resources such as wild plants and water fowl. Parts of the southern Fenland also have extensive burial fields, where barrows were constructed upon dry surfaces later inundated and buried by river-borne sediments and subsequent peat formation. Many of these monuments were built on low islands and peninsulas and at the entry of rivers and streams as they flowed into the Fen basin. The Bronze Age cemeteries of up to 25 mounds lie at some distance from the lithic scatters which indicate settlement, and, together with detailed environmental reconstruction, these provide a rare opportunity to view prehistoric landscapes with substantial surviving elements reflecting settlement, economy and ritual. There are many later prehistoric sites now known from the silt fens of the northern part of Fenland. The occupations show a form of co-existence with a severely flooded landscape, and are probably to be associated with salt-marsh grazing and with the production of salt. These Iron Age communities were as pioneering in their own way as were those earlier groups who first entered the low Fen basin to establish a farming and gathering way of life.

In addition to the discoveries of new Fenland sites by survey, excavation of selected monuments has also taken place, and one or two are referred to elsewhere in this book. One of the barrows at Haddenham near Cambridge has been excavated, as it formed a part of a Neolithic complex focused on a causewayed enclosure. The 50-m long barrow consisted of a turf and soil mound covering a wooden mortuary chamber and its attendant entry and ceremonial forecourt. Unlike other long barrows of the British Neolithic where postholes and stains survive, this barrow still held its wooden death-house, a long flat-roofed box rather like that of a megalithic chambered tomb. The roof, floor and sides of the structure were of huge oak planks up to 4 m long and possibly 1.3 m wide, split therefore from very old trees across the centre in order to obtain the necessary plank width. Heavy oak posts helped to hold the walls and roof in place. The chamber held the bones of at least five individuals, pottery was placed

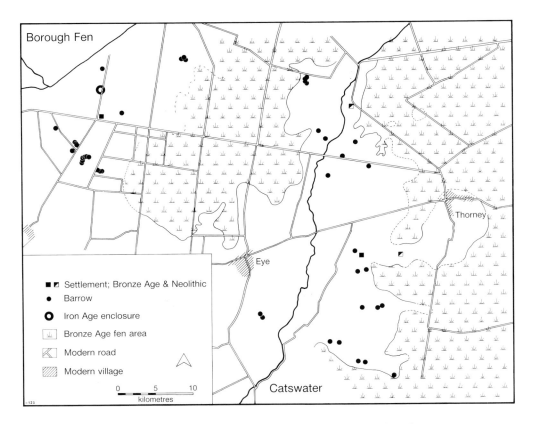

Borough Fen

Thorney

Eye

Catswater

Legend:
- ■ ◪ Settlement; Bronze Age & Neolithic
- ● Barrow
- **O** Iron Age enclosure
- ⟂ Bronze Age fen area
- ▨ Modern road
- ▨ Modern village

0   5   10
kilometres

100 Map of Borough Fen, England, showing the distribution of Bronze Age sites
in their contemporary landscape of marshy inlets and dryland peninsulas.

in the forecourt area, and red-coloured stones were brought in and laid in the
entry area to the chamber.

The archaeological work in the Fenland is the most ambitious wetland project
ever undertaken in Britain, and its results include new insights not only into the
prehistoric period but also into Roman, Saxon and medieval settlement and
activities. A measure of the new information gathered by the project field officers
is given by a single number: over 2,000 archaeological sites newly discovered
since 1981, an increase of over 80 per cent on what was known before. It is hard
to envisage what degree of confidence should be given to archaeological evidence
in other wetlands, where peats and silts will also have masked ancient sites,
without the kind of blanket surveys that have been completed by the Fenland
project. Comparison with the results of the Assendelver Polders Project
(Chapter 3), where a relatively small area was thoroughly surveyed leading to a
number of discoveries, reinforces the impression gained from the recent work in
the Fens, namely that chance discoveries reveal only a fraction of the
archaeological potential of such wetlands.

It was systematic survey of dyke sections by Francis Pryor and colleagues
which led to the discovery of Flag Fen in 1982. It is early years yet to give a full
outline of the site but some aspects of its character are emerging from the current
excavations (*ill. 101*). The settlement, of Late Bronze Age date, was set in
shallow marshes, probably dotted with carr woodland, in the narrows between

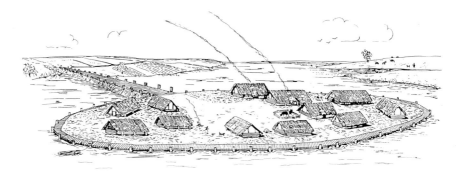

101, 102 **Reconstruction of two major settlements** (*Above*) Bronze Age Flag Fen, England. (*Right*) Iron Age Biskupin, Poland.

dryland and a large natural island. Effectively the site commanded the entrance to a lagoon of wetland, and probably controlled traffic from mainland to island as well. An area of about 0.5 hectare was built up with timbers and brushwood to make a platform. Alder, poplar, willow, yew and ash were used for this. In the excavated area a rectangular house has been identified, about 6 m wide and over 20 m long. The floor consisted of split oak planks. The walls were about 0.5 m thick and perhaps built of mud, peat and wattle supports; the house had been repaired several times, the woods used in its building being mainly ash and oak. The edge of the platform was revetted, and may have had a palisade in its initial stages. Around the perimeter was a 3.5 m wide road or walkway, a feature common to many wetland settlements of this period. Flag Fen has produced much worked wood, some of it in an excellent state of preservation, and several wooden artifacts including a willow-wood scoop and part of a wooden tub probably carved out of a block of alder wood. As excavation proceeds and lower levels of the site are exposed, further organic objects can be expected. Future work will also aim to establish the chronology of the site with some precision, and to determine how many buildings existed at any one time on the platform. Was Flag Fen a Wasserburg-Buchau with ample open space, or packed full of buildings like Biskupin?

Biskupin

Biskupin is one of several lake settlements of the mid-first millennium BC known from the area south of Gdansk. Sobiejuchy to the north covered about 6 hectares. Słupca was set on a man-made island apparently 2 km offshore in a large lake, and Biskupin itself covered about 2 hectares of an island 120 m offshore and linked to land by a bridge which later silted up into a peninsula. These and other similar and contemporary settlements were scattered across the watery landscape at about 20 km intervals.

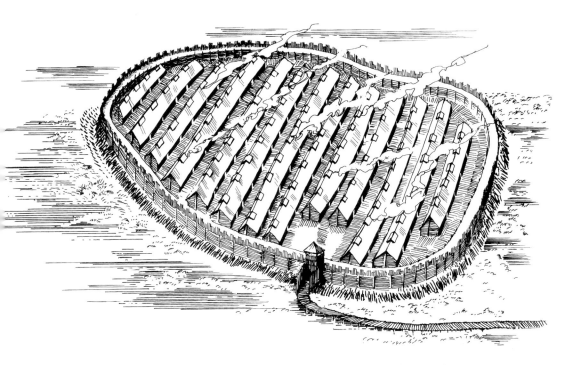

The settlement at Biskupin was heavily fortified and was apparently destroyed and rebuilt twice in its short existence of perhaps a century and a half in the early to middle first millennium BC (*ill. 102, ill. 37, ill. 38*). The outer defences consisted of a breakwater of 35,000 oak and pine stakes driven into the lake bed at 45 degrees, to point outwards and deter approaching boats as well as to deflect waves and winter ice; on the north-west, additional stakes were probably designed against wind-driven ice blocks. The settlement itself was protected by a rampart 6 m high and 3 m wide, frame-built of oak with earth packing, upon which a palisade stood. Entry to the oval area of 160 × 100 m (about 1.5 hectare) thus enclosed was restricted by a heavy gate tower with double swing doors, approached only by a funnel palisade of stakes. The approach to the gate was by an oak-built bridge 120 m long which curved from the south-west shore of the lake, where a freshwater spring existed, out to the settlement, and running in part alongside the rampart from where no doubt the inhabitants could have a good look at any visitors and take appropriate action. A 3-m-wide wooden road ran around the inside of the rampart; this was built of heavy oak and pine logs laid as a corduroy road on parallel beams beneath, and was covered by clay and stone. From this ring road there ran eleven narrow east–west streets, transverse to the long axis of the settlement, with a small open space left just inside the gate. The total length of roads was 1,300 m, mostly heavy enough to carry the weight of carts with solid wooden wheels, and 2 m wide; the carts could only pass one another in the village square, as the roads were too narrow for side-by-side vehicles. No one-way signs have been recovered from the site but some established direction signals must have existed.

The parallel streets provided access to 13 rows of terraced houses. These were built of horizontal wall beams slotted into vertically-grooved corner and side posts. The lowest wall beams were perforated to hold wooden bars which helped prevent the building from sinking into the damp earth of the island. There were 102–106 houses in the settlement, all of about 9 × 8 m in size and standing 6–7 m high with a pitched roof. Each house had an outer door facing south, which led into a hallway running the width of the building and about 2 m deep; here were spaces for overwintered animals, working areas and general stores. From the hallway a door led into the main room measuring about 6 × 9 m. On the left as you entered was a communal bed area, to the right was a stone and clay hearth, shelves and general living area. Such a house could have sheltered a family of 6–10 persons.

The inhabitants of Biskupin drew upon a wide territory for their supplies. Their arable land may have extended to 600 hectares, where wheat, barley and millet were grown. Plots were also cultivated for peas, beans, poppy, turnip, flax and other plants. Wild plants were collected from marshland and forest, which yielded hogweed, sorrel, hazelnuts, knotgrass and acorns, for food, and lilac and rennet for dyeing textiles. Honey and wax were collected from bees. Domesticated animals included cattle, sheep, goat, pig and horse, and probably dogs as well. Wild animals were actively hunted and gathered, including forest-dwellers such as deer, boar, bear, wolf, lynx and badger; beaver and otter were taken from the water's edge, and fish, fowl and mussels from the lake.

The artifacts made and used in the settlement include two-wheeled carts and four-wheeled waggons, logboats, ards and other agricultural tools, vessels and tubs, ladders, gates, beds, looms and handles, all of wood. Antler and bone were used for hoes, hammers, arrowheads, spearpoints, chisels and awls. The pottery included both coarse domestic wares and fine decorated dishes and jars; one of the dishes had a hunting scene inscribed, showing horsemen and deer. The heavier vessels include containers for 60–90 litres of, presumably, water. Amulets of clay, rattles, miniature chariots and the like were also produced. Bronze tools, weapons and ornaments were manufactured on site, but the iron objects were probably acquired by trade from outside sources.

Perhaps one of the more interesting aspects of the Biskupin settlement is the information yielded about construction in wood. The preservation of the lower parts of the houses, the roads, the base of the ramparts, gate, bridge, and the collapsed and partly burnt elements of the roofs, tower and so on all combine to demonstrate skill in carpentry and careful management of woodland. One of the houses alone required something like 50 trees of oak and pine, aged about 50 years for oak, less for pine; other estimates of the requirement are far higher, well over 100 trees. If we include the 100 houses, streets, ringroad, tower gate, rampart and palisade, bridge, and outworks, the quantity is immense. In addition, reed thatch for the houses might have required 200 hectares of reed beds to be harvested, and thousands of tonnes of clay, stone and sand were also required. Much of this material must have been transported to the island by waggon or sledge over the ice in winter. The whole enterprise speaks of careful planning in both design and execution. The first settlement lasted for 40 years, then was destroyed by fire. The second settlement, less well-built, lasted 80 years before it too fell. A third occupation was much slighter and undefended, a sequence paralleled at other wetland settlements of this period.

Glastonbury and Meare

Glastonbury and Meare belong to the final centuries of prehistory in southern Britain, a time when the environment of the Somerset Levels was probably at its most diverse both in the wetlands and on dryland. Within a 10 km radius the inhabitants could have found salt and brackish waters, tidal estuaries, reed swamp and shallow lakes, freshwater rivers, fen woodland and great expanses of raised bog, dryland forest at various stages of growth, some of it coppiced, and soils of sandy burtle and of lias island to cultivate or graze. The surrounding landscape was well-populated with dryland settlements, on islands, in the caves of the Mendips, and in hillforts.

The Glastonbury settlement was built in an area of the Levels where open water had always predominated, broken by occasional patches of willow, alder and reeds (*ill. 103*). The village was built on one such patch, using the felled trees as part of the foundation of a gigantic crannog, gigantic in the sense that most contemporary crannogs in northern Britain and Ireland supported only a couple of houses (see below), whereas Glastonbury was to comprise upwards of eighty structures. To east and north, across water, lay the dry grounds of modern Glastonbury and Godney, to south and west the lake was bordered by raised bog, beyond which lay the broad shallow Meare Pool, and Meare island, and further expanses of heather, moss and cotton-grass. The two adjacent villages of Meare East and Meare West were here, not surrounded by water and marsh as Glastonbury was but by island, raised bog, and patches of wet woodland as well as the reed-fringed waters of Meare Pool. The less-wet environment of Meare required less of a foundation for the settlement than at Glastonbury, and meant in due course less preservation of organic materials for future archaeologists.

At Glastonbury, the crannog-like foundations were surrounded by a palisade and within this was the village, a collection of buildings set upon clay floors, loosely grouped into four or five main areas, with open spaces and paths between. No two buildings from Glastonbury were identical, but a general pattern can be determined. They were circular, with a thick clay floor, vertical wattle and daub wall, and a fairly wide entrance; inside was a round raised hearth, and a central

103 Reconstruction of Glastonbury Lake Village as an Iron Age crannog.

post to carry the roof, which was probably thatched. At Meare East and Meare West, less structural evidence has been found, whether because of the drier conditions or because there never were substantial houses here is not certain. Bulleid during his early excavation, and the authors in their recent work, searched carefully for structures and reached the conclusion that the inhabitants of Meare probably lived in tents and other light structures, whereas at Glastonbury people were solidly housed. At Meare occupation was perhaps seasonal, at Glastonbury year-round.

Before we speculate further on the nature of the two sites, let us glance at the artifacts which were recovered from them. Because the sites were waterlogged and protected by overlying deposits, and never ploughed or otherwise seriously disturbed, artifacts of all types have survived in a much better state than is the norm on dryland sites and the quality of evidence is similar to that from Auvernier or Hornstaad-Hörnle. The pottery from Glastonbury and Meare is well known for its decoration and much fine but undecorated pottery has also survived. Occasionally, pots of almost identical shape and decoration have been identified from Meare West and Meare East, and also from Glastonbury, suggesting close links between the three sites. There is also similarity in the style of decoration on pots and on some of the wooden tubs from Glastonbury (*ill. 104*). Remains of fourteen tubs or smaller containers were found, some hollowed out of a solid piece of wood and others made of staves which were either dowelled together, or held by hoops like a barrel. One small tub, hollowed out of a block of ash, was 15 cm high and about 30 cm in diameter with sides and base 2 cm thick or less, and it may originally have had a handle. A delicate curvilinear pattern had been incised and burned on the outer surface, and this was a container of some beauty. Another well-finished wooden container was a little stave-built tub of oak, with four legs formed by a continuation of staves below the inserted base. Its

104   Reconstruction of baskets, wooden tubs and bowls from Glastonbury Lake Village.

height, including the legs, was just over 15 cm and it was nearly 25 cm in diameter. The staves were dowelled together with little oak pegs, and held by a bronze band around their middle.

Basketry was used for larger containers, fragments of which survived both at Glastonbury and at Meare. We suspect that leather containers were also in use, of the goatskin water bag or leather winebottle variety. The reason for this is that several wooden bungs or stoppers were found, but nothing to put them in. Had they stopped up pottery casks or wooden tubs, both container and stopper should have survived, but had the container been leather, no trace of the bag would have been left in the peat. The stoppers were made of oak, about 7 cm long and 3–5 cm at their maximum diameter.

The inventory of wooden household objects continues with ladles. Their bowls were from 7–10 cm across, and the handle of one complete specimen was 12 cm long, with a knob at the end. Wood was also used for the handles of knives, and other iron tools. On the whole the wooden handles are better preserved than the iron blades, but sufficient remains of the latter to gain an impression of the complete original object and its function. Many of the forms are familiar, with axes and adzes, billhooks, sickles, saws and files and knives of various sizes. Other finds are less easy to identify, like the wood described by Bulleid as 'sixty-three pieces of framework, presumably parts of looms or appliances for making textile fabric'.

Evidence for weaving is plentiful from Glastonbury and from the two Meare villages, although no woollen thread or piece of cloth survives. There are many bones from sheep which provided the fleece, antler combs to remove it and prepare it for spinning, spindle whorls of many and often decorative materials, and heavy clay loom weights for a vertical loom. Various other crafts were practised, most notably the production of glass beads. Glastonbury and Meare have proved rich sources of coloured beads, some plain yellow or blue or bluish green and others decorated with swirls of yellow on clear glass, or white on blue. The quantity of beads, especially from Meare, is such that the settlements have been interpreted as centres of production. But it was not until 1979 that evidence was uncovered at Meare West to prove that beads were made on the spot. The evidence came from beads that went wrong and were thrown away. One was made of blue glass, wound around a metal rod, and another was of multi-coloured glass encased in a mould. Bulleid and Gray recovered possible necklaces of beads from Meare East, and single specimens have been found scattered elsewhere, so it is likely that people were wearing as well as making these colourful ornaments.

In addition to the glass-makers, bronzesmiths and ironsmiths were at work, at times perhaps with disastrous results, for at Glastonbury it seems a smith burnt down his house. Wood and shale were turned, and wood, bone and antler carved into diverse objects. The evidence for all this activity is, if anything, greater from Meare than from Glastonbury. A similar diversity of crafts and industries practised in a domestic context was seen at Biskupin and at a number of circum-Alpine settlements.

The wet environment of the Somerset settlements has already been described. Why, one might ask, did people choose to live in such places? Choice it probably was, rather than necessity, for we have seen time and again that wetland settlements were placed to exploit the advantages of their environment rather than to escape the disadvantages of dryland. Recent work on the environment of Glastonbury has confirmed the diversity of wetland habitats around it, and it is clear from the evidence retrieved by Bulleid that these were fully exploited in addition to traditional Iron Age farming on dry land, which was however at some little distance from the settlement. The marshes were also protective, reeds and giant sedges, patches of alder and willow carr and a myriad of sluggish waterways concealing the Glastonbury village from strangers. Here people lived permanently, in a wealthy stronghold. At Meare, by contrast, the two adjacent and perhaps contemporary settlements were more in the open, on the edge of bleak raised bog and quite close to dry land. Resources were not lacking, but there was perhaps not the exceptional wealth that surrounded Glastonbury. The settlements were visible, open and seasonal, and a hive of industrial activity. We can envisage a bustling occupation at Meare, with a wide variety of specialists at work, able to devote time and energy to the manufacture of their wares, to talk and to barter, to give and to receive, and to use the summer season to the full whilst their flocks and herds grazed the moors. Soon enough they would be away to the late autumn and long winter occupations on the uplands, back to their own territories.

New work on crannogs

Anniversaries can be a useful stimulus to new work, and celebrations in Scotland in 1982 of the work of Munro and in Ireland in 1986 of that of Wood-Martin have revived interest in the archaeology of crannogs in both countries. Early investigations of these sites, described in Chapter 2, established that they were artificial islands, or natural islets artificially enlarged to accommodate a small settlement surrounded by a palisade. They normally occurred 100 m or so offshore of a lough (Ireland) or loch (Scotland) and were linked to dryland by a causeway or bridge (ill. 106). Occupation was thought to begin at the very end of the first millennium BC, with most crannogs built in the mid-first millennium AD and some occupied into early modern times.

The impetus to new work came a few years earlier in Scotland than in Ireland, and already surveys have established that crannogs were more common and more widely distributed across Scotland than previously thought. On Loch Awe 20 crannogs have been identified and on Loch Tay 18, where previously only a handful were known (ill. 105). A few excavations are under way, and at Eilean Domhnuill in Loch Olabhat on the Outer Hebridean island of North Uist (an island in a lake on an island in the sea) Early Neolithic material has been identified, considerably extending back in time the chronology of the Scottish crannogs.

At Oakbank, on Loch Tay, underwater excavations directed by Nicholas Dixon have identified a made-up island consisting of a 2-m thick layer of vegetable material overlain with stones, silt and gravel and capped by larger boulders, built in the mid-first millennium BC. The island was about 30 m across, and 50 m from the shore. One round house occupied most of its surface, leaving room for a walkway around the outside. This house was repaired, and then abandoned. A century or so later the island was reoccupied, a new building put up and a landing stage was added. A wooden causeway linked the island to the shore of Loch Tay, perhaps from the start. The preservation of wood is

105, 106 Crannogs in Scotland
(*Left*) Air photograph of Croftmartaig island, a crannog in Loch Tay, Scotland. (*Above*) Reconstruction drawing of the Milton Loch crannog, with bridge, landing stage and logboats.

excellent, both for structural timbers and for artifacts. Amongst the latter are flat wooden dishes, one still containing traces of butter, a wooden mug, a whistle, a paddle and part of what was probably an ard.

Bone was poorly preserved in the Oakbank deposits, but the presence of live animals on the small crannog is nevertheless suggested by the sheep droppings which have been excavated from the house floor. Cattle dung and human faeces may also be present, but are not preserved in such a recognizable state (Heer noted the same difference many decades ago, see Chapter 1). Net weights suggest fishing, and the paddle supposes dugouts or some other form of small boat for water transport. Pollen and plant remains indicate arable cultivation, and much evidence has been found for the exploitation of wild plants including hazel, cherry, blackberry and raspberry. The range of economic information may well be extended as the Oakbank excavations proceed, but already we can see elements of a classic full-blown wetland economy exploiting water and dry land, wild and cultivated resources.

In Ireland as in Scotland there is a renewed interest in crannogs. It seems likely that here too their distribution and their chronology will be extended. Already John Bradley's excavations at Moynagh Lough in Co. Meath have revealed Mesolithic occupation of two low knolls which were later to form the basis of a crannog. The site lies at the southern end of a former lake linked to the old course of the River Dee. The area is now wet pasture over peat and lake silts, the excavations are open-air, and it is unlikely that conditions of preservation will be quite as good as at underwater Oakbank. Nevertheless, Moynagh Lough is a rich and undisturbed site and its excavation under modern controlled conditions will give us a valuable record to set beside the often confused picture obtained from the earlier investigations of other sites.

At Moynagh Lough the old lake lay in a broad shallow basin surrounded by gentle hills. The two small knolls, 8–9 m across and barely 0.5 m above the then lake levels, were occupied some 6,000 years ago by Mesolithic peoples who consolidated the ground with stones, pebbles, hazel and bramble brushwood. They left, the lake rose, and muds and silts buried much of the knolls. About 4,000 years ago, in the Early Bronze Age, people again consolidated the small patches of dry ground and stayed a while, probably for fishing and fowling like their predecessors. A millennium later, in the Late Bronze Age, the knolls were used again, but it was not until the mid-first millennium AD (Early Christian) that the crannog was built.

The excavations at Moynagh Lough are still in progress, but already sufficient evidence has been exposed and published to indicate at least two phases in the occupation of the Early Christian crannog. Two lines of palisade can be traced, one built of young oak posts and the other of a mixture of very young oak, birch, hazel and ash. After the crannog platform was built over and around the knolls to give a dry area about 40 × 32 m, people lived on it who worked metals. Later a house was built over the metalworking area, a post and wattle round house about 10 m in diameter. Its occupants were a wealthy family, to judge by the debris they left behind. Bone survived well, and came mostly from domestic cattle, pigs and sheep with a few horses, dogs and cats and virtually no wild animals, apart from one or two otter, badger and wolf hunted perhaps for their pelts.

At Moynagh Lough, unlike Oakbank, the platform was considerably bigger than the house it supported; gravelled working areas and hearths indicate that the open air space was put to good use. Abundant evidence has been found for the manufacture of objects on site. Bronze and iron were worked, the bronze cast in delicately-ornamented clay moulds to produce ornaments. Leather snippets, wooden lathe-waste, unfinished wooden vessel staves, quernstones in the making and bone and antler pieces indicate that all these raw materials were used in the local production of artifacts, and some of the finished goods have also been recovered.

The wealth of industrial activity and the wealth of finished goods from Moynagh Lough are reminiscent of the richness of other Irish crannogs such as Lagore and Ballinderry, which have traditionally been interpreted as high status, even royal households. Glastonbury and Meare from the Somerset Levels were also wealthy, and the Late Bronze Age sites from around Zürich, or Auvernier-Nord on Lake Neuchâtel notably so. Two factors are at play here, first the wealth provided in antiquity through access to both wetland and dryland resources, and secondly the wealth provided to the modern archaeologist through the waterlogging and burial of sites in peats and sediments which has ensured so much better conditions of preservation and survival than on dryland sites of the same era and area.

Crannogs appear defensive, set out on the water, linked to land only by a narrow causeway or bridge, surrounded by a palisade. In historic times, they are known to have been used as refuges, and doubtless also served this purpose in their earlier days. But crannogs were also well placed to exploit good agricultural land, and to benefit from fish and fowl and other wild resources. It may be that just as the ameliorating effect of the Alpine lakes on local climate has been suggested as a factor influencing settlement there, so the crannog-dwellers benefited from a similar slight warming. It remains to be seen if their use can be correlated in any way with changes in climate of the meteorological rather than the military sort, although evidence from New Zealand (see below) indicates that the two were not exclusive.

Elsewhere in the world: a postscript on potential

The subject matter of this chapter has been European, and predominantly Alpine. This is a reflection of the state of archaeology and not of past patterns of wetland settlement: it is in this part of the world that most excavations have been funded and published. In this final section it is hoped to show, by brief descriptions of evidence available from elsewhere, the largely unrealized potential of worldwide freshwater wetlands.

In Russia, well to the east of the relatively well-known Estonian sites, peatbogs in the Ural mountains contain waterlogged sites of the Bronze Age and probably earlier. At Gorbunovo and at Shigir material has been recovered which relates to the widespread Turbino culture of the second millennium BC, and both sites contained organic materials. Shigir, the southern of the two sites, is best known for wooden sculptures of elk, goose and bear. At Gorbunovo, where a number of sites have been excavated, the one known as Section Six had three distinct cultural layers. The lowest, which was probably of Neolithic date, was found at the base of the peatbog on lake silts, associated with pollen from fir with some birch and hazel. The climate was relatively wet and cold. Wooden artifacts included paddles, netting needles, net sinkers made of clay wrapped in birch bark (in principle not unlike the pebble and bark sinkers of the circum-Alpine neolithic), birch-bark net floats, bows, a birch-bark bag or container, a long sled runner, and carved wooden figures of elk and duck and humans. The middle layer, of mid-to-later second-millennium BC date, belonged to a warmer and drier period with mixed oak forest, pine and birch. Remains of wooden floors were found in this level, along with wooden figures of humans, snakes and water-birds (*ill. 107*). The bird-figures included ladles with the bird's head and neck as handle, and body for the ladle bowl. There were also paddles, hooks and a boomerang, a copper axe, and wire fastening a wooden vessel. In the top layer the main finds were pottery and a spear mould of Late Bronze Age type.

107 Wooden figures from Gorbunovo, Russia.

From what little is known of Turbino people, it would seem they were well adapted to wetland exploitation. They had dugouts for summer travel by water and sleds for winter travel on the ice. They fished, judging by the Gorbunovo evidence for nets, and they hunted elk in the swamps and marshes. They were also farmers, with crops and domestic animals. Whether they were wetland dwellers as well as wetland users is uncertain. The Gorbunovo floors are not thought necessarily to belong to a house, but perhaps to some ritual structure given the wooden figures. However, western European evidence demonstrates the feasibility of houses with floors set directly on a peatbog surface, most notably around the Federsee, so Gorbunovo as a domestic settlement need not be ruled out.

Across the world, in North America, and at much the same time from the later second millennium BC onwards, there is also evidence for extensive wetland exploitation without as yet much indication of wetland living. In northeastern North America, around the Great Lakes, sites of the Woodland peoples abound around lakes, rivers and rapids but few waterlogged settlements are known, investigated and published. At Dawson Creek, a peninsula juts into the marshes at the southern end of Rice Lake. It was occupied in the earlier first millennium BC by people who visited seasonally, hunted deer and other mammals, and collected acorns and other nuts. The setting is wet, surrounded by marsh, but the site is dry and so is the economic information. From other sites, freshwater molluscs and fish are known, but again in dry or relatively dry contexts.

The Roebuck site lies in the Ottawa river by the city of that name, on an island. It was a village of the St Lawrence Iroquois, a group of late Woodland hunter-fisher-gatherers who had acquired some elements of farming and who lived on their fortified island in the years immediately preceding early European contacts. Within a palisade there were thirty or so long-houses each sheltering several families, and a population perhaps 2,000 strong. Organic materials are preserved in the marshlands ringing the site, known from early excavations. Current proposals to re-examine the settlement could yield significant information about pre-contact economy and material culture.

A site in Florida now under excavation offers a similar potential for establishing the nature of Indian economy and artifacts before Europeans arrived, for tracing their development over 1,500 years up to the time of contact and then noting the changes wrought by the arrival of Europeans. The site is Hontoon Island in northern Florida (*ill. 40*), which is being investigated by Barbara Purdy. The large island, which lies in the middle of freshwater marshes and lakes drained by the St John's River, has a number of shell middens, one of which lies adjacent to the water where waterlogged midden deposits are to be found. Preliminary trial excavations have yielded a vast amount of economic information showing the exploitation of wetland species of plant, fish, amphibian, bird and mammal, with very little from the dryland (not that much dry land was available in the immediate region). The animals included mussels and snails, seven species of turtle, water snakes and alligators, numerous species of fish, manatee or sea-cow, and several waterfowl. Agriculture was relatively unimportant in the pre-contact period, whereas after AD 1500, although there was no direct European presence, the Indians seem to have farmed more and to have made greater use of land resources in general. The reasons for this somewhat enigmatic change, together with evidence for development in material culture to set alongside the excellent range of economic information, should emerge from future seasons of excavation.

A third region of the world where wetland sites document the state of affairs prior to European invasion is New Zealand. Here, archaeological survey and investigation of Maori sites offer some important corrections to the written record and corroborate other observations. This shows, incidentally, that what on the face of it are records of first contacts are in fact records of a society already altered by European expansion. The best-known of Maori sites are the *pa*, defended forts usually thought to be hillforts but also occurring in swamps. A number of waterlogged *pa* have been investigated, including those around Lake Mangakaware, described by Peter Bellwood (*ill. 108*). Lake Mangakaware is on North Island, about 25 miles (40 km) in from the west coast, and about 40 acres (16 hectares) in extent with swamps around. Three *pa* were built on its shore, two have been examined and numerous wooden artifacts have been recovered from the lake bed. The *pa* were heavily defended with wooden palisades on the shore side. Excavation at one of the three revealed a narrow entrance in the palisade leading to a large open area, with a group of houses in one corner of the enclosure. Evidence survived for the plank construction of the houses and details of superstructure came from house timbers retrieved from the lake bed: upright wall planks had a notch which held the tenon on the end of slanting roof planks (*ill. 108*). There were 5 houses and shelters, for 30 or so people, who lived in the *pa* for most of the year but went off on short seasonal trips to exploit other parts

108 Lake Mangakaware, New Zealand, showing the location of the defended fort or *pa* and a reconstruction of the house frame.

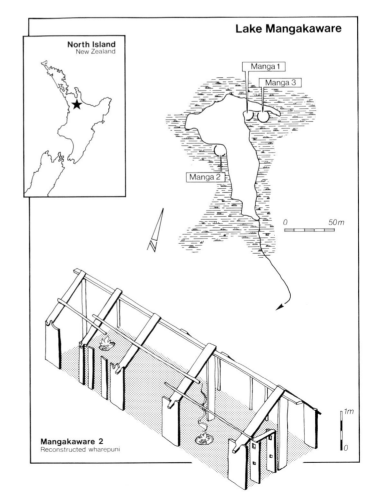

Lake Mangakaware

North Island
New Zealand

Manga 1

Manga 3

Manga 2

0   50m

Mangakaware 2
Reconstructed wharepuni

1m

0

of the region, including the seashore. Subsistence evidence showed the use of marine molluscs and probably eels, alongside horticulture. The numerous wooden artifacts include equipment for cultivating the ground and for processing foods, various clubs and spears, canoes and paddles, weaving sticks and children's toys, in addition to the house timbers noted above. Other waterlogged sites which have yielded significant Maori wooden objects are Waitore Swamp with its decorated canoe prow and small human head, Kohika where a canoe prow, combs, matting and cordage were found, and Kauri Point Swamp where plain and decorated bone and wooden combs were recovered.

Maori society is known to have been a warrior society, and the *pa* were attacked by enemies. The swamp location can therefore be seen as defensive. Some of the waterlogged sites are effectively crannogs, manmade islands; their building was described by the Reverend R. Taylor in 1872:

> first by driving long stakes into the lake to enclose the required space then by large stones being placed inside them, and all kinds of rubbish being thrown in to fill up the centre, upon which an alternative stratum of clay and gravel was laid until it was raised to the required height, on which the houses were then erected, and the *pa* surrounded with the usual fence.

Swamp *pa* and crannog *pa*, being undoubtedly defensive, give credence perhaps to the defensive nature of similar European settlements. But just as the European sites were noted to be well placed to take advantage of mild lake climates, so too were the *pa*. Bellwood notes that alongside a wealth of resources such as eels and freshwater mussels for food, flax and raupo for cordage and matting, and the wetland manuka tree for palisade stakes, the swamp *pa* inhabitants had the benefit of soils warmer than elsewhere. This was particularly important to the Maori, whose cultivated plants, like themselves, came from warmer Polynesian islands. Their crops were not easy to grow in temperate New Zealand, and deliberate efforts were made to raise soil temperatures. Soils that were naturally warmer like those around Mangakaware must have been particularly welcome.

The sites described here are but a sample. There must be many other freshwater wetland sites around the world, known only locally, perhaps excavated and unpublished, or unexamined for lack of funds and other resources. At times, the sheer bulk of information which pours out of a good waterlogged site undoubtedly deters investigation. One example known to the authors remains buried for other reasons: it is the core of Mexico City, where massive stone pyramids and other structures of late Aztec times rest on the waterlogged deposits of earlier peoples who built in the lake basin. A few wooden posts stick out of the ground to catch the unwary tourist and to invite speculation from wetland archaeologists on the undoubted wealth of cultural and economic information that lies buried, safe from development but perhaps at risk from the ever-increasing drainage, and the pollution, of the largest city in the world.

6 · Reaching the far side

A horrible desert, the foul damps ascend without ceasing,
corrupt the air and render it unfit for respiration . . . never
was Rum, that cordial of life, found more necessary than in
this Dirty Place.

SUCH A DESCRIPTION, written of an unidentified bogland in America by
Colonel William Byrd III in 1736, exaggerates the uncompromising
character of marshes, bogs and fens, and to many people, these always
damp and often bleak wetlands have a fascination that does not require that
sustaining cordial. Many of the wetlands so far encountered in this book are
physically halfway between the water and the land, whether that be ocean or
lake, coastland or shore, and yet they are distinct, participating in the wealth in
natural resources of each. Bogs are a different kind of halfway world, neither
water nor land yet a part of both, some bogs benefiting from the relationships,
others seemingly disadvantaged by their ambivalent position. Many varieties of
bogland exist, but the most significant for us are peat-filled wetlands where
human remains, wooden roadways, boats and other objects have come to rest and
been preserved from decay.

Peatlands can build up for thousands of years, accumulating organic matter in
the form of dead plant litter. The waterlogged conditions inhibit the influx and
flow of oxygen, slowing down the bacteria and other agencies that normally
decompose organic matter. Thus the plant debris builds up, and compresses by
its own waterlogged weight into peat, which may be loose or firm, light or dark.
Evaporation of water from the surface of the mire cools the peat and thereby
restricts the growth of the organisms that would otherwise decompose the plant
litter. The whole system is, in a way, self-activating, and over time, if the annual
rainfall is sufficient, there can develop bogs that are raised above the surface of
the surrounding land, and well above ordinary water table.

These *raised bogs* (*Hochmoor* in north-western Europe) may be several
kilometres across, and several metres high. They require cool wet climates, and
nutrient-poor water supplies. So do *blanket bogs*, well named as the acidic bog
covers entire landscapes of many hundreds of square kilometres. Up mountain
slopes and down valley sides, the peaty shroud depends on rain for its formation
and somehow, acting like a sponge, prevents it from flowing downslope. Very
occasionally, where the water becomes too heavy, the bog will burst and a thick
black peat will flow inexorably downslope, burying all in its path; a recent bog
flow buried part of the coast road in Co. Mayo, Ireland, and there are earlier
reports of houses being submerged overnight by the soaking black peats.

Raised bogs are fed only by rainwater and become very acidic; they are
carpeted by a rather restricted yet still vibrant plant life, particularly the

Sphagnum mosses, in colour from bright green to deep red. Low shrubs and various sedges may also grow at the bog edges, and cotton grass as well as members of the heather family will colonize the bog surfaces. The water table is generally high and the plant hummocks are separated by dark pools where little vegetation can survive. The overall effect of a raised bog is not immediately attractive, and there were few reasons in the past for communities to settle on, or to try to farm, such nutrient-poor and oxygen-starved wet regions. These bogs were more of an obstacle than a benefit, and yet they were entered, utilized and in some cases accepted as a vital part of the life of societies living near.

Fens are also peatlands but they are often fed by nutrient-rich waters from the surrounding land and thus support a more varied and richer stock of plants, and the animals that fed from them. Dominant plants are the sedges, mosses and flowers like the flag iris. Shrubs and trees such as willow, alder and birch will flourish. The peats of such a fen or *Niedermoor* may well have preceded a raised bog; a characteristic bog such as we will be discussing in this chapter may have started to form in a poorly-drained basin, at the bottom of which are silts and other sediments laid down in standing water. Above are fen peats, representing the formation of plant communities attracted to the flow-fed nutrients from the surrounding mineral lands, and living and dying in a peat-forming system. Where rain-fed water is sufficient, the fen plants may be succeeded by raised bog plants, dominated by *Sphagnum* moss.

The surface of peatbogs is a mosaic of plant life of distinctive types (*ill. 109*). Sedges may grow in tussocks and form in time a dense fibrous peat in hummocks. Bog beans and some wet-loving mosses form thin carpet-like covers, with watery pools. The cotton grass sedges have roots that seek scarce nutrients. The bog moss *Sphagnum* is the most characteristic plant to be found in bogs; some of these mosses prefer very wet conditions, others less wet, and most like nutrient-poor acidic waters. They store usable inorganic substances in their long stems, which stretch down into the peat beneath and suggest that the same plant may flourish for hundreds of years. *Sphagnum* is superficially fragile, and it is said that a footprint impressed in a moss may still be recognizable a year or more later, so

109 (*Left*) The surface of a peat bog, a mosaic of moss and other plants of the acidic wetland.

110 (*Right*) Part of the North European plain and southern Scandinavia, showing the location of bog sites mentioned in the text (Chapters 6 and 7).

delicate yet so tenacious are its strands of life. Equally so are the evergreen leaves of the plants of the heather family that conserve both moisture and nutrients. More unusual plants of the bogs are the insectivorous sundew and the underwater bladderwort which sucks in passing organisms.

The extent of boglands is very great in northern latitudes. In Ireland, for example, over 17 per cent of the whole land is or was peatland; that is almost 1.2 million hectares. Canada is over 18 per cent peatland, with 150 million hectares; Alaska has 30 million hectares. In the United Kingdom, the figure is over 6 per cent and 1.5 million hectares, and in West Germany, about 4.5 per cent and 1.1 million hectares. That is a vast amount of peat, even without the huge peatlands of Russia, Finland, China and the United States. From early postglacial times, peatlands exercised their control over the landscape, many inhibiting movement yet some at the same time offering rich resources to hunters, gatherers and early farmers. Reeds and alder, willow and birch for houses and fences, wild plants to harvest for leaves or berries, fish and eels, waterfowl both permanent and seasonal, and mammals that grazed and fed in the watery pools and sluggish streams of the fens, swamps and marshes, all provided easy supplies for energetic humans. Indeed, by medieval times, the church was in the habit of complaining that the poor peasant could manage so well from his wetland living that he needed little guidance from on high, and sought even less. Fenland was described in 1603 as 'the fatness of the earth gathered together at the time of Noah's Flood'. In contrast, raised and blanket bogs were far less rich in life forms useful to man, and one such derelict bog was described as a wild expanse of reeds in 'an atmosphere pregnant with pestilence and death'.

The archaeological evidence from the bogs is varied and extensive. Part of it speaks strongly of offerings made to propitiate and placate the deities or other forces that prehistoric people relied upon for their safety and well-being. Other parts of the record indicate the enormous efforts that went into transport and communication across the bogs. And yet other discoveries speak of darker deeds, of which we have little comprehension. In this chapter, and in Chapter 7, we will look at some of these events miraculously preserved for us in the bogs. (*ill. 110*).

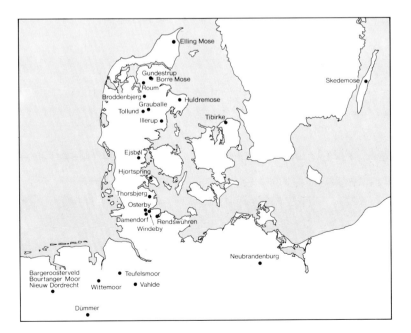

Travel and transport over the bogs

Bogs are notoriously treacherous places for the unwary and uninitiated. Many are the tales of travellers vanishing in the dark waters, or sucked down by quaking peats, as they ventured out onto the treacherous bog surfaces. Many bogs are of pool and hummock type, with plant tussocks separated by small areas of standing water. Raised bogs are particularly uneven and they posed problems for communities settled on the bordering drylands. Some could be easily solved. The Irish monk, St Maedoc, was set the task of harnessing wild oxen to a cart for the gathering of firewood. He tamed the oxen and set off in pursuit of other monks already at work. In order to reach them he had to cross 'a large spongy and uneven bog', and by making the sign of a cross 'God made a smooth and easy road, and a firm and level path through the soft and yielding surface of the bog for Maedoc and his oxen. The road still remains . . . and has been of great use and profit to both men and oxen.'

In the absence of such intervention, ordinary folk had to make do with their own facilities, and the archaeological record of bog finds demonstrates their degrees of success. Bogs could sometimes be crossed on foot, by jumping from one drier hummock to another, but on many occasions and seasons of the year the bogs were impassable. They were almost endlessly long obstacles to foot traffic which in the prehistoric period had to rely upon natural passages along ridges, beside shallow streams, and over dry terrain. Peninsulas of sand or rock where settlers could take advantage of the resources of both wetlands and drylands were cut off on three sides by bogs, and island-based communities were surrounded by a 'wetscape' that prevented access by both boat and by dryshod foot. Where bogs were very common, in Ireland, in Britain, in the Netherlands and in northern Germany, much energy went into the work of track and roadway building to provide those links essential if early settlements were not to be cut off from their contemporaries across the bogs.

The construction and use of such ancient paths and roads has gone on for 6,000 years in north-western Europe, and the bogs still hold ample evidence of the endeavour, and will continue to do so until drainage destroys the waterlogged matrix of peat. Bog surfaces are wet and soft, and any objects, particularly heavy objects, placed upon the surface will sink under their own weight. Thus any track or road must be built to withstand this tendency. Furthermore, as bog plants continue to grow, to die and not to decay, more and more plant remains will build up, forming layer upon layer of peat, which will gradually and inexorably engulf anything lying on the old bog surface, as the bog literally grows upwards. This is why, buried at different levels in the peatbogs of the north, there lie tracks and roads and other objects, once on the surface but now buried deep in the cold dark peats of past centuries.

Archaeological discoveries in the peatbogs are very much at the whim of those who work the land. Today, many fens have been drained and are now under intensive cultivation. Raised bogs are also being worked, but this time for peat fuel and fertilizer. The deep drains, ditches and cuts in both fen and raised bog peats have often revealed timbers of ancient tracks and roads that once snaked across the bog surfaces, or of the platforms and dwelling-places of fenland settlers (*ill. 111*). One advantage of landscapes that are repeatedly 'sectioned' by deep ditches is that the archaeologist is presented with an opportunity to see

111 An ancient peatbog now cut by machine. The oblique lines of the section
mark the passage of the machine blade, cutting and lifting the mumps of peat which
are stacked on the surface. The machine has chopped through a Neolithic trackway,
which lies sectioned at the base of the cut, with hundreds of fragments lying in the
bottom of the mumps.

beneath the surface, and to trace the alignments of any tracks or roads that are
encountered. In this way it has been possible to plot the exact lines of many
prehistoric routes, thereby giving a precision of direction which is sometimes
absent on dryland where no built roads were necessary and thus where routes are
only vaguely known through the distributions of objects dropped along the way.
The bog paths and roads also demonstrate a real intention on the part of the
builders to provide an easy passage, and this shows not only the exact direction
but also the degree of interest in the route; enormously heavy and repaired
roadways must signify a well-organized and established communication system.

From Ireland, Britain, the Netherlands, Denmark and North Germany there
are perhaps 1,000 prehistoric tracks and roads known to have existed, and this
probably represents only a small fraction of what there once were. There have
been sporadic records of wooden paths, called toghers, in Irish peatbogs, but the
first real effort to look for them, by a systematic search in 1987 and 1988 of
drainage ditches in the peatfields, revealed about 40 wooden structures in only
one small bog of central Ireland. In the Somerset Levels, a few tracks were long
known but these were quadrupled in the first season of organized search.
Consistent survey in Lower Saxony over the past 30 years has recorded over 200
tracks and roads. What is yet to be discovered in the deepest peats of all these
areas will depend on archaeological responses to the opportunities offered by
commercial exploitation of the bogs.

The Sweet Track

A pattern of construction and use, and of the periods when built paths and roads were needed, has only now begun to emerge. The earliest set of wooden tracks in Europe is known from the Somerset Levels, where a bog began to form about 6,000 years ago. The area where the first structure was built was a wet reed-filled swamp, separating a long peninsula of rock from a large island set in the middle of the wetland. The early farmers and gatherers of the Levels built an elevated footpath, now called the Sweet Track, for almost 2 km across the swamp, using large quantities of oak, lime and ash planks from trees growing on the dryland, and supporting them with long rails and pegs of other species from both the dryland and the wetland (*ill. 112*).

Studies on the tree-rings of the track wood show that two stands of oak were exploited, one of mature 400-year-old oaks on the northern island, and one from younger forest at the southern end, where only 120-year-old oaks were available; the latter indicates that woodland clearance had taken place about 120 years prior to the track-builders' activities. The trees were felled, debarked, cut and split into long planks in the forests, and branches and young trees also collected for use as pegs and rails. Other wood was gathered nearer the wetland edges. Once assembled at both northern and southern terminals, the construction work began. The track was made by placing long heavy poles on the marsh floor, probably mostly or wholly underwater, and pinning them into place by driving pairs of pegs in a criss-cross pattern over the poles. The upper part of the crossed pegs, projecting well above the poles and above the water, created a V-notch for planks which were wedged in place between the pegs. The planks, laid end to end, provided a long very narrow plank walk over the marsh waters. In experimental reconstructions of this track, it was found that the components fitted together so well that the 600 planks, 3,600 pegs and 350 poles that made up the whole track could possibly have been assembled by a small gang of about 10 people in only one day! Of course, felling trees, splitting planks, sharpening pegs, and transportation down into the wet, would have taken far longer. It is a good example of pre-fabrication and Neolithic engineering.

The archaeological evidence for this event is based in part upon extensive analysis of the tree-rings. The work demonstrated that almost every piece of oak and ash, making up a majority of the planks, had been felled in the same year, and that the hazel and other pegs had equally been felled as one single episode, presumably the same episode as the plank production. This must indicate an agreed plan on the part of the settlers, i.e., the need for a route, its precise position, a structural 'diagram' with a trial demonstration perhaps, the organization of labour to fell and prepare the required number of planks, rails and pegs, the transportation to stockpiles, and then the event itself – the building by a concerted effort of a raised walkway through the swamp. Tree-ring evidence further suggests that the track served its purpose for only a short period of time. With seasonal floods, which led to the continued formation of peat and the preservation of the wooden track, there would have been damage to the walkway and occasional floating-off of planks. Where damage was extensive, repairs would be made. Only a few planks, of ash, and some pegs of hazel, show a felling-date later than that of the bulk of the wood, and this only extends to a single decade after the building of the track. It suggests that the continued flooding and

112   The oldest road in Europe: the Sweet Track, Somerset, as excavated, showing the plank walk timbers lying in disarray along the foundation wood.

the relentless growth of reeds and formation of decayed reed peats beneath and around the track eventually caused its abandonment, not because the track itself was buried but because the swamp was gradually overwhelming the track level, and could no longer provide a walkway raised sufficiently to make it useful, and feasible to repair. Hence we think that a child observing or helping to build the track would be barely an adult when the track was finally abandoned and left for the reeds and then peats to hide it, until exposed by modern peat-cutting.

The extensive environmental analyses carried out on the track wood and the peat have provided many insights into the local conditions in and around the swamp. The wing cases and other hard parts of beetles include those of species now extinct in Britain, but still found on the continent where winters are colder and summers warmer than today in Britain; they suggest that Britain, 6,000 years ago, had summers 2–3 degrees warmer, and winters 3–4 degrees colder, than today. The forests surrounding the swamp consisted of oak, elm, ash and lime trees, with hazel and holly as understorey species. Some of the trees were huge like those at Ehenside Tarn (Chapter 2). Plants growing in the swamp on the line of the track tell us of the exact conditions encountered by the builders. At one point on the line, water-lilies flourished, and whirligigs and water-skimming spiders suggest a deeper pool of water to be crossed by the track; here the workers had to overbuild, to increase the height of the walkway.

The track was merely a footpath, barely 20–30 cm wide, stretching away through high reed beds which masked the ends once a traveller had begun his or her walk. Hazards of high water, obscuring reeds and projecting pegs all combined to make the walkway precarious. Passing places for chance encounters were not a feature of the construction. Hence, along the line we find the residues of swampland activities as well as accidental losses and breakages. Flint flakes, unmoved since loss and cushioned by the peat, lie along the track sides. Some were used to cut wood, others for reeds and other plants, and a single flake was used to cut hide. Arrowheads of flint point to hunting expeditions; traces of glue, or of arrowshafts, or of binding string, were preserved on several of them, and a number of bow fragments were also recovered. A fine flint axe was also found beside the track timbers, and an axe-head of jadeite. These two unhafted unused axeheads suggest either accidental losses or deliberate acts of deposition for a purpose unknown to us. Pottery is also found along the track, including heaps of sherds making almost complete pots accidentally broken by clumsy travellers; in one case, a pot had held hazelnuts; in another a wooden spurtle or stirrer was being carried along with, perhaps, gruel. Other artifacts found along the track line represent other objects discarded during use in the swamp. Bows, digging sticks, spades or paddles, wedges, handles, pins, a spoon, mattock, comb, toggles, and a carved bowl are in no way spectacular or even carefully fashioned; they are the common variety of artifacts that have perished on all dryland sites of the Neolithic.

Because of the environmental conditions, the track structure itself, and above all its tree-ring studies, we can say with confidence that everything found on, in or beside the track was contemporary. This is not archaeological 'contemporaneity', which may with luck be only a century, but it is real-time. Everything, artifacts of stone, flint, pottery and wood planks and pegs, the swamp, the forests, fields and coppices on the dryland around, was in existence and in operation, either passively or actively, at one moment in time. One group of unnamed people saw it all, and were a part of it all. Their settlement and all their other works have perished, leaving only their footpath as witness to their presence.

We have described the Sweet Track in some detail here because it well illustrates the amount of information that a seemingly-simple object, a mere trackway, can yield. Although there are many hundreds of prehistoric trackways now known from north and western Europe, not many have been studied so extensively as the Sweet Track, but in the following pages we will point to a few other examples of particularly informative tracks.

Corlea: an Irish roadway

A further example of the opportunities offered by such sites and precision comes from recent work in the central bogland of Ireland. Here, the vast raised bogs that formed over many hundreds of years are being systematically and one might say ruthlessly cut away for fuel. Many were the finds made in the past by the bog workers, from human bodies to wooden houses (Chapter 1), and from gold ornaments to kegs of bog butter, and there is some argument for saying that the Irish bogs still hold more information about the past than any other wetland in Europe; but time is running out. In 1957 the peat cutters discovered a heavy wooden road in Derraghan bog. It was rapidly examined before being totally destroyed over its entire length of 960 m. The road was made of oak planks and halved stems laid transversely upon a substructure of long poles and other debris. The plank ends were perforated for long stakes that pinned the timbers to the bog surface. The road ran westwards from a small island in the middle of a huge bog, and it was dated by radiocarbon to the 2nd century BC. By 1985, the bog of Corlea, to the east of the island, was yielding 200,000 tonnes of peat to fuel a nearby power station, and a heavy timber roadway was uncovered and demolished by the enormous ditching and milling machines that scour the peatlands *(ill. 113)*. Archaeological work by Barry Raftery has established that the roadway is the same as the Derraghan track, the whole representing an enormous undertaking in the year 148 BC to build a track across both bogs, linking the edges to one another and to the island. The split oak sleepers forming the surface of the road were 3–4 m long and in width up to 60 cm. In one place a 7-m stretch was broken, or dismantled, and nearby, beneath the oak timbers, was a jumble of carved wooden objects including staves from a bucket, and parts of a waggon. One of the longitudinals beneath the track was 5 m long and had one end axed to a point, the other notched around to form a typical flagpole-top; what this could be is a puzzle, but it seems possible that it was just that, a discarded flagpole. Other artifacts found under the timbers include handles, tent pegs, and a flat piece of oak with a chiselled mark like an Ogham (the earliest evidence for writing in Ireland), four parallel lines from one straight line. Such marks are not unique as we will see. But why was such an enormous roadway built across the bogs? There are no known settlements on the edges of the bog, nor many Iron Age artifacts in the area. Yet the dendrochronological date of 148 BC for the work of building is very close to that of other major works in Ireland, including the construction of huge linear earthworks, and the erection of a great temple-like building at Navan, ancient capital of Ulster. In the ancient Irish tales, which may reflect back to earlier episodes in the island, there are several references to bog

113 A heavy wooden roadway at Corlea, Co. Longford, Ireland, dated to 148 BC.
The planks are 3–4 m long.

roadways or causeways or toghers, and these may either suggest ancient discoveries of wooden timbers in the bogs, or the actual construction of certain roads. In the Tochmarc Etaíne, the wooing of Etaín, Midir was set the task of constructing a causeway over an impassable bog:

> All the men in the world from sunrise to sunset had come into the bog. They all made one mound of their clothes and Midir went up on that mound. Into the bottom of the causeway they kept pouring a forest with its trunks and roots, Midir standing and urging on the host on every side . . .

This could be a togher like the Corlea road. Indeed, there is another tale that may speak of the exact bog – wherein two groups of people were set to make a roadway, and having met midway in the bog from their opposite ends, they quarrelled over its completion, fought and left the road unfinished. Could this be the unmade portion of the Corlea road? It would be almost too good to be true. Be that as it may, the road and the many other tracks found in the area speak of a very considerable human presence over long periods of time in an area that has barely any other surviving evidence for occupation; such is the unique character of the archaeology of raised bogs.

The Tibirke roads

It is a feature of many areas of bogland that a favoured crossing place in one period will continue to be preferred in subsequent times. This may be a reflection of the narrowness of bog to be traversed, and thus economic decisions based on the amount of wood required, or the recollection of a long-buried passage over the bog that for no practical reason was still preferred, or the influence of a shallowly-submerged road that provided a slight measure of dryness on an otherwise inhospitably wet bog. In several areas of north-western Europe, bog routes survived over centuries. A group of roads in northern Zealand, Denmark, is a good example of this trend. The Tibirke roads were excavated long ago but have recently been re-examined and dated. Just inland from the open waters of the Kattegat, a wide expanse of present-day bogland separates many peninsulas and small islands of dryland. In the Neolithic, much of the low-lying area was a tidal inlet of the sea, and a finger stretched inland, creating a narrow but wet channel and isolating a small island at high tide. The island was occupied by a Neolithic community about 3000 BC, and a heavy post-built causeway 150 m long was laid across the muds to link the settlement with the southern shore. Two rows of hazel posts set 2.5–3 m apart created a passageway suitably wide for waggons; the actual road surface has barely survived but is thought to have been of hazel hurdles, laid down as and when traffic was proposed. In periods of high tide, the hurdles could have floated unless they were held firmly in place by pegs or by stone weights. The road was abandoned while the inlet was still tidal. Thereafter, uplift of the land excluded the sea and the inlet turned to freshwater bog, with the small island still providing a dry and safe haven. In the first millennium BC, the Neolithic route, now well buried by peat, was adopted as the safest passage across the bog. A wooden track was built first, then a post and stone causeway just beside the original line. This was succeeded by a row of stepping stones, set one pace apart and supplanted by a raised plank walkway held upon stone heaps in the wettest part of the bog where flat stones were inadequate. Just beside this, and along the entire length of the buried Neolithic road, a heavy stone road was finally built about 200 BC, with a kerb serving as pedestrian way beside the 3m-wide stone-paved road. We thus see a continuity here stretching over 2,500 years.

Bourtanger Moor

One of the best-studied trackway regions in north-western Europe is the Bourtanger Moor, spanning the border between the province of Drenthe in the Netherlands and Lower Saxony in Germany. The moor was formerly a raised bog sprawling between two areas of higher ground about 13 km apart. From the southern end of one of these drylands there was built a massive log road now called after the village of Nieuw-Dordrecht (*ill. 114*). Over 1,000 m of this Neolithic road have been traced, but it seems certain that it never extended the whole 13 km across to the eastern dryland; it may have gone only to a small bog stream, or to a terminal in the wettest part of the bog. The track was made about 4,000 years ago of heavy logs of oak, lime, birch and alder laid transversely on the bog surface or on birch stems laid along the track line. The track itself was 2.5–3.5 m wide but there are places where shorter logs were used. It is significant that at least part of the road was deliberately placed upon a rough line of hummocks in the bog, where conditions were a bit less wet than elsewhere. The logs were not split into planks but were whole stems with bark or stems split into halves or roughly squared off into beams. The rough bumpy surface these created was somewhat modified by putting small branches or splinters of wood into the gaps between the heavy pieces. The track was certainly wide enough for wheeled vehicles but was nonetheless very unstable, and overturns would be a constant hazard. The Nieuw-Dordrecht track remains something of an enigma, a massive undertaking but for an unknown purpose; however, a number of bog finds may provide a hint.

The bog itself has been extensively cut over, and from it there has come a number of artifacts that could well be contemporary with the track. These include a hoard of flint blades and one axe, an oak disc wheel, and an axe-haft of yew and club of rowan; several were found under the track timbers and must surely be ritual deposits; the wheel may have been abandoned at the western end of the track. The road was built in one season and lasted only for about a decade before it was overwhelmed by the bog. Those archaeologists who have examined the track suggest that the builders did not comprehend how unstable a raised bog can be; they should have pinned the track wood to the bog instead of merely placing it loosely upon the surface. Yet there are few examples of the ancients misinterpreting their environment, and we prefer to think that the Nieuw-Dordrecht builders built what they wanted and needed – an impressive road into the deepest bog, and never mind the bumpy ride.

The oak wheel found near the end of the Nieuw-Dordrecht track is only one of about 15 disc wheels from the raised bogs of the region, and to this should be added a number of wheels from Lower Saxony just to the east (*ill. 115*). Some have been found in pairs, and may thus represent carts rather than waggons. Many of these are of the later Neolithic, of the third millennium BC. Some were damaged, and abandoned in the bogs, and others were unused, perhaps kept fresh by deliberate burial in wet peat. They have integral naves worked by stone

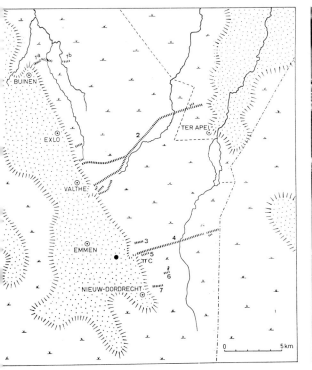

114, 115 **Wheels and trackways** (*Above left*) Map of the Bourtanger Moor, the Netherlands, showing the lines of prehistoric trackways. 2, the Valtherbrug road (Chapter 1); 7, the Neolithic Nieuw Dordrecht road; C, the Bargeroosterveld 'temple'; the other tracks are of the Bronze Age and Iron Age. (*Above right*) Disc wheels of the Neolithic period from Lower Saxony, just to the east of the Bourtanger Moor area.

axes out of massive oak planks. The fact that the Nieuw-Dordrecht track appears to have gone nowhere, except into the bog, may suggest that its wheel as well as the axe haft and club were ritually deposited.

In the same Bourtanger Moor, at least six other trackways are known, as well as other structures (*ill. 114*). Three trackways are of the Bronze Age and dated by radiocarbon to about 1500 BC and one by dendrochronology to 1350 BC. All are plank-built footpaths and exhibit careful selection of oak from the drylands and pine from the moor. By the time they were built, the peatbog was over 12 km wide and over 6 m thick, thus presenting an enormous barrier to anyone wanting to cross from ridge to ridge, or to get into the bog for its resources. The three footpaths are narrow plank or pole-built structures, pegged or slotted into the bog, and they would have provided adequate support for humans or sure-footed animals. They do not extend across the whole bog and must relate to areas where bog-iron ore could be extracted. The discovery of an iron punch on one of the tracks is a clear indication of a Bronze Age interest in such deposits, and must help explain the efforts to gain access into the bog. The bog-iron was probably carried to a settlement at Angelsloo, on the dryland ridge to the west. The settlement here was a large one with houses, barns, fenced enclosures, and a nearby cemetery. One of the houses was 18 m long, and built of wattle-and-daub; cattle were stalled in the middle part, people lived in the south end, and iron-working and other activities were carried out in the other end.

Another track in the area, of the Iron Age, was made entirely of woven panels, or hurdles. The concept is obvious, a wide flat raft-like trackway built of panels dropped on the surface of the bog, and probably held in place by pegs or ties. Another hurdle track, but from the Somerset Levels, required over 1,000 Bronze Age hurdles to provide a walkway from a dryland hill to an island in the middle of the bog (*ill. 116*). Neolithic hurdles are also well known from the Levels, demonstrating that some form of woodland management existed as early as 3000 BC; this would take the form of regular coppicing of hazel and other trees to ensure supplies of uniform rods and poles for hurdles and other purposes. Their use in many prehistoric houses, in wattle-and-daub building, is documented elsewhere in this book.

During peat-cutting in the Bourtanger Moor in 1957, a Bronze Age structure was found at Bargeroosterveld and has been called a 'sanctuary'. Situated 300 m out on the bog, the site lies midway between two of the Bronze Age tracks, and is slightly older than them. The structure consisted of a small setting of oak planks pinned to the bog and surrounded by a ring of stones brought from the dryland. The collapsed upper pieces of wood included carved horn-like timbers, perhaps forming extended eaves, but the exact appearance of the building is uncertain. It does however suggest that the bog was considered a fit place for activities of a ritual nature as well as for industrial work.

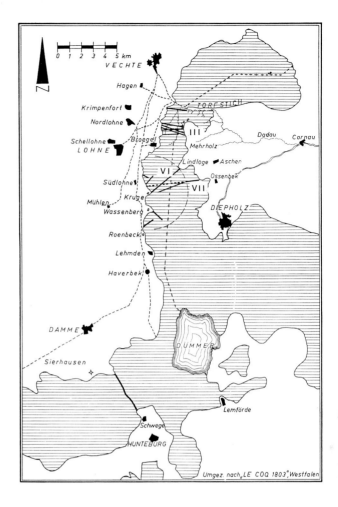

116 (*Left*) Prehistoric hurdles. The Bronze Age Eclipse Track, Somerset, originally made of 1,000 hurdles woven from hazel rods, now destroyed.

117 (*Right*) Map of the Grosse Moor, Lower Saxony, showing the lines of many trackways which traversed the moor. Bohlenwegen (roadways) III, VI and VII, mentioned in the text, are identified.

Lower Saxony

Ancient tracks and roads are also known throughout the vast peatlands of Lower Saxony right across to the River Elbe. Almost a quarter of this area was once covered by raised bogs, but today these are reduced by drainage and cutting to a fraction of the original. A number of the moors are elongated in a general north-south direction, and wooden tracks and roads were built in great quantity to cross these obstacles. Most of them are of the Bronze and Iron Ages, but there are several Neolithic roads as well. The Grosse Moor am Dümmer, for example, has more than twenty tracks, all providing links across the narrow parts of the bog (*ill. 117*). They range in date from about 3500 BC to the fourth century AD and indicate a continued occupation of the drylands on either side of the moor, an interest in the rich wetland margins and a requirement to establish and maintain contact between communities.

A Neolithic road across the Grosse Moor, Bohlenweg (roadway) VII, still lies in places beneath 4 m of peat. It was first seen in 1894 and has recently been rediscovered. Another early road in the Meerhusener Moor, Bohlenweg XV, is of comparable construction, built of heavy logs laid transversely to the road line, and resting upon long poles laid along the line of the track. Some of the logs were split into halves, but most were complete stems axed to sharp points in the felling

118 Reconstruction of disc wheels
and other elements of a Neolithic cart
from Klosterlund, Denmark.

operations of the birch and alder. The tracks were 3–4 km long, and were used by
cattle as well as wheeled vehicles, but problems must have existed. Many hooves
were trapped in the logs and snapped off. Track XV also had parts of one-piece
disc wheels and both tracks had fragments of axles with a gauge of 1.5 m; when
the axles were too thin for the wheels, birch-bark was wrapped around to enlarge
the shaft, but the wheels had to turn freely on the fixed axle. Parts of a draught
pole and yoke for oxen were also found, and fragments of the waggon body too. It
all speaks of heavy waggons, well-laden with produce, labouring across the
bumpy wooden road, the oxen straining against their yokes, catching and
damaging their hooves, and in time one of the waggons breaking up and being
abandoned in the same way as the many disc wheels which split when
inadvertently jammed and jarred by the massive wooden log surfaces (cf ill. 118).

Very elaborate roads were constructed in the Grosse Moor from about 1500
BC to the time of Christ. Several provided links across a narrow part of the bog, a
distance only of about 2 km, but the roads were now quite densely packed with
timber and must still have demanded large supplies of oak and other trees.
Bohlenweg III, for example, was 2,100 m long with timbers forming a road
3.2–3.4 m wide (ill. 120). It was a very complex structure of oak planks laid on a
dense substructure; the planks were perforated to receive heavy vertical stakes
which were themselves perforated to hold longitudinal stringers. The amount of
carpentry is quite remarkable in this track which from its discovery was known as
a 'Roman Pioneer' road, because no locals were considered capable of producing
such a fine piece of engineering. The road is now dated by dendrochronology to
640 BC. Beside it were found wooden shovels and mallets used in the work, and
parts of the vehicles that were pulled along the road.

We know very little about how these finely-carpentered roads were planned.
Who made the decisions about the need for a road, its route and its design? The
felling and carpentry involved are more readily apparent, and two heavy roads
from Lower Saxony provide intriguing information about the methods.
Bohlenweg IX and XII are plank-built roads, each made of oak felled in 713 BC
according to dendrochronological work (ill. 121). Furthermore, the wood used in
both roads came from the same trees, yet the two roads are 40 km apart. Some of
the planks have enigmatic 'makers' marks' upon them, as if designated for
particular places in particular roads (ill. 122). It suggests that in 713 BC a network
of roads was required, and a group of experienced woodsmen was employed to

BOHLENWEG XLII (Jp)

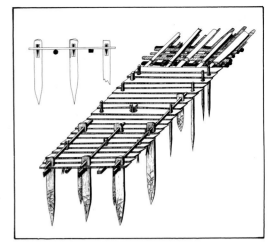

119, 120 **Complex trackways from Lower Saxony** (*Left*) Reconstruction of trackway XLII in the Wittemoor, with possible archway and wooden figures placed beside the track. Track width 3 m. (*Above*) Trackway III from the Grosse Moor, with elaborate carpentry and jointing. Width 3.2 m.

121, 122 **Makers' marks and prehistoric roadmen?** Photograph of trackway IX (*above*) and (*right*) marks cut into some of the planks from this trackway and from track XII, 40 km away. The tracks were made from the same trees, in 713 BC. Plank lengths 3 m.

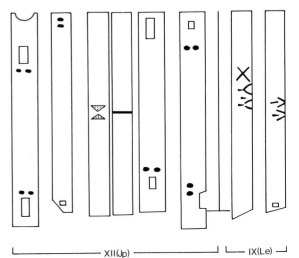

XII (Jp)   IX (Le)

undertake or oversee all of the work. The men selected some good-quality oak in a forest, felled, split and trimmed the timber, marked them and transported them to the sites. It was no mean undertaking; Bohlenweg XII was 6,500 m long, and thus required over 20,000 planks.

In the Grosse Moor, the Neolithic, Bronze Age and Early Iron Age tracks were succeeded by a very substantial Bohlenweg VI which extended for over 4,200 m from a promontory on the west to another on the east. This road was first discovered in 1817 and was thereafter seen by peat-cutters and others at intervals until it was well explored by H. Hayen in recent decades. Its heavy timbers were regularly perforated at the ends to hold narrow stakes, and there was a substructure of long poles or planks. Oak and ash were felled on the higher lands, and pine, birch, alder and poplar nearer to the bog. About 2,000 waggon loads of timber went into the building operation about 100 BC, and the track is believed to have been kept in use for about 200 years. Various waggon parts were found beside or near the road, including fragments of disc wheels, spokes, axle and parts of the body. Also found were several 'measuring sticks', like ranging poles but with heads notched or ribbed. These sticks are 70–90 cm long; they could of course be decorated waggon poles or emblems.

The waggons by now had either spoked or tripartite disc wheels, either of which could be repaired after breakage unlike the earlier one-piece disc wheels. Wooden rims could be attached. Axles were perfected to allow front axle swivel on a vertical pivot. Double oxen or horses were used as draught animals, and now the swingle-tree was in use, holding the traces behind the animal and transmitting power to the front axle. Single yokes for individual animals were also made. All these artifacts have been found in the bogs, as abandoned pieces or as seemingly deliberate offerings.

From a number of the German tracks there have been reported carved wooden boards, in the shape of humans, and it is suspected from the Neolithic onwards that some form of statue or emblem was erected by some tracks to ensure their survival and success against floods and bog subsidence. The best example of this practice is from Bohlenweg XLII which traversed the Wittemoor, and provided a link between a southern dryland and a navigable stream which flowed northwards to the River Weser. The southern part of the 3,200 m long track was built of oak from the dryland, and the northern part was of alder growing at the bog edge and the stream edges: where the two building parties met, an excess of alder logs was abandoned beside the track. The condition of the track timbers suggests that the vehicles were laden more heavily on the outward journey to the stream, returning with lighter loads. The bog was particularly treacherous at a small watercourse, and here the track had soon broken up in use, by vehicle weight and by subsiding unstable peat. The broken short stretch of track was marked by fires set beside the track, and two oak posts were erected on the track sides, possibly forming a sort of gate or even an archway (*ill. 119*). On either side of the track were placed two tall carved wooden figures, one on a small peat hummock, the other set in a perforated plank. Various small sticks and stones encircled the hummock. The track was abandoned soon after it was built about 129 BC and the figures were removed and placed flat on the peat surface and covered by loose peat. Other parts of the same track probably had similar wooden figures placed at broken areas, perhaps to mark them for the unwary waggon driver or even pedestrian. The effort put into this track and a contemporary road to the west may have been directed towards the transport of bog iron. Deposits of this are abundant in the Wittemoor, and a settlement and industrial site is known from the lower slopes of the hills to the south. We might thus envisage extraction and collection of the ore from the bog, its carriage and working at the settlement, then the transport across the heavy road to the landing stage and the water route to the Weser River. The Dutch Bronze Age footpaths represent an earlier attempt to get into a bog for the same purpose.

We may well wonder why so many tracks and roads were built in these regions. Their presence should not be surprising if we recognize that ancient communities may have been self-sufficient but were not content to be isolated. Contact for ideas, for artifacts, for food, and for new partners would have been essential if ancient societies were to flourish. There would always have been the desire to participate in the outside world, to partake of its luxuries as well as its necessities, and to meet new people. The prehistory of European and other societies is full of trade and exchange, contact and communication, and for these, travel and transport had to be made possible. Dry routes existed and were extensively used. More difficult terrain had to be negotiated, whether it was the mountain passes of the Alps or the boglands of northern Europe. Like the many inventions and developments that we can see in the Neolithic, Bronze Age and Iron Ages of Europe, the trackways and roads also demonstrate the energy and ingenuity of ancient people in maintaining contact whether that be with their neighbours or with their gods.

Travel and transport upon the water

Almost from the first discoveries of wetland settlements in the Swiss lakes, and in the crannogs of Ireland, the excavators recorded log boats found embedded in the lake muds, or abandoned at the adjacent shore. These craft, carved and burnt-out from a single tree stem, often of oak, are the simplest form of floating carrier that could be propelled and directed (*ill. 123*). Logboats or monoxylous boats have been found in many wetland deposits throughout Europe and America, for example, over 100 from the Swiss Lakes, and the same from the Florida swamps and peatlands. Early logboats made by hunters and gatherers probably existed by about 9,000 years ago over all of north-western Europe, and large numbers of the boats are known from later prehistoric wetlands and particularly from the early historic crannogs of Ireland and Scotland. Oscar Paret was one of the first to list and describe European logboats, and his study of the Federsee boats, published in 1930, is still a classic work; by 1930 the Federsee had already yielded 25 logboats from its shrinking peats. There are many varieties in these simple boats, with a basic division into double-bowed and transom-sterned craft. Poled or paddled across smooth waters, in difficulty only in heavy water, they provided easy passage for heavy loads across wide rivers, small lakes, estuaries and, perhaps, along coasts of larger bodies of water. Most have been found in river beds, an outcome of preservation conditions perhaps, and many are finely carpentered such as the logboat from Sainte Anne, one of the 25 or so from the basin of the Loire in western France. The now-destroyed logboat from Brigg in eastern England was almost 15 m long, carved from a huge tree stem, of which about 90% was removed to leave the boat shell. This boat could have carried 28 men and drawn only 36 cm of water, and with a heavy cargo of 10 tonnes the draft would be only 88 cm, thus leaving a freeboard of 12 cm.

Drainage works in 1984 at Hasholme, East Yorkshire, led to the discovery of another huge logboat probably capsized and abandoned about 250 BC in a small creek leading into the River Humber. The oak tree felled to make this boat was a forest giant 600–800 years old and with a straight stem clear of branches for 11 m, and a girth of over 5 m at 11 m height. It had a transom at stern, beam-ties to hold the sides of the boat together and elaborate bow damaged both in the ancient unsuccessful attempt to drag it from its submerged position and by the modern drainage machine. The boat could have held 9 pairs of paddlers, standing (the sides were too high for kneeling and paddling), and one or two helmsmen. The carrying capacity of the boat was enormous; for example, with a crew of only 5 men she could carry up to 8 tonnes depending on the load density and thus its storage height on board. A number of bones of cattle, with a few of sheep, horse and deer were recovered from around the boat and its seems likely that these were once the cargo, or part of it; they were lost in the water as butchered joints of meat. Some timbers were also probably being transported when catastrophe ensued. The greatest loss was undoubtedly the boat itself.

Other types of watercraft from the prehistoric past are less well known. Coracles are inferred from decayed traces in the soil, and rock carvings of the Bronze Age are thought to represent either planked boats or frame and skin boats, but there are few survivors in the muds and silts of Europe. The North Ferriby boats, found abandoned in a Bronze Age shipyard or breaker's yard on the bank of the River Humber in eastern England, are still unique coasters or ferry boats, but not for sea-going passage (*ill. 126*). The circumstances of recovery of these boats deserve an entire book, and the boats themselves are the oldest known planked craft in Europe, dated to about 1500 BC. The river muds had preserved a number of oak planks with yew withy bindings and moss caulkings. One boat could have carried 3 tonnes with a draft of only 30 cm and a freeboard of 36 cm, with a maximum load of 5.5 tonnes in clear calm conditions. They were freshwater craft, and there is still little evidence for any prehistoric craft capable of undertaking the long maritime voyages that archaeological evidence asserts took place.

A war-canoe from Hjortspring on the island of Als in Denmark is an exceptional craft. It had a lime wood hull of seven planks, sewn with lime bast cord through drilled holes sealed by resin. Hazel branches and ash boards were used to help firm the strakes. The canoe would have been propelled by 20 double-banked paddlers with a steersman and oar. The boat was about 13 m long and is the oldest known craft with overlapped strakes. It was deposited around 200 BC in a small bog on the island as a votive offering, and is briefly discussed in Chapter 7.

When water-based travel was necessary in the north, the bark canoe was almost certainly preferred to the logboats so ubiquitous in other regions, but surviving boats of any kind are extremely rare in the far north of Europe. Rock carvings of the prehistoric hunter-gatherers may provide some indication of the size of boats, but not much of their character. From the north, however, various paddles have been recovered which are over 9,000 years old. The Mesolithic paddles from Tybrind Vig in Denmark have been noted in Chapter 3, and there

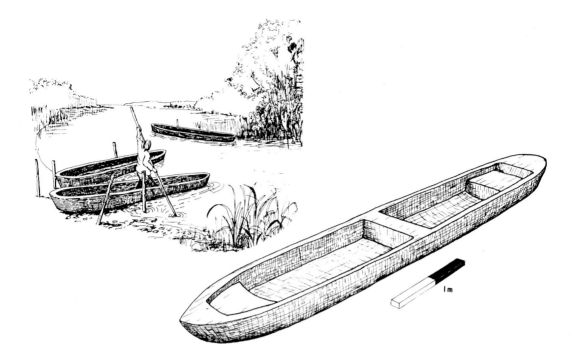

123–126 **Boats, paddles and skis** (*Above*) Prehistoric logboat from the Loire, France, together with reconstructed scene of logboats in use. (*Left*) Travel across the snow and over the water in prehistoric Finland. Far left, a decorated ski from Kinnula. Near left, a paddle from Konginkangas. (*Below*) Reconstruction drawing of the Bronze Age boat from North Ferriby, England. Length *c.* 15 m.

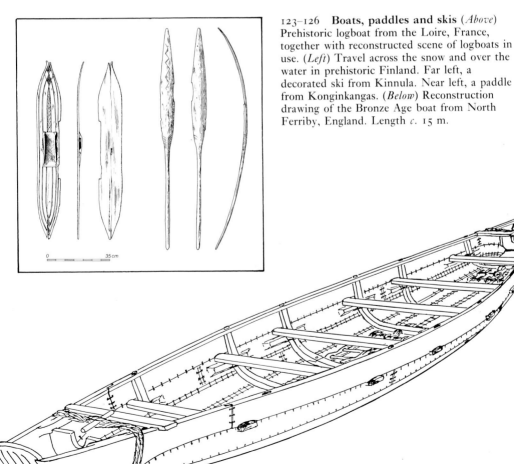

are many others of almost all ages, found with dugouts and canoes in north-west and central Europe. Decorated paddles with lance-shaped blades were found in an inlet of Lake Keitele at Konginkangas in central Finland, and are dated to about 2000 BC (*ill. 125*). Others are earlier and come from peatbogs or swampland in the region. These paddles, and others of equal antiquity, suggest something more than gentle paddling with fat blades, and were probably prized artifacts, posssibly used for poling in shallow waters as well as for paddling in deeper lakes and rivers.

In the far north of Europe, and Russia and Canada too, travel by lake and stream waters was far easier than on land choked by trees or impassable treacherous bogs. But in these northern lands, travel was facilitated most by climate, so that the winter months became the preferred season for long-distance journeys. Ice-clad lakes and rivers, snow-clad bogs and forests, all were more easily traversed in winter than in summer when water was at its least accommodating. For winter travel, skis and sledges were needed, and the boglands, lake muds and river silts of Finland, Sweden and Norway have yielded many finds of these ancient wooden artifacts. Some came to rest when broken and abandoned, but others are considered to be deliberately deposited in bogs as some form of propitiation. Skis are known from about 2500 BC in the north and are a far cry from the slender elongations of today; some are elaborately decorated, as on the Kinnula ski of about AD 800 from central Finland (*ill. 125*). These short wide skis were in effect two-thirds of the way towards the fast-running skis of today, one-third towards flat expanded snow shoes, but they would have served well in hunting down animals such as the elk in heavy snows. They could also have been used in summer over the treacherous bog surfaces.

Transport of heavy loads, such as furs, was easier on snow and ice than on fast-running water or saturated land, and parts of sledges have survived from about 7000 BC. Various double-runner and single-runner sledges are inferred from the wooden runners often found, and may well relate to the trading network established in early times between the inland hunters and trappers, and the coastal rural settlers and farmers of Finland and elsewhere. The Rudanmaa pine sledge runner from south-west Finland, dated to about 3500 BC, probably relates to Stone Age settlement in the immediate area, and two other sledge runner finds nearby, of later date, are also closely linked with later prehistoric activities. In central Finland the runner from Laukaa bears carved decoration of about 300 BC. Simpler sledges could have been made out of animal skins stretched over wooden frames; one was found in 1880 in the Teufelsmoor (the Devil's Moor) near Bremen in north Germany.

Possibly the oldest known sledge from Denmark was one discovered near the end of the Second World War in Zealand. According to the account, a German soldier was digging a trench when he encountered a bundle of birch branches covering a sledge made of wood and bark strips, including a plaited rope and a wide runner of birch fibres. The sledge carried a prehistoric pot, set on a small heap of sand, and associated with a hafted antler axe, a fish-hook and a greenstone axe. Unfortunately this unique find was consumed in flames en route to the museum when the lorry bearing the sledge was involved in an accident; the finder also perished. Perhaps the story is apocryphal.

7 · Bogs and bodies

AMONG THE MANY OBJECTS, both human and artifactual, that came to rest in the wet boglands in the prehistoric period, there are some that provide exceptionally detailed information about the past. This is because they were deliberately deposited directly into water under circumstances that assured their survival. The best examples of this phenomenon are the bog bodies of north-west Europe, and the burial swamps of Florida. In this section we will look at several Florida sites which have only recently been explored. The oldest of these is at Windover, near Cape Canaveral.

Into the pool

The burial pool at Windover was originally a shallow depression in the calcareous bedrock, now filled by freshwater peats which have preserved both the environmental record and also the human and cultural remains that came to rest in the waterlogged peats. Over 7,000 years ago the pond was used by prehistoric Indian hunter-gatherers as a burial ground, the bodies wrapped in grass mats or other coverings, placed in the water and fastened to the pond bottom by stakes (*ill. 128*). Peats gradually filled the pond and sealed the burials until recent drainage and excavations for a housing development exposed them. Work has now succeeded in recovering over 160 bodies, of which half are children. The waterlogged peats have preserved some of their clothing, their wooden and other grave-goods, and brain tissue of over 90 individuals; flesh, skin and hair have not survived the 7,000 years of waterlogging; the peats are nearly neutral, and the water as well. The twined and woven fabrics of plant fibres have perhaps been the most important discoveries, as they are by far the oldest surviving fabrics in eastern North America, and demonstrate quite sophisticated tight weaving. Children seem to have been favoured, at least in death, by generous artifacts placed with them; they include wooden, bone and antler objects. One child had suffered in life from a degenerative spinal disorder, and probably would have required special care during the 12–15 years of life. Some of the adults were as much as 65–70 years old, a quite remarkable age to achieve at such a time and place, and with such a life-style as we often assume hunters and gatherers to have had. The teeth of some of the humans show that plants such as cabbage palm were regularly chewed, but better evidence of diet has survived in the abdomens of some individuals. One body still retained thousands of seeds of edible fleshy fruits, particularly elderberry, with some grape and prickly-pear cactus. There are also a few seeds of holly and black nightshade, both traditionally parts of other drinks, the holly featuring in the ritual Black Drink of the historic south-eastern Indians, the nightshade a medicinal plant. The seeds suggest that this individual died in late spring or summer, and other bodies show similar seasonally-distinct foods. Two other bodies, however, show a different pattern. One adult male and a 2-year-old child had eaten little or no fruit but had large amounts of crushed bones of fish in their abdomens. The Windover burial pond has only been partially examined; the remainder is now sealed again to await future refinements in recovery and analysis.

The wetlands of Florida are extensive and there are, or were, many other sites where human remains and their accompanying grave-goods survived in exceptional condition. An interest in burial ritual can nowhere be better served than in such sites. At Fort Center in the basin of Lake Okeechobee, communities of Indians contemporary with the later Bronze Age inhabitants of Europe practised maize horticulture on earthworks raised above floodwater levels. The settlement persisted and in time an elaborate burial ritual was developed. The bodies of the dead were prepared, perhaps defleshed and parts possibly extracted on a low mound before being wrapped in textiles and placed on a wooden platform erected over a pond 20 × 12 m newly scooped out along a creekside. The edges of the mortuary were embellished by carved pine totem poles sunk into the pond bottom and standing well above the 150 bundled bodies. The thirty totems bore the effigies of eagle, turkey, owl and duck, as well as otter, bobcat and other animals (*ill. 127*). These elaborate burial practices were only a part of the well-established life of this prehistoric community, which became engaged in long-distance exchanges for maritime objects and other materials. The settlement and its closely-associated middens and raised plots ultimately extended for almost 2 km along the creek, and almost 1 km inland. The inhabitants consumed turtle, fish, deer and turkey, all readily to hand in the creeks, rivers, swamps and forests. Maize was also a staple in their diet, grown and stored on the site. The Fort Center complex still has many unexplained features but its waterlogged burials and decorated platform remain as unique evidence of burial ritual in the later prehistoric past of Florida, just as Key Marco (Chapters 2 and 3) is unique in its marine-based settlement debris in the Court of the Pile Dwellers.

Although there are several other burial ponds known from the Florida wetlands, their investigation has left much to be desired due to the rate of drainage and dredging that has taken place. The site of Little Salt Springs, on the Gulf Coast, is an exception to this, however. About 12,000 years ago a spring-fed natural well 60 m deep existed in the rock, with projecting rock shelves near the surface of the ground. Leading into the spring was an old depression about 400 m long and 30–90 m wide. Human occupation of the site began during a period of low water when a Palaeo-Indian encampment was established on one of the rock shelves within the great shaft; turtle, snake, ibis and a giant land tortoise were killed and eaten. The tortoise had a wooden stake driven between its carapace and plastron. By 9,500 years ago the well waters had risen to cover the shelves and flood into the upper sloped basin at the top of the shaft, and further occupation by hunters and gatherers took place around the freshwater pool. Hearths were made, deer hunted, and wooden and other artifacts were manufactured; one object is an oak boomerang or throwing-club, the oldest known from America. By 8,500 years ago, rising waters flooded into the long depression turning it into a swamp and peat began to form. About 7,000 years ago new people arrived and settled along the edge of this slough. They buried their dead in the shallow waters, pinning them to the soft peat bottom, where

127, 128 **Prehistoric burial ritual in Florida** (*Above*) Reconstruction of a burial platform with carved totems of eagles, turkeys, owls and other creatures from a swamp at Fort Center. (*Right*) A 7,000-year-old burial pool at Windover has so far yielded over 160 bodies, many of them wrapped and staked to the pool bed, as shown here.

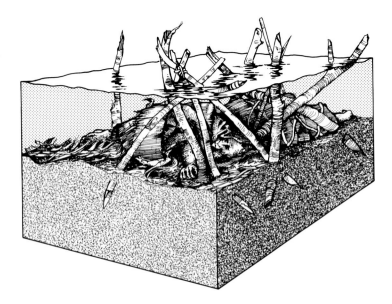

129 Two wooden heads (and a side view of the second) from les Sources de la Seine, France. Heights *c.* 20 cm.

their preservation by water and by peat formation was exceptional. The dead were laid to rest on biers of leafy wax myrtle branches, or were partly wrapped in grass or with leaves. Artifacts from the settlement were deposited in the swampy waters, among them deer bone points and wooden tools including digging sticks and a wooden tablet with an engraved design of a long-necked, long-billed bird. The bodies decayed slowly, and at least one, buried 6,000 years ago, still retained its brain when recovered in 1979. It is believed that over 1,000 burials were put into the swamp.

A rather different use of a spring-fed pond is documented by the extraordinary groups of votive effigies in Gallo-Roman France, dating to about 2,000 years ago. Two main sites have been discovered where spring-fed pools were used as some sort of sanctuary, not for humans but for their effigies. Around the springs were set carved wooden representations of both naked and clothed persons, their separate heads, legs and arms, and other figures. At les Sources de la Seine near Châtillon, a Gallo-Roman sanctuary of the 1st century BC contained about 200 figures, of semi-naturalistic humans, legs, arms, schematic figures, horses and other shapes. Included were some long sticks with sets of heads carved upon them, like a totem pole (*ill. 129*). At les Sources des Roches near Clermont Ferrand a later sanctuary set around a spring-fed pool had hundreds of figures set around its edge, later to be washed into the pool by rising waters, and subsequently sinking to lie in disarray in the wet silts. The figures, of beech, include the same range of subjects as in the Seine find, complete humans, legs, arms and other effigies. The figures may represent the same kind of relationship between humans and the life-giving and taking waters that is attested in other regions. Deliberate deposits of worldly goods were made in a sacred pool or Ywai Tapu associated with the pa of Kauri Point, New Zealand; valuable objects were placed in a sacred spring at Isokyrö, Finland; and prestigious bronze artifacts went into the lake of Lough-na-Shade beside the Celtic ritual centre at Navan, Co. Antrim. There are many other examples of swamps and ponds used for acts of deposition of wealth from at least the Bronze Age onwards in Europe, and well into the historic era here and elsewhere.

Gifts to the bogs

The wetlands of north and western Europe in particular have yielded not only wooden roads and tracks, waggons, boats and skis, but also human remains, and these have always posed problems of interpretation as well as providing us with lurid thoughts and tales of dark deeds done long ago.

Bog bodies are a widespread phenomenon. Hundreds of bodies have been recorded from the peatbogs in Germany and Denmark in particular, with other examples known from all the other countries of the north and west (*ill. 130*). Many of these are no more than skeletons, parts of skeletons, or fragments of clothing, and it is difficult to consider them all as representing any one particular cultural or chronological episode. Very few of the human remains have been investigated scientifically, and hardly any have been preserved for modern examination.

The earliest authenticated discovery of a bog body is 1773, and the first photographic record of a bog body dates to 1871, in Rendswühren Fen, Germany (Chapter 1). All these early finds were made by peasants cutting peat, and there were and are many traditions and tales about these discoveries. Some were lifted from the peat, boxed and buried in the local churchyard; others were destroyed, deliberately or by accident. Some were abandoned and left to rot away in the air, through ignorance, neglect or fear and superstition, some were hastily covered up and treated as if never found.

Some of the reasons for people of whatever period to feel uneasy about the human remains were that often the bodies were incomplete, like the single hand at Hørby Mose, a leg at Tved Mose or a pair of hands and lower legs at Søjards Mose; these probably represented the remains of complete bodies truncated by earlier peat-cutting or decayed away differentially. But notwithstanding these logical explanations the discoveries, made often by a lone person working in the peatbog, probably caused some surprise, perhaps fright. Less startling perhaps were the discoveries of dogs buried deep in the bogs; one animal from the Dreiechsmoor of Lower Saxony was like a dachshund, with short brown hair; it had been killed and buried in the bog about 2,000 years ago.

130   A bog body at Windeby, Germany, held down by stakes and branches.

The existence of these bodies in the bogs is due to a variety of circumstances as we will see (*ill. 131*). Bogs can be treacherous places and it is likely that some of the bodies found in the peat were those of travellers who slipped into bog pools and were trapped. Some ancient bodies found in the peat were supposedly found clutching heather or sticks, as if attempting to haul themselves out. A body from the Vehne bog (near Cloppenburg) in north Germany held tufts of heather in his hands, and lay on his front with arms outstretched; perhaps he was one of these accidental deaths. A French abbot has recounted how he suddenly sank into a bog, and after an hour of fruitless struggle was up to his neck before help arrived.

Other bodies found in bogs are deliberate burials. In 1857, peat cutters came upon three bodies buried in a bog at Getelo on the border of Germany and Holland. A man, woman and child had been laid fully clothed upon animal hides, with bunches of flowers placed upon the bodies. Records also exist of the burial of suicides in the bogs. 'And early next morning, as expected, the assistant county court judge came and gave permission for the burial of the woman who had committed suicide . . . the body was wrapped in a torn bast cover, put on a cart and taken to the swamp'; so reads a report of 1850 in Russia. And in 1988, reports from China tell of the burial of suicides on wasteland in the belief that they would become ghosts; other suicides were nailed into their coffins to prevent their spirits escaping, so it is said. Clearly there have been, and are, many fears about suicides and the afterlife.

And others were also consigned to the bogs. Strangers who died in rural communities in the Middle Ages were sometimes buried in unconsecrated ground, and so were women who died in childbirth. Bishop Burchard of Worms records the 11th-century belief that such burial would help prevent the newly-born child being dragged by the dead mother into the grave. A 12th-century woman from Peiting in Bavaria was put in her coffin in a bog very soon after giving birth, judging by her physical condition; her woollen gown had been converted into a maternity dress by the addition of an extra panel of cloth.

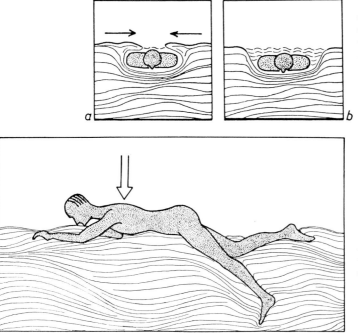

131 (*Left*) Sketches of bodies submerged in a bog hollow (a) and a bog pool (b). Below, a characteristic position for a body laid upon a raised bog surface (see ills. 109 and 141).

132 (*Right*) The remains of a decapitated man from Dätgen, Germany, with only skin, traces of flesh and bones surviving.

Less explicable are the remains of individuals who are represented only by parts of bodies, or even with extra limbs. The 1848 discovery at Vahlde (near Rotenburg) in north Germany is a case in point. Two complete bodies with skulls split and arrowheads embedded lay with four arms and two legs apparently belonging to several different persons, all the limbs severed by axe, sword or knife. Possibly this was the scene of a battle, or even a field hospital, with amputated limbs and expired patients abandoned. The date of this particular event is uncertain, but it could be of the medieval period. An earlier find, from Bentstreek in the same region, consisted of a left tibia of an adult male, whose hairy leg had been chopped off just below the knee. The leather shoe still worn on the foot dates the find to the first millennium BC.

These remains may have been the result of battles or executions (*cf ill. 132*), but there are other records and discoveries that are more explicit if even less pleasant to contemplate. A man buried in a bog at Neu Verssen (near Neppen) in north Germany about 2,000 years ago was found without his ears and nose. This might have been due to differential, if unusual, decay, or to damage upon discovery. However, 13th-century Mongol soldiers collected rewards for enemies killed by submitting the ears of the slain, and earlier still the penalty for sacrilege was to lose one's ears. A discovery at Driesen in Brandenburg pulls it all together, or apart; an adult male found in a bog had been scalped, and had skin stripped from his back. He was buried with his ears and lips placed in his hands. Other dastardly deeds are also recorded from the bogs. A man from Schwendt near Berlin was found in a barrel studded inside with nails and tipped into a bog pool. Another man, a medieval soldier judged by his clothing, had been hanged at Nienburg in Germany, with two dogs also strung up by their hind legs right beside him; his thighs and stomach were badly bitten by the dogs as they thrashed about. All of the bodies had hung for a time before being thrown into the bog; their eyes had been pecked, probably by ravens. A grisly find made near Hamburg in 1859 was of a man whose intestines had been drawn out and wound

on a pole. The crimes of these people are unknown, but punishments like these were sometimes inflicted in medieval times for seemingly, to us, minor sins.

It is very difficult now to determine the nature of much of the clothing that was deposited with many bodies. There are numerous records of naked bodies, and also of bodies with only scraps of clothing, a fragment around the neck, or underneath the buttocks or stomach, or around the ankles or knees. In these latter cases, it is highly likely that the bodies were clothed, but that most of the textiles or skins have decayed away. The 'rags of infamy' need not have accompanied all of the naked or near-naked bodies found. A report in southern Germany in 1955 describes the discovery of a naked body in a bog ditch, with traces of a collar of a type worn by soldiers of 1945, and fragments of army socks on the feet; in only ten years this body had remained well-preserved, yet almost all of the clothing had disappeared.

These remains, and hundreds of others from the bogs of northern and western Europe, are of varying ages. Yet within this haphazard assemblage there is a group of bog bodies, dated to the centuries from about 700 BC to AD 200, which seems to make a coherent picture, even if a number of puzzles remain, and we now turn to this evidence.

Because of the peculiar conditions that bogs create, the survival of these bodies too is extremely varied. A male from Damendorf, for example, survived only as a skin with hair, and no trace of bone or flesh (*ill. 133*); his leather shoes and belt lay beside him. And many were the opposite, only the bones and hair remaining, with no skin or flesh, as at Vester Thorsted. Other partial remains, however, seemed more deliberate and less accidental. In Roum Mose and Stidsholt Mose human heads were found; at Roum a male head had been chopped from the body at the 2nd–3rd vertebra, the blow carrying through to chop away part of the chin.

Tollund man

The most famous bog body was found in 1950 in Tollund Mose in Jutland. The bog area, called Bjaeldskovdal, had been cut for peat for many centuries, and in 1927 a body was found and abandoned under a collapsed peat bank; in 1938 another body was found at a site called Elling, and then in 1950 the Tollund Mose yielded its body. About 60 m out from the edge of the small bog, and at 2.5 m depth, the body was clearly not recent and it received prompt treatment and care. The body lay on its right side, legs drawn up and arms bent; it was naked except for a leather cap and belt. The peat upon which it lay was undercut and it was then lifted *in situ* for transport to the National Museum of Denmark. In its removal from the fen, one of the helpers suffered a heart attack; the bog 'claimed a life for a life'.

The parts of the body uppermost in the peat were partly decayed, and the arms and hands had relatively little flesh remaining; the body itself was collapsed, due to bone and flesh deterioration, so the skin lay in folds. The feet were well preserved, and the right sole bore the scars of cuts probably caused by thorns or stones. Only one finger retained its print, and this fitted unobtrusively into those of the modern Danish population. The head was in excellent condition, and the stubble on chin, the leather cap, and the preservation of the sexual organs, showed that the body was that of a man; he was aged about 30–40

133 The Damendorf man, surviving only as a skin with hair, leather belt and shoes (see also ill. 149).

years and just over 1.6 m tall. His face was startling to behold, and many spoke of his tranquil expression, lips closed together, forehead barely wrinkled, eyes shut (*ill. 134*). But around his neck was a noose of braided leather which had left a furrow on the skin at the sides and throat, but not at the nape. From this it is deduced that he was hanged, not strangled. All his internal organs were intact, including the gastro-intestinal tract, with the remains of his last meal, eaten 12–24 hours before death. This was a gruel or porridge, of barley, linseed, *Camelina sativa* (gold-of-pleasure) and pale persicaria or willow herb seeds, with smaller amounts of about thirty different kinds of wild seeds, including fat hen, corn spurrey, black bindweed, violet, hemp nettle and mustard; none of the plant remains indicated a time of the year when fresh vegetation was available. Radiocarbon tests suggest that the winter or early spring thus indicated occurred about 2,000 years ago.

Two years after the discovery of Tollund man, a further well-preserved body was found by peat-cutters in Nebelgårds Mose near Grauballe. The bog is small, only 140 m across and the body had been placed near the centre, in an old peat cut. The body, again male, was naked with hair about 5 cm long and a stubble on the chin. Aged about 30, the man was 1.75 m tall, and his skin had almost been tanned by the bog acids. The bones were soft and the inner organs were partly decayed. Unlike Tollund man, the face of Grauballe man was not in repose, and for good reason; his throat had been cut from ear to ear. In addition, he had probably been struck on the right temple and his left shin was fractured. His hands were well preserved, and showed a lack of wear on the fingers surprising in one who might have been considered to be a land-worker. His teeth were worn, three lost during life, and several had caries. Just before death, he had had a meal, perhaps like that of Tollund man, a gruel with barley, willow herb and brome grass, 'chess' seeds, some emmer and oats, and about fifty species of wild seeds several not of local character. Among the seeds were clover, spelt, rye-grass, lady's mantle, camomile, smooth hawksbeard, goosefoot, buttercup, yarrow and

134 (*Overleaf*) The face of Tollund man, Denmark. 'The dead and the sleeping, how they resemble one another' (Epic of Gilgamesh).

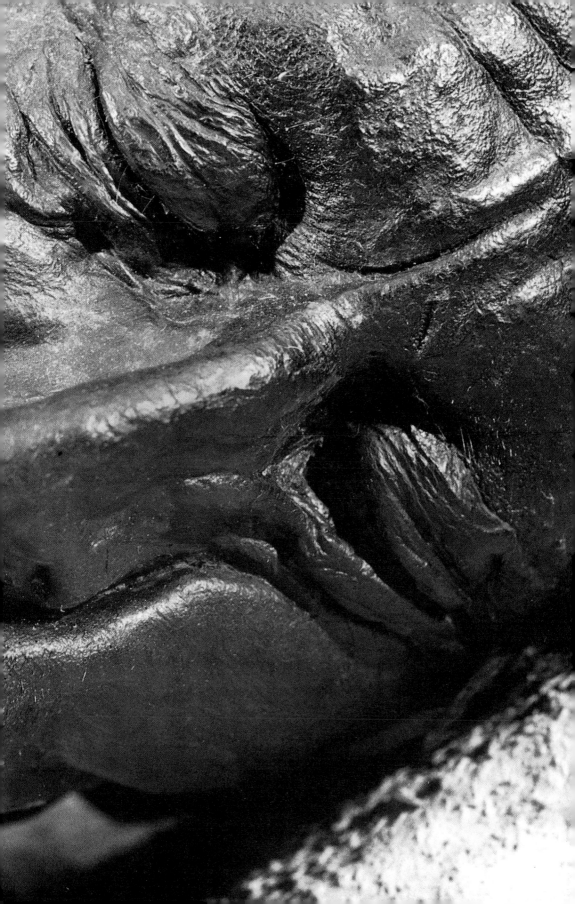

black nightshade, perhaps gathered during the harvest of grown crops. There were also slight traces of meat and some animal hair. Again there were no summer or autumn fruits, berries or apples or hips, nor were there any traces of 'greens'. Grauballe man was put to death at about the same time as Tollund man.

Because of the great interest of these 'last meals' of Tollund and Grauballe man, a rather light-hearted television experiment was organized by the BBC. After much scurrying around botanic gardens and bird food shops, the gruel was assembled; it included many of the species noted above, but not apparently the fragments of *Sphagnum* moss and teaspoonful of sand that Tollund man had also swallowed with his meal. The seeds were boiled slowly and eventually produced a rather oily porridge, greyish-purple in colour, with flecks of orange and black. After a taste, one of the experimenters, Sir Mortimer Wheeler, exclaimed 'Tollund man probably committed suicide to escape his wife's cooking'; and his colleague Glyn Daniel explained later that it was necessary to wash it down with good Danish liquor. A fair description of the gruel in modern terms is farmhouse mash, and Pliny describes the peasant foods of Greece and Rome as a gruel made of barley, linseed, coriander seed and salt, not much different; salt if present would not have been detectable in the Tollund and Grauballe intestines.

Preservation

The preservation of these two bog bodies, and many others less well known, is due to a combination of circumstances only now becoming clear. The varying conditions of the hundreds of human remains from Danish and North German bogs demonstrate the range of survival, and thereby point to the exceptional circumstances that permitted some bodies to survive almost intact. In essence, the preservation of bodies depended on three factors:
(1) Deposition of the body in water deep enough to prevent attack by organisms such as fly maggots, rodents and foxes, and still enough to be oxygen-deficient, as most raised bog waters are, to inhibit decay by bacteria. Thus the records of bodies placed in old peat cuttings, i.e. in deep holes or pits, are relevant.
(2) The bog pools contained water with tannic acid of sufficient strength to begin to preserve the outer layers of the body by tanning; Grauballe man was noted as partially tanned upon discovery, and has been conserved by tanning with oak-bark. If the water was non-acidic, the bones would survive but the flesh would rot away.
(3) The temperature of the water in the bog pool was below 4 degrees Celsius; this (normal refrigerator temperature) prevented decay and inhibited rot. If the water was warmer, the flesh would rot, and the acids in the water would decay the bone as well. If the burial pit was filled in at once, the temperature would be prevented from rising to decay-levels, and rodents would be excluded.

Therefore, it appears that the bog bodies were probably deposited in acidic bog pools in winter; if put in open pools in summer, they would not be likely to survive. This conclusion is supported by the stomach contents of Tollund and Grauballe men, which had no remains suggesting summer plants. The skeletal remains, or part remains, of many other humans from the bogs may represent deposition under different conditions, seasonally or environmentally. The Vester Thorsted skeleton with hair, and with hide coat, but no flesh, must represent one of these other conditions. And the observation that some of the better-preserved bodies were decayed in the parts protruding above the rest, such as shoulder, or uppermost arm, suggest that these were within the decaying zone of the particular conditions of tannic acid and water in the bog pool. There is of course a corollary to this basic conclusion, and it is that many bodies may have been placed in bog pools in summer but have not survived at all.

Clothing

Both Tollund man and Grauballe man were naked (apart from a cap and belt at Tollund), and other bog bodies dating to the same general period, the pre-Roman Iron Age, are rarely clothed. Some, however, have clothing placed nearby. From Borre Mose, three such bodies have been recovered. The first, found in 1946, was a naked male, with two sewn sheepskin capes at his feet; one of the capes had a collar. In 1947 a female was discovered, naked on a sheet of birch-bark and covered by a skirt of 4-strand twill and a fringed shawl. It is worth noting that the skirt had previously been worn as a cape, judging by the pin holes and wear on it; such capes are generally found with males. A year later, the bog yielded a third body; this prompted a note accompanying it to the National Museum, stating 'I have great pleasure in sending you the customary annual bog body from Borre Fen'; since then, no more have been found. The third body was a female covered by a blanket-shirt like that of the other Borre Mose female; there was also a leather strap (*ill. 138*).

The male had been put into an old peat cutting in a sitting position with legs bent and crossed; he was bent forward so that his right shoulder almost touched the left knee. There was stubble on the chin, and the left eyeball was well preserved, yellow-white with a black iris. The hands were unworn. The back of the skull was crushed, and the right thigh-bone was fractured, but the cause of death was a hemp rope about 1 m long with a slip-knot tied around his neck; he had been strangled or hanged. The last meal of Borre man had a been a gruel with corn spurrey and knotweed, as well as many other weed seeds, and he may have eaten this just before his execution about 700 BC.

The woman found in 1947 at Borre Mose lay on her front in a deep old peat-cutting. Around her neck was a leather strap with an amber bead and a bronze disc, and her hair was 2–3 m long. Her right leg was broken, perhaps before death, and just above the body were several small sticks and the bones of an infant. An associated potsherd was of a type identified in an Iron Age bog settlement in the same fen; the date of her death is about 400 BC.

In 1948 the final body was found, lying face down and covered by a blanket-skirt, her right arm bent up against the face and her left arm beneath her left leg which was bent up. Aged 20–35 years, her face was smashed and she had been in effect scalped at the back of the skull. There is some discussion about these injuries, which will be considered below. The date of this body is about 700 BC.

From these and other bog bodies it would appear that males of the period had skin capes, woven coats or kilt-like garments, possibly leggings, shoes and a cap. Females had woven skirts, scarves and skin capes which reached to the hips or below (*ill. 135, ill. 136*). None of these clothes and coverings shows signs of cuts or blood; the victims may have been stripped before execution. But not all were, and a body only recently reunited with its clothing is particularly informative in this respect

135 Reconstruction of a skin cape on the female from Elling Mose, Denmark.

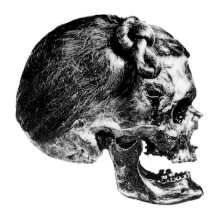

136–138 **Coiffure and costume of the bog bodies** (*Left*) Woollen skirt from Damendorf, Germany. (*Above*) The 'Swabian knot' on a beheaded man from Osterby, Germany. (*Below*) One of the Borre Mose bodies, wrapped in a blanket.

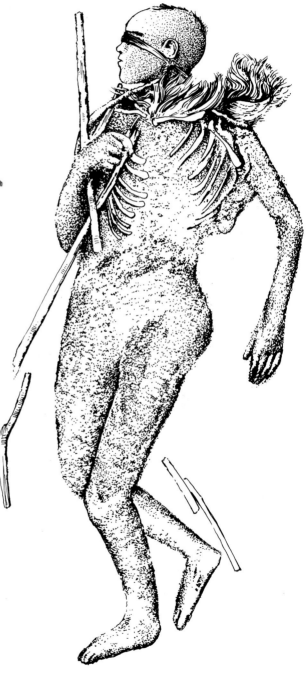

139, 140 **The young girl of Windeby, north Germany** Head (*above*) and reconstruction drawing (*right*) of the body as found. This 14-year-old girl showed no sign of a wound or strangulation. Instead, some 2,000 years ago she was blindfolded and perhaps drowned in a bog pool, her naked body held down by branches.

The bog of Huldremosen in Jutland was cut for peat in 1879 and a body was discovered, one hand severed by the peat-cutter's spade. A schoolteacher interested in antiquarian matters forbade all the soon-assembled onlookers to touch the body, which was clad in a skin cloak and other garments darkened by age and peat. The police were called in, as a man dressed in a leather coat had recently gone missing from the area. The corpse was hauled up from its peatbed, and taken on a stretcher to a nearby barn where it was undressed and cleaned. In so doing, it was found that the body was female, so the police departed. In attempts to clean the hair, the whole scalp came off. The body was then put in a coffin and buried in the churchyard, and the clothing was washed and hung out to dry. The museum in Copenhagen requested that the finds be sent for study, so the coffin was dug up and sent with the clothes by steamship to Copenhagen. Here there were problems of space, and in 1904 the Museum of Nordic Antiquities asked the Museum of Normal Anatomy if it could take the body, as otherwise it would be buried again in a cemetery. The transfer was done, and the body forgotten by the archaeological world. The clothing remained as one of the best-preserved Iron Age examples from Denmark. Only in 1978 was the body traced to the anatomy museum, and it now takes its place alongside the other preserved bodies from the bogs.

The body had been buried in the deep peats, and the early investigators reported that it was dried out, looking rather like a smoked ham and greatly wizened. The woman lay on her side, with legs drawn up; her left thigh bone had been broken in life and grown crooked, so she had a limp. The left arm was tied by a leather strap to the body. The right arm had been broken by an axe blow so fierce that the bone was nearly severed, and the lower arm dangling only by the remains of skin and tissues. What the woman had done, or not done, to deserve this frightful fate we cannot know. She went to the grave with two skin capes on her upper body. The outer cape was made of pieces of sheepskin in two colours with the hair outside; this was lined with sheepskin with hair facing inwards, which went around the neck and shoulders, and down the sleeves. This cape was closed at the neck so had to be pulled on over the head. The seams were particularly finely-stitched, and the cape looked almost new. The inner cape was open and fastened over the left shoulder. It was of lambskin with hair inside, and was well-worn. Under this was worn a chequered woollen cloth like a scarf, wound over the shoulder and under the left arm where it was fastened by a bone pin. A leather strap went around the body between the two capes. The skirt was of chequered cloth, ankle-length and very full (cf ill. 136), with a decorative feather-stitch seam probably worn down the front, and it was held up by a leather thong drawn through holes in the waistband, and with a button and loop attachment to keep it closed. The woman's hair, before it was pulled off her head, was long and dark, drawn back and held by a long woollen string wound several times around her neck, where there was also a necklace with two amber beads. Inside the inner cape, in a lining, were some small objects: leather thongs packed in a piece of bladder, a horn comb, and a narrow woven hair band of bright colours. All this was consigned to the bog about AD 100.

The hair of women was sometimes elaborately coiffured. The Elling Mose female had a cloak of sewn pieces of sheepskin, gathered at the front by leather thongs, and a woven wool belt. Her hair was c.90 cm long and arranged as follows: all the hair except that on the back, was combed up and braided in a 3-

strand plait down to the back hair; all the hair was then divided into 7 switches, each twisted, and braided together in 2 pairs and one triple, to make a 3-strand plait. At the end of the plait, the hair was twisted into 2 switches. Then the plait was wound twice round itself above the nape of the neck. This was the coiffure worn by the Elling Mose girl when she was hanged about 100 BC. Males occasionally wore their hair in a comparably elaborate fashion. The Kohlmoor, Osterby, find consisted only of a head wrapped in a sewn cape of roe deer skin; the male, aged 50–60 years, had been beheaded with an axe, and although little skin survived, the hair, originally blond with some grey, was well preserved. It was *c*.25 cm long, parted at the back and gathered at the right temple into a knot, called a Swabian knot after the recorded male coiffure of Classical times in that area of Germany (*ill. 137*).

The hair was combed and parted at the back. The left half was drawn low across the forehead to the right side. The left and right strands were wound tightly around one another, to keep the strand across the forehead, and the long strand-ends were plaited. The plait was then coiled high up, and the remainder turned to form a loop which was pushed through and drawn tightly by the coil. The loop hung down on the side of the head.

At Dätgen in Schleswig-Holstein, a head with hair dressed in Swabian fashion was found in a peat bog in 1955. The head was of a 30-year-old man whose body was buried about 3 m away. A wooden axe haft was also found, possibly part of the weapon that had decapitated the man. His legs had been broken before burial, probably after he was stabbed in the heart with a sharp dagger. The man was naked other than a woollen cord tied around his left ankle, and a woollen cloak from the same bog may once have been his.

Death in the bog

A particularly evocative discovery was made at Windeby, in north Germany, which casts some light upon the whole assembly of death that we are witnessing in this region in the few centuries before and after the birth of Christ. The Windeby bog was barely 0.5 hectare in area and during its cutting in 1952 two bodies were found. One was a naked elderly male, only represented by skin and hair, laid on his back, arms crossed, and held down in an old peat-cutting by thick branches, forked sticks and turves (*ill.*); there was a hazel withy around his neck, possibly a strangling bough. Several metres away, in another old peat-cutting, was the body of a young girl, lying on her back, head turned to one side and left arm outstretched (*ill. 140*). Between this arm and her hip was a heavy stone and some branches of wood lay over her body. The girl was aged about 14 years, and her body appeared rather thin; her bone structure suggests she had been under-nourished for much of her life. She was naked except for a double collar of ox-hide and a woven band tied tightly over her eyes (*ill. 139*). This band was probably a brightly-coloured headband, of 38 threads in tablet weave of brown, yellow and red repeat, ending in twisted strings. The girl's hair, light blonde in colour, was about 5 cm long on the right side of the head but had been shaved off with a razor on the left, where it was only 3 mm in length. Her brain when exposed for examination in the laboratory was extraordinarily well preserved, perhaps due to the presence of water-insoluble chlorestin.

141   The body of the man from Lindow Moss, England, lying face down in the peat (see ill. 131).

The excavations at Windeby revealed groups of heavy branches, forked sticks and stones which were a part of the act of deposition. A find made near Jelling a century earlier had also included branches; here an elderly female had been pinned into the bog by wooden crooks driven over her knees and elbows, and branches had been laid across her chest. The body was identified in the mid-19th century as that of Queen Gunhild, the beautiful, shrewd and cunning Norwegian consort of King Erik Bloodax. The Danish Harald Bluetooth invited her to marriage but on her arrival in his land, she was met by Harald's men who maltreated her and drowned her in a deep bog. The story was soon disputed and it seems clear that this woman was yet another Iron Age victim. The Jelling woman and the Windeby girl may have met death in the same way – pinned into a bog pool and drowned, for there was no sign of wound or strangulation on the Windeby girl.

No marks have been found on another bog body, from Gallagh, Co. Galway Ireland. This body, of a man lying on his back, was discovered in 1821 under 9 ft (3 m) of peat. It was apparently covered up again and re-exposed from time to time; this did not help its preservation. The body was clothed in a deerskin cape, tied at the neck with twisted withy or some sort of fibre. The body was held in the bog by wooden stakes. Perhaps the cord at the neck was a strangling rope. A sample of the body has been dated by radiocarbon, and suggests that the Gallagh man met his death just over 2,000 years ago.

Finally we come to the recent discovery of a bog body in Lindow Moss, England (*ill. 141*). In 1984, peat workers discovered a human lower leg on the factory conveyor, and called in the police and the archaeologists. This led to the peat section in Lindow Moss, where a flap of skin was seen still in place; the machine cutting peat had removed all the lower part of the body, and the lower leg was all that survived. The rest of the lower body is presumably now in numerous bags of peat, or spread as fertilizer on the rose beds or the mushroom beds of England. The upper body was found to be that of a male, aged *c*.25 years, perhaps 1.67 m (5.5 ft) tall, with a short beard and moustache; he wore nothing on his upper body other than a fox fur band on his arm. In his intestine were the remains of a meal of breadcake, made of spelt and emmer, and barley. There was also pollen of mistletoe; this last may have had Druidic connotations. The sequence of his death is particularly gruesome. He was hit on the top of the head twice, the blows crushing through the skull; at the same time he may have been kneed violently in the back, breaking a rib. A thin rope, tied around his neck, had been twisted to throttle him and perhaps his neck was thus broken. When death finally came, his throat was slit, severing the jugular vein, in an act possibly of bloodletting (exsanguination). He was then tipped into an old bog pool which filled with water and effectively sealed and preserved his body until truncated by peat machine some 2,000 years later.

There are now about ten bodies which have been radiocarbon dated to the Iron Age period in north and western Europe, but there are many others which can also be assigned to this general time-range on the basis of bog stratigraphy, proximity to Iron Age settlements or watery votive offerings, association with Iron Age artifacts or clothing, or context of death and deposition. One view is not so restricted as this, and sees humans in bogs whether skeletal, partial or fleshed bodies, as part of a very long tradition of sacrifice to fertility which was manifest from at least the Neolithic to the Viking Age in Denmark, that is, for about 4,000 years. This interpretation sees the bog bodies of the Iron Age as merely one element in this cult, more vividly demonstrated for us by the conditions of burial at the time.

Ritual deposits

Another view is that the human lives sacrificed to the bog waters were but a part, and perhaps a small part, of the dominating practice in the Iron Age of ritual deposition of objects of value in watery places. These may be pottery vessels containing food, or bronze or silver vessels, torcs, weapons, parts of carts, or animals, or war booty, cast or laid in lakes, marshes and pools in order to propitiate the gods or demonstrate the power of those who chose to, or were allowed to, dispose of property. In Denmark and north Germany, where many of the finds have been made, special studies of the composition of the hoards and deposits suggest that there are several different types of find, each of a ritual character but probably made for dissimilar reasons.

One group consists of offerings, small in quantity and varied in character. Such might be leather shoes, singly or in pairs, from sites at Pinneberg and Lottorf in north Germany; the skeletons of ten dogs and potsherds at Barsbeker moor, cowhorns in pairs or multiples at Wees, a wooden hammer at Wanderup, and many groups of pottery vessels at Rüde, Wattenbek and Süsel are all dated to about the time of Christ. Some of these finds may be accidental losses, such as the shoes or tools, but others seem more deliberate. A wooden beehive from

142 Wooden beehive from Edewechter-damm, Germany. Height *c*. 1 m.

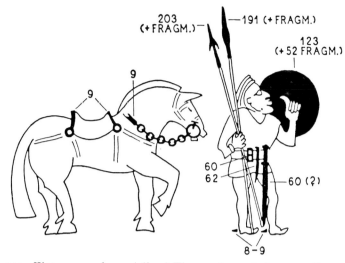

143, 144 **Weapons and war** (*Above*) The number and character of weapons and harness (e.g. 203 spears; 123 shields) found in the ritual deposit at Ejsbøl, Denmark, seeming to indicate that about 200 men had fought and lost a battle near here in the 4th century AD. (*Right*) Part of the ritual war booty thrown into the pond at Thorsbjerg, Germany.

Edewechterdamm is an unusual object to be found buried in a bog; made of a hollowed-out beech trunk, with a number of flight holes and a lid, it contained plaited twig ring-frames for the honeycombs (*ill. 142*).

In Chapter 6 we referred to the discovery of a number of carved wooden sticks, possibly measuring rods, associated with a heavy wooden roadway of about 100 BC. The purpose of these stave-like objects is unknown, but perhaps they too are a part of the ritualistic deposition of valuables. In Shakespeare's *Tempest*, Prospero renounces sorcery by declaiming:

> But this rough magic
> I here abjure; . . . I'll break my staff,
> Bury it certain fathoms in the earth,
> And, deeper than did ever plummet sound,
> I'll drown my book.

Perhaps here we detect the memory of distant acts of which we can now know little, other than to muse upon the physical artifacts laid deep beneath the surface.

War booty

When large quantities of objects are found in the bogs, it would seem that some powerful incentive was at work. One of the identifiable groups of artifacts consists of warlike implements. Among the earliest of these deposits is the Hjortspring war canoe, submerged with iron swords, spears, shields, and chain-mail, in a small bog on the island of Als. It dates to the 3rd or 2nd century BC. One of the main episodes of disposal of weapons and associated artifacts is between AD 200 and 400 when vast arrays of weapons and other valuables were

put into small lakes or onto wet marshland (*ill. 144*). The artifacts were bundled together and often put into special areas marked off by wooden posts or woven panels. The objects thus presented to the gods are considered to be the booty of battle, with the weapons often 'killed' by bending or breaking. The quantities can be vast; six such finds in Denmark together contained between 15,000 and 20,000 objects of iron, bronze, gold and other substances. And there are other such sacrificial finds, at Skedemosse in Sweden for example.

Caesar wrote of the practice:

> When they have decided to fight they dedicate their war booty to the god of war. After victory they offer the captured animals; the remainder they pile up in one place. With all tribes, whole heaps of such articles of booty can be seen in their sacred places. Only rarely does anyone so disregard the religious customs that he dares to hide booty in his house, or take anything from the heap of spoils. Such a crime is punishable by a cruel death.

The great votive deposit at Thorsbjerg in south Jutland is believed to represent booty from battles involving invaders from the south, from the lowlands between the Rhine and the Elbe rivers. The Illerup bog contained at least 3 separate sacrifices of booty, and the Ejsbøl bog yielded one large and several smaller deposits. At the latter site, the quantities found suggest that about 200 men had fought and lost a battle near here in the 4th century AD, with 60 foot-soldiers and 9 horsemen killed (*ill. 143*). The investigations at Skedemose suggest that the watery fen chosen to receive the sacrificial offerings was used only for the purpose and was otherwise left untouched. The objects brought from the scenes of battle or other sites were mutilated deliberately and with great force; swords were bent double, bracelets were rolled up, other objects were chopped into pieces, shields were hacked. The weapons were sometimes bundled up in separate parcels, and were then thrown into the waters at selected places and from particular platforms, or carried out in boats and dumped. During the ceremonies, fires were lit, meat was cooked and probably consumed, and some parts of animals such as horses' skulls and feet were collected and deposited in special places.

Another group of deposits in the bogs of the north consists of non-military finds, often of pottery but also sometimes of wheels, yokes and waggon parts, or ploughs, the former possibly connected with wooden and stone roads built at this time, crossing wet bogs just as in northern Germany and elsewhere. And there are also hoards of precious metal objects, of gold, bronze and iron, laid in the ponds and bogs particularly in the 5th and 6th centuries AD and which emphasize to a remarkable degree the attraction, the fascination, and the pull of the wetlands to the societies from at least 500 BC for over 1,000 years. Unusable they may have been for agriculture and other ordinary pursuits, but the wetlands were a focus for the spiritual life that drove the societies forward into production, acquisition and ritual disposal of their wealth.

Among the huge quantities of offerings, one in particular links wealth in precious metal, warfare, and human sacrifices in an extaordinary manner. The Gundestrup silver cauldron (*ill. 148*) is a unique artifact, with its 1st-century BC representations of supernatural beings, sacrifices and processions, in a fascinating juxtaposition of ideas and beliefs which may reflect upon the whole concept of sacrifice and renewal in Iron Age Europe; but whether this was by way of initiation of ideas or depiction of old traditions is uncertain. The cauldron was found stacked in pieces near a vantage point overlooking Borre Mose, a bog containing a formidable and protected Iron Age settlement and the three bog bodies already noted. Strabo, writing not far removed in time from the deposition of the Gundestrup cauldron, records the practices of the Cimbri, a people of the north:

> Their women who went to war with the men were accompanied by priestesses who possessed the gift of prophecy . . . These, sword in hand, walked through the camp towards the prisoners, decorated them with garlands and then led them to a cauldron of bronze . . .; they had a ladder up which they climbed and, bending over the cauldron, they cut each prisoner's throat as he was lifted up to them. They read the signs from the blood which flowed into the cauldron. Others cut open the prisoners' bellies and read the omens from their intestines announcing victory for their people, with loud voices.

Wooden figures

And there is yet another group of finds from the bogs of north and west that reflect other ideas. This is a widely disparate series of carved wooden figures and human representations that seem to belong to the period of bog burials and deposits of weapons and other valuables. From the Aukamper moor of north Germany a pair of human effigies 2.25–2.75 m tall was recovered from the peat (*ill. 145*), and a double-bodied effigy 1.7 m tall is known from Neubrandenburg in East Germany; four figures are from Oberdorla in the same region. A Danish figure from Broddenbjerg is distinctly phallic, unless he is kicking a football (*ill. 146*), and was deposited beneath a cairn of stones, and another figure, of female form, was similarly deposited at Foerlev Nymølle. The Danish saga of Ragnar

145 A pair of wooden figures, 2.25 and 2.75 m tall, from the Aukamper moor, Germany.

146–148 **Offerings and effigies**
(*Left*) Wooden figure from
Broddenbjerg, Denmark. Height
88 cm. (*Right* and *below right*)
Wooden figure from
Kingsteignton, England. Height
34 cm. (*Below*) The 1st-century
BC silver cauldron from
Gundestrup, Denmark, with
representations of supernatural
beings, sacrifices and processions.
Diameter 69 cm.

Lodbrok refers to the landing of Ogmund on an island where he found an old man of wood fully 14 m high, overgrown with moss; even Ogmund could not answer the question – who might have sacrificed to this god?

Such representations of humans are widespread in the prehistoric past, and in many media such as paint, pottery, stone and wood. The wooden effigies of the north and west of Europe are remarkable for their dramatic appearance, their burial in bogs and pools, and their apparent narrow chronological period, from the closing centuries BC to about AD 500.

From Ireland and Britain there are a number of carved wooden figures, including one in pine from the Dagenham marshes, Essex, a group of five from Roos Carr, Yorkshire, and a large figure from Ralaghan, Co. Cork. These all have facial features shown and a hole positioned to receive a separate penis, if indeed they were meant to be male. The Roos Carr group of pine figures was found with an animal-headed boat-like curved piece of wood with 8 holes, possibly for 4 figures. There are also 2 round shields, and the figures have holes for the insertion of arms. A different and much larger figure, 1.5 m tall, was found deep in a peatbog at Ballachulish, Argyll, lying on its face and covered with wickerwork; the oak figure was described upon discovery as 'very slim in figure, but no more so than some young ladies of the present day', 1880. And it is supposed to represent a female. Both the Ballachulish figure and the Roos Carr figures have eyes of quartz, and others may have had once. Other wooden figures from Britain include a finely-carved oak image from Kingsteignton in Devon (*ill. 147*). All of these figures, and there are more from Britain, Germany and Denmark, suggest a particular interest in the association of humans and bog or pool or other wet place.

It will be clear that powerful forces were at work in the Iron Age society of northern Europe, and the bog bodies of the period must have had a special place in this episode. The number of individuals apparently executed may represent only a small part of the seemingly wholesale sacrifice of wealth, or the burial of ritually important artifacts, in this period. Perhaps human sacrifices, disposal of wealth, discard of war booty, and concealment of effigies formed a coherent pattern of appeasement to the forces of nature and of the other world, so that societies and individuals could feel more comfortable with their unequal lives, their uncertainty of survival and their acceptance of a fate over which they had little control.

But there are other views as well, which see some of the bog bodies as unconnected to the votive offering and sacrificial cult of the north. One receives strong support in the writing of Tacitus, who described in some detail the practices and beliefs of certain of the Germanic tribes with which the Romans were in contact, if only in an unfriendly way. Tacitus was writing in the late 1st century AD and part of his texts refer to Germanic law:

- traitors and deserters are hanged on trees.
- cowards, shirkers and sodomites are pressed down under a hurdle into the slimy mud of a bog.
- wives guilty of adultery are taken from the house, stripped, shaven and flogged by their husbands.
- criminals are taken to the place of execution, and the body from the execution, on a cow-hide so as not to touch cultivated land.

From these comments we may envisage hanging and the noose, pinning into a bog pool, victims naked and shaven, and cow-hides laid beside the bodies, all elements of which are recorded at the sites of Tollund, Borre, Windeby and Lindow. Tacitus also refers to the ritual offerings made by the Germanic peoples, with both material possessions and human lives sacrificed to propitiate the gods and ease the passage of the seasons. The Gundestrup cauldron depicts what seems to be a bloodletting, with the victim held over a cauldron, and the throat-cutting of the Grauballe and Lindow men may relate, if distantly, to the practice of letting of blood for ritual purposes. Nonetheless, the image of punishment for misdeeds is strongly projected by some of the bog bodies, and the original report on the second Borre Mose female makes harrowing reading. It envisages the unfaithful wife being shaven and driven by her husband out of the village into the bog; 'out there in the bog, the walkers slowly formed a circle around the two, and while the men began to dig her grave in the black peat the man came forward . . .'; after the final crushing blow to the head she was thrown into the grave, and it was then filled in. It is necessary to note here that modern forensic examination of the Borre body does not support all of this scenario; her smashed face might be post-mortem damage, and she certainly did not attempt to fend off any blows with her arms. Yet she, and her fellows over a number of centuries from c.700 BC, did end up in the bogs of the north and west, slain under unusual circumstances, and they provide us with our first real look at our European ancestors – their flesh and blood, their physical condition, their clothes (*ill. 149*), some of their food, and their precise manner of death. It hardly makes one yearn for olden times. As R. B. Sheridan said, 'Our ancestors are very good kind of folk but they are the *last* people I should choose to have a visiting acquaintance with.'

We hope that this book has provided some degree of acquaintance with the people of the bogs and lakes, rescued from the waters of oblivion.

149   Tailpiece: leather shoes from Damendorf, Germany.

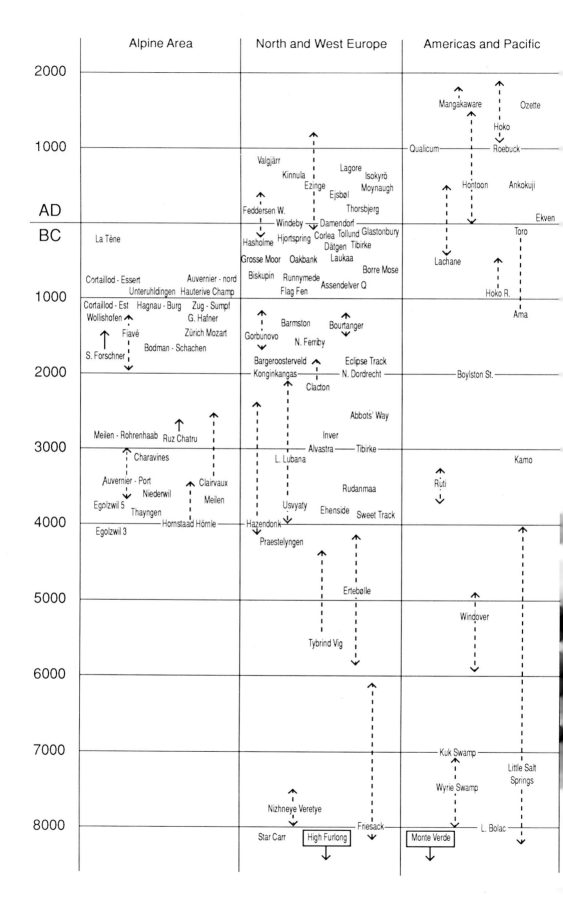

Brief guide to sites and museums

Many wetlands of the world are now drained or being drained. Most of these were once utilized by people who could obtain a wide variety of raw materials and foods from the fertile wetlands. An appreciation of the importance of these areas to ancient peoples can be best obtained by visits to surviving wetlands.

Some of the wetlands listed below are nature reserves or are otherwise on restricted property. Potential visitors are advised to seek permission before entering any of these reserves where wildlife may be disturbed. Almost all the locations noted here have been visited by the authors.

Many small museums hold artifacts from local wetland sites, and only some of the museums with large collections or particular displays are listed here.

BRITAIN AND IRELAND

The Somerset Levels. Sites are mostly buried or gone, but the local Peat Moors Visitors Centre, south of the village of Westhay, about 7 km west of Glastonbury, will have information about visible monuments. A reconstruction of the Abbot's Way can be seen, and walked upon, on the road between Westhay and Burtle, behind a peat factory. The Glastonbury and Meare Lake Villages can be seen as mounds in pasture fields, the former north of the town of Glastonbury, the latter just north of the village of Meare. The Sweet Track is visible as a reconstruction in a Nature Reserve for which permission for entry should be sought from the Nature Conservancy Council, local office at Meare.

The Fens of East Anglia and Lincolnshire. The visitor should start at the Flag Fen, 3 km south-east of Peterborough, where exca-vations and exhibits can be seen. A good impression of flat Fen landscape can be obtained by driving from Flag Fen to Wicken Fen, by way of March or Ramsey and Chatteris. Wicken Fen is a National Trust-owned nature reserve with artificially main-tained high water tables.

A number of Bronze Age burial mounds can be seen emerging from the shrinking peats at Borough Fen, 4 km north of Peterborough, about 1 km to the south-west of the hamlet of Newborough, and south-east of the Peakirk Wildfowl refuge. Nearer the coast of the North Sea, mounds and ridges left by sea salt extraction processes, mostly medieval, can be seen near Gosberton on the A16 road between Boston and Spalding. North-east of Boston, at Wrangle on the A52, a series of sea reclamations, salt marsh grazing, and the 'tofts' (areas of raised ground) left by salterns show many of the former attractions of such coastlands. To the north of the Fenland, the river Witham has yielded many prehistoric finds including structures at Fiskerton, east of Lincoln city.

North-west England. A number of archae-ologically important mosses and peatbogs still exist although wetland monuments are no longer visible. Among the important wetlands are the following: Lindow Moss near Wilm-slow, just south of Manchester. This small peatbog is commercially worked and enquiries should be made at the local office. Several bog bodies have been recently found in the peat. Chat Moss, 10 km west of Manchester, is only one of a number of much reduced bogs in the area. Pilling Moss, 8 km west of Garstang, is a peat wetland with many dry settled islands; 'God's Grace and Pilling Moss are endless' (Fylde proverb) may give an impression of its former appearance and extent.

North-east England. Thorne Waste and Hatfield Chase are large areas of peatbog south of the river Humber, between Doncaster and Scunthorpe. Parts are being cut for horticultural peat and access is restricted, but the area gives a good impression of a lowland raised bog. Various prehistoric trackways have been recorded but the structures are gone. Hatfield Chase has also yielded a number of bog bodies: 'We then found the Skin of the Arms, which was like the top of a Muff or Glove, when the Bones were shaken out . . .', but obviously nothing remains today of these ancients.

British estuaries. Many archaeological discoveries have been made in estuaries such as the Humber and the Severn, but soft muds and a wide intertidal range make such places dangerous to visit without expert local guidance and supervision. The local museums will be able to offer advice – please take it. The Ferriby boat site lies in such a zone, and the boat is undergoing conservation at the National Maritime Museum, Greenwich. The very large Hasholme logboat is being conserved while on display at the Town Docks Museum, Hull.

Crannogs in Scotland and Wales (information from Dr N. Dixon and A. Lane). Among the hundreds of artificial islands known to exist, only a few have been examined. A few easily visible from the shores of lochs include:
Cherry island near Fort Augustus, Loch Ness, a crannog with trees in a small bay. Blundell excavated here in 1908, and timbers are still visible in the silt underwater.
Priory island, east end of Loch Tay. Historic crannog with ruins of the Campbell stronghold.
Strathcashel Point, east side of Loch Lomond. Submerged crannog with oak timbers exposed. Reached by a walk from the Forestry Commission caravan park.
Duddingston Loch, Edinburgh. Submerged crannog, and site of Bronze Age 'ritual' deposit of metal artifacts. Best view from the road in Holyrood Park.
Lochrutton, Kirkcudbrightshire. Small island

in the middle of the loch, a medieval crannog occupation in the upper layers, with timbers projecting underwater of possible earlier date. The adjacent peninsula is defended, perhaps by the crannog builders.
Llangorse, 10 km east of Brecon, Wales. Small crannog off the north shore of the lake. Nature reserve.

Ireland. The Midlands of central Ireland are characterized by very extensive raised bogs which are now being heavily worked by peat-cutting machines. A few nature reserves have been established. Visitors might commence a tour at Clonmacnoise on the River Shannon where information can be obtained. Or a journey from Athlone down the Shannon to Clonmacnoise and Shannonbridge Power Station, and thence eastwards into the bogland, will show the nature of the boglands and their present levelling. The area round Keenagh in Co. Longford is now yielding many prehistoric structures on commercially worked peatland. Access permits should be sought from local Bord na Mona offices.

Other wetland sites and areas to visit include the reconstruction of a crannog at Craggaunowen, north of Limerick; another crannog of modern date can be seen in the National Heritage Park, Ferrycarrig, near Wexford in south-east Ireland. Lough Gur, south of Limerick, is a small lough and marshland with archaeological exhibits of finds made from the lough and its shores. In the north of the island, the Iron Age ritual lake at Lough-na-shade west of Armagh lies next to the Navan fort, but is partly buried by quarry spoil. The royal crannog sites of Ballinderry and Lagore are now silted up and lie on private lands. The excavated crannog at Moynaugh Lough, near Nobber, north-west of Dublin, lies in a pleasant valley.

Museums in Britain and Ireland
The British Museum, London (*Lindow man, Sweet Track*)
County Museum, Taunton, Somerset (*Somerset Levels*)

National Museum of Ireland, Dublin (*bog finds*)

National Museum of Wales, Cardiff (*wooden artifacts*)

Royal Museum of Scotland, Edinburgh (*wooden artifacts*)

University Museum of Archaeology and Anthropology, Cambridge (*Fenland and Somerset Levels finds*)

DENMARK

Many waterlogged sites are known, but few still have traces visible on the ground. The Mesolithic settlement of Tybrind Vig, off the west coast of Fyn, 12 km south of Middlefart, is submerged but the small bay is beautiful. Vedbaek, on the north-east coast of Zealand, between Copenhagen and Helsingor, was the site of a Mesolithic cemetery with good preservation. The Illerup bog with Iron Age sacrificial deposits lies north-west of Skanderborg; the bog is being restored as a wetland. The Ertebølle midden in north-west Jutland lies on the east coast of the Limfjord, opposite Nykøbing.

Borre Mose and the site of the Gundestrup cauldron find are in north Jutland near Aars, west of the road from Viborg to Aalborg. This small bogland has the stone outline of an Iron Age settlement; bog bodies were found nearby.

Tibirke, in north-west Zealand near the coast, north-west of Helsinge, has the traces of a former Neolithic island occupation, linked to the shore by trackway.

Museums in Denmark
Forhistorisk Museum, Moesgård, nr Aarhus (*Tybrind Vig, Grauballe man*)

National Museum of Denmark, Copenhagen (*Gundestrup cauldron, bog finds*)

Silkeborg Museum, Silkeborg (*Tollund man*)

FRANCE

The French Alpine lakes of Chalain, Clairvaux and Paladru (Charavines site) are worth visiting, and reconstructions of prehistoric houses may be visible. These small lakes lie east of the river Saône.

Wetlands in western France to visit include the Brière, north-west of Nantes, and the Marais Poitevin, east of La Rochelle, which has a number of prehistoric sites scattered around its edge such as Champ Durand.

Museums in France (all with material from the lakes and rivers of Alpine and eastern France)
Musée archéologique, Dijon
Musée d'Archéologie, Lons-le-Saunier
Musées Denon, Chalon-sur-Saône
Musée municipal, Dole
Musée savoisien, Chambéry

GERMANY

South Germany. On the Bodensee, the sites of Hornstaad-Hörnle and Unteruhldingen are in the north-west part of the lake. Other sites are now more or less land-locked, including those on the Federsee, a shrinking lake north of Bad Buchau, west of Biberach.

The Wetterau region, north of Frankfurt, is being restored as a wildlife wetland sanctuary. A number of separate wetlands will be connected to form a varying series of habitats for the rich plant and animal life. The region should provide a good example of past wetland environments that were once exploited by ancient people.

Museums in south Germany
Federseemuseum, Bad Buchau (*Federsee sites*)

Pfahlbaumuseum, Unteruhldingen (*lake-dwelling reconstruction*)

Rosgartenmuseum Konstanz, Konstanz (*Bodensee material*)

Württembergisches Landesmuseum, Stuttgart (*Wasserburg Buchau and other sites*)

North Germany. The small hamlet of Ziallerns, north-west of Wilhelmshaven, 1 km north of Tettens, is a good example of a terp, lying in a coastal flatland; many of the terps are occupied today, like Ziallerns and Olddorf, 3 km east of Tetten. There are other terps in the Dithmarschen region, on the west coast of Schleswig-Holstein, west of Heide, and especially between the hamlets of Heuwisch (hay meadow) and Haferwisch (corn meadow), 9 km north-west of Heide.

The sites of Flögeln and Feddersen Wierde are on the east side of the Weser mouth. Flögeln lies beside the Flögelner See, an inland lake.

In the triangle formed by Oldenburg (east), Elisabethfehn (west) and Wiesmoor (north) are moorlands from which prehistoric trackways and other finds have been discovered. Little is visible on the ground today. The Teufelsmoor, north of Bremen and south of Vollersode, will give a good impression of an isolated and desolate moor, especially in the mist. From moors such as this have come many finds of bog bodies. The sites of Windeby, Damendorf, Österby and Dätgen, from which bodies have been recovered, lie in small moors west and south of Eckernförde, east of the E3 motorway.

The Duvensee moor, 11 km east of Ratzeburg, south of the road from Bad Oldesloe to Ratzeburg, had a Mesolithic partly waterlogged settlement, now excavated. The wetland is now being restored by blocked drainage.

Haithabu (Hedeby), near Schleswig, is the site of a waterlogged Viking fortress settlement on the Schlei inlet. There is a museum at the site.

Museums in north Germany
Archäologisches Landesmuseum der Christian-Albrechts-Universität, Schloss Gottorf, Schleswig (*bog bodies and offerings*)
Bachmann-Museum, Bremervörde (*material from terps*)
Deutsches Schiffahrtsmuseum, Bremerhaven (*boats*)
Heimatmuseum, Weener (*material from terps*)
Küsten-Museum der Stadt Wilhelmshaven, Wilhelmshaven (*material from terps*)
Moor und Fehn Museum, Elisabethfehn (*peat moor history*)
Morgenstern-Museum, Bremerhaven (*Feddersen Wierde*)
Museum Burg Bederkesa, Bederkesa (*Feddersen Wierde, Flögeln*)
Staatliches Museum für Naturkunde und Vorgeschichts, Oldenburg (*trackways and waggons*)

ITALY
Fiavé and the Lake Carera bog, north of Lake Garda in Italy, south-west of Trento, is another former lake settlement, now landlocked. The finds are at the Museo Provinciale d'Arte, Castello del Buonconsiglio, Trento.

THE NETHERLANDS
Most of the Netherlands are by definition lowland and wetland, but almost all is drained. The Veenmuseumdorp 't Aole Compas' at Barger-Compascuum, east of Emmen, is an open-air museum of peat-cutting and archaeology, with numerous reconstructions of prehistoric trackways.

Museums in the Netherlands (all with wetland material)
Fries museum, Leeuwarden
Groninger Museum voor Stad en Lande, Groningen
Museum voor Scheepsarcheologie, Ketelhaven
Provincial Museum van Drenthe, Assen
Rijksmuseum van Oudheden, Leiden

NORTHERN EUROPE
There are many sites in the north that were once in wetlands, but many are now lost, and most are barely visible on the ground. The Alvastra Neolithic occupation site, on the east coast of Lake Vättern, Sweden, north of Gränna, has been partly reconstructed. The small bogland of the Skedemose, scene of ritual deposits in the Iron Age, lies south-east of Borgholm, on the island of Öland, Sweden. The Iron Age fortress of Biskupin, north-east of Poznan, near Znin in Poland, has massive reconstructions and current excavations and other displays, depending on local conditions.

Museums in Northern Europe
National Museum of Sweden, Stockholm (*Alvastra*)
Państwowe Muzeum Archeologiczne Oddzia W Biskupinie, Warsaw (*Biskupin*)

SWITZERLAND
The lake-shore prehistoric villages are no

more visible than many a wetland site but their setting can be appreciated particularly by boat from the lakes. On Lake Neuchâtel, the sites of Cortaillod, Auvernier and Hauterive-Champréveyres are on the north shore, and excavations are likely to be in progress at or near the last-named site. On Lake Zürich, the main sites are clustered around the harbour area of Zürich itself.

Museums in Switzerland (all have material from the lakes)
Bernisches Historisches Museum, Berne
Musée cantonal d'Archéologie, Neuchâtel
Musée cantonal d'Archéologie et d'Histoire, Lausanne
Musée d'Art et d'Histoire, Fribourg
Musée Schwab, Bienne
Naturhistorisches Museum, Lucerne
Schweizerisches Landesmuseum, Zürich

JAPAN
The site at Toro in Shizuoka City has reconstructions of Yayoi Period houses. Wooden artifacts can be seen in the National Museum, Tokyo.

UNITED STATES AND CANADA
Two main areas of wetland in North America – in Washington State and in Florida – possess interesting sites and extensive swamp, marsh and coastland. The prehistoric settlements of Ozette and Hoko River in north-west Washington State, are particularly important for visitors to the region.
Ozette. The Makah Indian Reservation has a museum display and a reconstructed house from the Ozette site. Take the ferry from Seattle to the Olympic Peninsula and travel west along the north edge to the town of Neah Bay, at the end of highway 112. The museum is in Makah Village. The Ozette site itself can be visited by turning left on the Hoko–Ozette road a few miles past Sekin on highway 112. After 28 miles, the road ends at Lake Ozette; hike down a planked trail 3.3 miles to the Pacific coast. Turn right and walk up the beach $\frac{1}{2}$ mile to Cape Alava. A Makah Ranger station is located next to the site, with a small

replicated longhouse on top of the excavated area. The house has a fire pit, benches and a bronze plaque dedicating the site as a World Heritage Site. The Ranger can provide further details about the site and the Makah heritage.
Hoko River. This site is under excavation in the summer, and visitors are welcome. Travel on highway 112 past the Hoko–Ozette turnoff for about $\frac{1}{2}$ mile and turn right up Eagle Point Road (a signpost for the site is here). At the end of this road, park and walk a short distance along a track to the site. At the river, excavations can be seen and explained, and across the river, the prehistoric camp is being reconstructed; dugout canoe rides may be available.
Florida. Apart from the major wetlands noted below, there are many small peatbogs and swamps in Florida; some are being cut for commercial peat, and others are being drained and dredged for development. Most are privately owned.

There are many wetlands to see in Florida, such as the Everglades, Big Cypress Swamp and, to the north, Lake Kissimee. In the more northern part of Florida, Hontoon Island, on the St John's River, is a nature reserve with an extensive prehistoric settlement now surviving as a series of middens, some waterlogged. Fort Center, along Fisheating Creek by Lake Okeechobee, has a series of mounds representing part of the elaborate settlement and burial complex. The waterway of St John's River and Lake George, with many small tributaries and interfingered lakes, contains many middens along its shores, and local catfish are delicious.

Museums in North America
Florida State Museum, Gainesville, Florida (*Fort Center, dugouts*)
Heye Foundation Museum for the American Indian, New York (*wood carvings*)
Makah Cultural and Research Center, Neah Bay, Washington State (*Ozette*)
Museum of Anthropology, University of British Columbia, Vancouver (*totem poles*)
Museum of Canadian Civilization, Ottawa/Hull (*Northwest Coast finds*)

Museum of Florida History, Tallahassee, Florida (*Florida wood carvings*)

National Museum of Natural History, Smithsonian Institution, Washington (*Key Marco*)

Royal British Columbia Museum, Victoria, British Columbia (*Lachane and other material*)

The Sequim Museum, Sequim, Washington State (*the Manis Mastodon site*)

University Museum, Philadelphia (*Key Marco*)

Select bibliography

GENERAL READING

BOCQUET, A. (ed.) 1984. *Archéologie des lacs et des rivières*, 1984. Musée d'Annecy, Annecy.

COLES, J. 1984. *The Archaeology of Wetlands*. Edinburgh University Press.

COLES, B. and J. 1986. *Sweet Track to Glastonbury: the Somerset Levels in Prehistory*. Thames and Hudson, London and New York.

COLES, J. M. and LAWSON, A. J. (eds) 1987. *European Wetlands in Prehistory*. Clarendon Press, Oxford.

DIECK, A. 1965. *Die Europäischen Moorleichenfunde*. Neumünster.

GLOB, P. V. 1969. *The Bog People. Iron Age Man Preserved*. Faber, London.

LOUWE KOOIJMANS, L. P. 1985. *Sporen in het land. De Nederlandse delta in de prehistorie*. Meulenhoff, Amsterdam.

MORRISON, I. 1985. *Landscape with Lake Dwellings: the crannogs of Scotland*. Edinburgh University Press, Edinburgh.

MUNRO, R. 1890. *The Lake Dwellings of Europe*. Cassell & Co. Ltd., London.

PÉTREQUIN, A-M. and P. 1988. *Le Néolithique des Lacs. Préhistoire des lacs de Chalain et de Clairvaux (4000–2000 av. J.-C.)*. Editions Errance, Paris.

PÉTREQUIN, P. 1984. *Gens de l'eau, gens de la terre*. Hachette, Paris.

PURDY, BARBARA (ed.) 1988. *Wet-site Archaeology*. Telford Press, Caldwell NJ.

SCHLICHTHERLE, H. and WAHLSTER, B. 1986. *Archäologie in Seen und Mooren*. Konrad Theiss Verlag, Stuttgart.

Preserved. Faber, London.

GODWIN, H. 1978. *Fenland: its ancient past and uncertain future*. Cambridge University Press, Cambridge.

GUYAN, W. U. 1954. Das Jungsteinzeitliche Moordorf von Thayngen-Weier, in *Das Pfahlbauproblem*, 223–72. Schweizerische Gesellschaft für Urgeschichte, Schaffhausen.

JOHNSON, F. 1942. *The Boylston Street Fishweir*. Papers of the Peabody Foundation for Archaeology 2. Andover.

KELLER, F. 1878. *The Lake Dwellings of Switzerland and other parts of Europe*. 2nd edition. Longman, London.

MUNRO, R. 1882. *Ancient Scottish Lake-dwellings or Crannogs*. Douglas, Edinburgh.

— 1890. *The Lake-Dwellings of Europe*. Cassell, London.

— 1912. *Palaeolithic man and Terramara settlements in Europe*. Oliver and Boyd, Edinburgh.

RAJEWSKI, Z. 1970. *Biskupin*. Warsaw.

SPECK, J. 1981. 'Pfahlbauten: Dichtung oder Wahrheit? Ein Querschnitt durch 125 Jahre Forschungsgeschichte', *Helvetia Archaeologica* 45–48, 98–138.

TROYON, F. 1860. *Habitations lacustres des temps anciens et modernes*. Bridel, Lausanne.

VOGT, E. 1954. Pfahlbaustudien, in *Das Pfahlbauproblem*, 119–219. Schweizerische Gesellschaft für Urgeschichte, Schaffhausen.

WOOD-MARTIN, W. G. 1886. *The Lake Dwellings of Ireland: or ancient Lacustrine Habitations of Erin, commonly called Crannogs*. Hodges Figgis, Dublin.

WYSS, R. 1976. *Das jungsteinzeitliche Jäger-Bauerndorf von Egolzwil 5 im Wauwilermoos*. Archaeologische Forschungen, Schweizerischen Landesmuseum, Zürich.

1 The decades of discovery; 2 Extending the search

History of wetland archaeology

BULLEID, A. and GRAY, H. S. G. 1911, 1917. *The Glastonbury Lake Village*, vols. I and II. Antiquarian Society, Glastonbury.

CUSHING, F. H. 1896. 'Exploration of Ancient Key Dwellers' Remains on the Gulf Coast of Florida', *Proc. American Philosophical Society* 35, 329–448.

DARBISHIRE, R. D. 1874. 'Notes on discoveries in Ehenside Tarn, Cumberland', *Archaeologia* 44, 273–92.

EGLOFF, M. 1980. 'Etapes de la recherche archéologigue dans le canton de Neuchâtel', *Helvetia Archaeologica* 43–44, 92–116.

GASTALDI, B. 1865. *Lake Habitations and Pre-Historic Remains in the Turbaries and Marl-Beds of Northern and Central Italy*. Longman, London.

GILLILAND, M. S. 1988. *Key Marco's buried treasure. Archaeology and adventure in the nineteenth century*. University of Florida Press, Gainesville.

GLOB, P. V. 1969. *The Bog People. Iron Age Man*

3 Living by the sea

Environmental background

BAILEY, G. and PARKINGTON, J. (eds) 1988. *The Archaeology of Prehistoric Coastlines*. Cambridge University Press, Cambridge and New York.

CLARK, J. G. D. 1975. *The Earlier Stone Age Settlement of Scandinavia*. Cambridge University Press, Cambridge.

JENSEN, J. 1982. *The Prehistory of Denmark*. Methuen, London.

JONES, MARTIN 1986. *England before Domesday*. Batsford, London.

MALTBY, E. 1986. *Waterlogged Wealth*. Earthscan.

ODUM, E. P. 1971. *Fundamentals of Ecology*. Saunders, Philadelphia.

OELE, E. SCHÜTTENHELM, R. T. E. and WIGGERS, A. J. (eds) 1979. *The Quaternary History of the North Sea*. Uppsala.

SUTCLIFFE, ANTONY J. 1985. *On the Track of Ice Age Mammals*. British Museum (Natural History), London.

TANSLEY, A. G. 1968. *Britain's Green Mantle* (chs 15–17), 2nd edition, revised by M. C. F. Proctor. Allen and Unwin, London.

America

CROES, DALE R. (ed.), 1976. *The excavation of water-saturated archaeological sites (wet sites) on the northwest coast of North America*. National Museum of Man Mercury Series. Archaeological Survey of Canada Paper No. 50. Ottawa.
FLADMARK, KNUT R. 1986. *British Columbia Prehistory*. National Museum of Man, Ottawa.
GILLILAND, MARION SPJUT. 1975. *The Material Culture of Key Marco*. The University Presses of Florida, Gainesville.
MCKILLOP, HEATHER and JACKSON, LAWRENCE. 1987. 'Excavations at a waterlogged coastal Maya island site in Belize, Central America', *NewsWarp 3*, 10–12.
PURDY, BARBARA (ed.) 1988. *Wet-site Archaeology*. Telford Press, Caldwell, N. J.

Europe, Stone Age

ALBRETHSEN, S. E. and BRINCH PETERSEN, E. 1977. 'Excavation of a Mesolithic Cemetery at Vedbaek, Denmark', *Acta Archaeologica* XLVII, 1–28.
ANDERSEN, SØREN H. 1987. Tybrind Vig: a submerged Ertebølle Settlement, in Denmark, in J. M. Coles and A. J. Lawson, (eds) *European Wetlands in Prehistory*, 253–80. Oxford University Press.
ANDERSEN, SØREN H. and JOHANSEN, ERIK. 1986. Ertebølle Revisited. *J. Danish Archaeology 5*, 31–61.
ANDERSEN, SØREN H. and MALMROS, C. 1984. '"Mads-korpe" pä Ertebøllekar fra Tybrind Vig', *Aarbøger*, 78–95 (English summary pp. 93–5).
BOOKER ENGHOFF, I. 1986. 'Freshwater fishing from a Sea-Coast Settlement – The Ertebølle *locus classicus* Revisited', *J. Danish Archaeology 5*, 62–76.
COLES, J. M. 1971. 'The early settlement of Scotland: excavations at Morton, Fife', *Proc. Prehist. Soc. 37(1)*, 284–366.
FISCHER, ANDERS and SORENSEN, SØREN A. 1983. 'Stenalder pä den danske havbund', *Antikvariske studier 6*, 104–26 (English summary 125–6).
GILBERTSON, G. 1984. *Late Quaternary Environments and Man in Holderness*. BAR British Series 134. Oxford.
HAZZLEDINE WARREN, S., PIGGOTT, S., CLARK, J. G. D., BURKITT, M. C. and GODWIN, H. and M. E. 1936. 'Archaeology of the Submerged Land-Surface of the Essex Coast', *Proc. Prehist. Soc. 2*, 178–210.
LARSSON, L. 1984. 'The Skateholm Project. A Late Mesolithic Settlement and Cemetery Complex at a southern Swedish Bay', *Meddelanden från Lunds Universitets historiska Museum*, 1983–1984. New Series, Vol. 5, 5–38.
LOUWE KOOIJMANS, L. P. 1974. *The Rhine/Meuse delta. Analecta Praehistorica Leidensia VII*. Leiden University Press.
— 1987. Neolithic Settlement and Subsistence in the Wetlands of the Rhine/Meuse delta of the Netherlands, in J. M. Coles and A. J. Lawson (eds) *European Wetlands in Prehistory*, 227–51. Oxford University Press.
MELLARS, P. 1987. *Excavations on Oronsay*. Edinburgh, University Press.
SKAARUP, JORGEN. 1983. 'Submarine stenalderbopladser i det sydfynskeøhav', *Antikvariske studier 6*, 137–61 (English summary, 159–61).
SMITH, R. A. 1911. 'Lake Dwellings in Holderness', *Archaeologia 62*, 593–610.
TOOLEY, M. 1978. 'The history of Hartlepool Bay', *International Journal of Nautical Archaeology and Underwater Exploration 7*, 71–5.
VARLEY, W. J. 1968. 'Barmston and the Holderness Crannogs', *East Riding Archaeology 1*, 12–23.
WILKINSON, T. and MURPHY, P. 1986. 'Archaeological Survey of an Intertidal Zone: the Submerged Landscape of the Essex Coast, England', *Journal of Field Archaeology 13(2)*, 177–94.
— 1988. Wetland development and human activity in Essex estuaries during the holocene transgression, in P. Murphy and C. French (eds) *The Exploitation of Wetlands*, 213–33. British Archaeological Reports, British Series 186. Oxford.

Europe, Iron Age

BRANDT, R. W., GROENMAN-VAN WAATERINGE, W. and VAN DER LEEUW, S. E. (eds) 1987. *Assendelver Polders Papers 1*. Cingula 10. Amsterdam.
BRANDT, R. W. and VAN DER LEEUW, S. E. 1987. The Assendelver Polders of the Netherlands and a Wet Perspective on the European Iron Age, in J. M. Coles and A. J. Lawson (eds) *European Wetlands in Prehistory*, 203–26. Oxford University Press.
HAARNAGEL, W. 1979. *Die Grabung Feddersen Wierde*, 2 vols. Franz Steiner Verlag. Wiesbaden.
SCHMID, P. 1977. New archaeological results of settlement structures (Roman Iron Age) in the north-west German coastal area, in B. Cunliffe and T. Rowley (eds) *Lowland Iron Age Communities in Europe*, 123–46. BAR International Series 48, Oxford.
— 1982. 'Landliche Siedlungen der vorromischen Eisenzeit bis Volkerwanderungszeit im niedersachsischen Kustengebiet', *Offa 39*, 73–96.
ZIMMERMAN, W. H. 1977. Economy of the Roman Iron Age settlement Flögeln, Lower Saxony, in B. Cunliffe and T. Rowley (eds) *Lowland Iron Age Communities in Europe*, 147–66. BAR International Series 48, Oxford.

4 Pioneers of the inland waters
Early Europe, including Russia

Andresen, J. M., Byrd, B. F., Elson, M. D., McGuire, R. H., Mendoza, R. G., Staski, E. and White, J. P. 1981. 'The deer hunters: Star Carr reconsidered', *World Archaeology 13*, 30–46.
CLARK, J. G. D. 1975. *The Earlier Stone Age Settlement of Scandinavia*. Cambridge University Press.
— 1954. *Excavations at Star Carr*. Cambridge University Press.
— 1972. *Star Carr: a case study in Bioarchaeology*. Addison-Wesley Modular Publications, Module in Anthropology no. 10, 1–42.
COLES, J. M. and ORME, B. J. 1983. 'Homo sapiens or Castor fiber?', *Antiquity 57*, 95–102.
DOLUKHANOV, P. 1979. *Ecology and Economy in Neolithic Eastern Europe*. Duckworth, London.
— 1986. 'Natural environment and the Holocene settlement pattern in the north-western part of the USSR', *Fennoscandia archaeologica 3*, 3–16.
DOLUKHANOV, P. and MIKLYAYEV, A. M. 1986. 'Prehistoric lacustrine pile-dwellings in the north-

western part of the USSR', *Fennoscandia archaeologica* *3*, 81–9.

GRAMSCH, B. 1987. 'Ausgrabungen auf dem mesolithischen Moorfundplatz bei Friesack, Bezirk Potsdam', *Veröffentlichungen des Museums für Ur-und Frühgeschichte Potsdam 21*, 75–100.

HALLAM, J. S., EDWARDS, B. J. N., BARNES, B. and STUART, A. J. 1973. 'A Late Glacial elk with associated barbed points from High Furlong, Lancashire', *Proc. Prehist. Soc. 39*, 100–28.

OSHIBKINA, S. V. 1982. 'Wooden artifacts from the Mesolithic site of Nizhneye Veretye', *Archaeologicke Rozhledy 34*, 414–29. (English summary).

ZVELEBIL, M. 1981. *From Forager to Farmer in the Boreal Zone*. BAR International Series S115, Oxford.

Early sites outside Europe

AIKENS, C. M. and HIGUCHI, T. 1982. *The Prehistory of Japan*. Academic Press, New York.

ARUTIUNOV, S. A. and SERGEEV, D. A. 1975. *Problem of ethnohistory of the Bering Sea region* (in Russian). Nauka, Moscow.

DILLEHAY, T. 1984. 'A Late Ice-Age settlement in southern Chile', *Scientific American* 251, 106–117.

ELISSEEFF, V. 1974. *The Ancient Civilization of Japan*. Barrie and Jenkins, London.

GORECKI, P. P. and GILLIESON, D. S. 1985. 'The highland fringes as a key zone for prehistoric developments in Papua New Guinea', *Bull. Indo.-Pacific Prehistory Assoc. 5*, 93–103

GILLIESON, D., GORECKI, P. and HOPE, G. 1985. 'Prehistoric agricultural systems in a lowland swamp, Papua New Guinea', *Archaeol. Oceania* 20, 32–7.

LUEBBERS, R. A. 1975. 'Ancient boomerangs discovered in South Australia', *Nature*, *253*, 39.

Circum-Alpine Neolithic

BILLAMBOZ, A. 1985. 'Premières investigations archéodendrologiques dans le champ de pieux de la station de Hornstaad-Hörnle 1 sur les bords du lac de Constance', *Berichte zu Ufer-und Moorsiedlungen Südwestdeutschlands 2*, 125–47.

BILLAMBOZ, A. *et al. La station littorale d'Auvernier-Port: cadre et évolution.* Cahiers d'Archéologie Romande No. 25, Lausanne.

BILLAMBOZ, A. and SCHLICHTHERLE, H. 1985a. Pfahlbauten-Häuser in Seen und Mooren, in D. Planck (ed.) *Der Keltenfürst von Hochdorf. Methoden und Ergebnisse der Landesarchäologie*, pp. 248–66 plus catalogue pp. 272–85. Katalog der Ausstellung, Stuttgart, Kunstgebände vom 14. August bis 13. Oktober 1985. Landesdenkmalamt Baden-Württemburg.

— 1985b. Le Néolithique des bords de lac et des tourbières du Sud-Ouest de l'Allemagne, in *Première Céramique, Premier Métal: du Néolithique à l'âge du bronze dans le domaine circum-alpin*, pp. 23–35. Exhibition guide-catalogue, Musée Municipal, Lons-le-Saunier, France.

BOCQUET, A. (ed.) 1984. *Archéologie des lacs et des rivières.* Musée d'Annecy, Annecy.

BOCQUET, A. 1985. La civilisation Saône-Rhône dans les Alpes du Nord, in *Première Céramique, Premier Métal: du Néolithique à l'âge du bronze dans le domaine circum-alpin*, 147–51. Exhibition guide-catalogue, Musée Municipal, Lons-le-Saunier, France.

BOCQUET, A., BROCHIER, J. L., EMERY-BARBIER, A., LUNDSTROM-BAUDAIS, K., ORCEL, C. and VIN, F. 1987. A submerged Neolithic village: Charavines 'Les Baigneurs' in Lake Paladru, France, in J. M. Coles and A. J. Lawson (eds) *European Wetlands in Prehistory*, 33–54. Oxford University Press, Oxford and New York.

BOCQUET, A. and HOUOT, A. 1982. 'La vie au Néolithique: Charavines, un village au bord d'un lac', *Histoire et Archéologie 64*. (Issue devoted to Charavines, many illustrations and reconstruction drawings.)

DIECKMANN, B. 1985. 'Die neolithischen Ufersiedlungen von Hornstaad-Hörnle am westlichen Bodensee. Die Grabungskampagne 1983–84', *Berichte zu Ufer-und Moorsiedlungen Südwestdeutschlands 2*, 98–124.

KOKABI, M. 1985. Vorlaufiger Bericht über die Untersuchungen an Tierknochenfunden aus Hornstaad-Hörnle I am Westlichen Bodensee. *Berichte zu Ufer-und Moorsiedlungen Südwestdeutschlands 2*, 148–63.

MAGNY, M. and SCHIFFERDECKER, F. 1980. 'Essai sur l'occupation du sol au Néolithique: le groupe de Lüscherz', *Bulletin de la Sociéte Préhistorique Francaise 77(1)*, 18–25.

PÉTREQUIN, P. 1984. *Gens de l'eau, gens de la terre*, Hachette. (espec. chs. 3–5).

— 1986. Recherches récentes sur les habitats lacustres de l'Est de la France. In J. P. Demoule and J. Guilaine (eds) *Le Néolithique de la France*, 291–304. Picard, Paris.

— (ed.) 1986. *Les sites littoraux néolithiques de Clairvaux-les-lacs* (Jura), Vol. I: Problématique générale. L'exemple de la station III. Editions de la Maison des Sciences de l'Homme, Paris.

PÉTREQUIN, A-M. and P. 1988. *Le Néolithique des Lacs. Préhistoire des lacs de Chalain et de Clairvaux (4000–2000 av. J-C)*. Editions Errance, Paris.

PÉTREQUIN, P., PÉTREQUIN, A. M. and PASSARD, F. 1982. *Villages néolithiques des lacs du Jura.* Centre Universitaire d'Études Régionales, Besançon (well-illustrated booklet).

RÖSCH, M. 1985. Die Pflanzenreste der neolithischen Ufersiedlung von Hornstaad-Hörnle I am westlichen Bodensee. *Berichte zu Ufer-und Moorsiedlungen Südwestdeutschlands 2*, 164–99 (English summary p. 186).

SCHLICHTHERLE, H. and WAHLSTER, B. 1986. *Archäologie in Seen und Mooren*. Konrad Theiss Verlag, Stuttgart (well-illustrated account of recent work in southern Germany).

WYSS, R. 1959. *Anfänge der Bauerntums in der Schweiz. Die Egolzwilerkultur*. Verlag Paul Haupt, Bern (small booklet with artifact photographs).

— 1973. *Wirtschaft und Gesellschaft in der Jungsteinzeit*. Francke Verlag, Bern (good for site plans and illustrations of artifacts).

— 1976. *Das jungsteinzeitliche Jäger-Bauerndorf von Egolzwil 5 in Wauwilermoos*. Schweizerischen Landesmuseum, Zürich.

Alvastra

BARTHOLIN, T. H. 1978. Alvastra pile dwelling: tree studies. The dating and the landscape, *Fornvännen 73*, 213–19.

MALMER, M. 1980. The Explanation of a Pile Dwelling, in L. K. Königsson and K. Paabo (eds) *Florilegium Florinis Dedicatum. Striae 14*.

Material culture

BAUDAIS, D. 1985. Le mobilier en bois des sites littoraux de Chalain et Clairvaux, in *Chalain-Clairvaux, Fouilles Anciennes*. Présentation des Collections du Musée de Lons-le-Saunier No. I, 177–99.

BAUDAÍS, D., CORBOUD, P. et NIERLE, M.-C. 1986. Un site littoral lémanique, Corsier-Port (GE), in *Première Céramique, Premier Métal: du Néolithique à l'âge du bronze dans le domaine circum-alpin*, 91–7. Exhibition guide-catalogue, Musée Municipal, Lons-le-Saunier, France.

BILLAMBOZ, A. and SCHLICHTHERLE, H. 1986. Le Néolithique des bords de lac et des tourbières du Sud-Ouest de l'Allemagne, in *Première Céramique, Premier Métal: du Néolithique à l'âge du bronze dans le domaine circum-alpin*, pp. 23–55. Exhibition guide-catalogue, Musée Municipal, Lons-le-Saunier, France.

BOCQUET, A. 1984. *Archéologie des Lacs et des Rivières*. Musée d'Annecy, Annecy.

BOCQUET, A., CAILLAT, R. and LUNDSTROM-BAUDAIS, K. 1986. Alimentation et techniques de cuisson dans le village néolithique de Charavines-Isère, in J. P. Demoule and J. Guilaine (eds) *Le Néolithique de la France*, 319–29. Picard, Paris.

EGLOFF, M. 1989. 'De Cotencher à Auvernier: l'âge de la Pierre dans le canton de Neuchâtel', *Helvetia Archaeologica 43/44*, 101–116.

FELDTKELLER, A. and SCHLICHTHERLE, H. 1987. 'Jungsteinzeitliche Kleidungsstücke aus Ufersiedlungen des Bodensees', *Archäologsiche Nachrichten aus Baden 38/39*, 74–84.

HÖNEISEN, MARKUS. 1986. Vue d'ensemble sur le Néolithique dans le Nord-Est de la Suisse, in *Première Céramique, Premier Métal: du néolithique à l'âge du bronze dans le domaine circum-alpin*, 37–67. Exhibition guide-catalogue, Musée Municipal, Lons-le-Saunier, France.

HUNDT, H.-J. 1986. Tissus et sparteries néolithiques, in P. Pétrequin (ed.), *Les Sites Littoraux Néolithiques de Clairvaux-les-Lacs (Jura)*. Vol. I Problématique générale. L'exemple de la Station III, 233–42.

MASUREL, H. 1985. Vanneries, tissus, réserves de fil et liens trouvés à Chalain et conservés au Musée de Lons-le-Saunier, in *Chalain-Clairvaux, Fouilles Anciennes*. Présentation des Collections du Musée de Lons-Le-Saunier No. I, 201–10.

MÜLLERBECK, H. with contributions from SCHWEINGRUBER, F. 1965. *Seeberg, Burgäschisee-Süd. Teil 5: Holzgeräte und Holzbearbeitung*. Acta Bernensia II. Verlag Stämpfli, Bern.

MUNRO, R. 1890. *The Lake-Dwellings of Europe*. Cassell & Co. Ltd., London.

PÉTREQUIN, P. 1984. *Gens de l'Eau, Gens de la Terre*. Hachette, Paris.

PÉTREQUIN, P., PÉTREQUIN, A.M. and PASSARD, F. 1982. *Villages Néolithiques des Lacs du Jura*. Université de Franche-Comté, Besançon.

RAMSEYER, DENIS. 1986. Le Néolithique dans le canton de Fribourg, in *Première Céramique, Premier Métal: du néolithique à l'âge du bronze dans le domaine circum-alpin*. 69–77. Exhibition guide catalogue, Musée Municipal, Lons-le-Saunier, France.

RUOFF, E. 1981. 'Stein-und bronzeitliche Textilfunde aus dem Kanton Zürich', *Helvetia Archaeologica 45/48*, 252–64.

RUOFF, U. 1981. 'Die Ufersiedlungen an Zürich-und Greifensee', *Helvetia Archaeologica 45/48*, 19–61.

SCHLICHTHERLE, H. and WAHLSTER, B. 1986. *Archäologie in Seen und Mooren*. Konrad Theiss Verlag, Stuttgart.

WINIGER, J. 1981 'Ein Beitrag zur Geschichte des Beils', *Helvetia Archaeologica 45/48*, 161–88.

— 1981. 'Jungsteinzeitliche Gefässschnitzerei', *Helvetia Archaeologica 45/48*, 189–98.

WYSS, R. 1973. *Wirtschaft und Gesellschaft in der Jungsteinzeit*, Monographien zur Schweizer-Geschichte Band 6. Francke Verlag, Bern.

— 1976. *Das jungsteinzeitliche Jäger-Bauerndorf von Egolzwil 5 in Wauwilermoos*. Schweizerischen Landesmuseum, Zürich.

— 1983. *Die jungsteinzeitlichen Bauerndörfer von Egolzwil 4 im Wauwilermoos. Bande 2: Die Funde*. Schweizerischen Landesmuseum, Zürich.

5 The lake-dwellers

Circum-Alpine, later prehistory

ARNOLD, B. 1983. Les 24 maisons d'Auvernier-Nord (Bronze final). *Jahrbuch der schweizerischen Gesellschaft für Ur-und Fruhgeschichte 66*, 87–104.

— 1986. *Cortaillod-Est, un village du Bronze final, 1. Fouille subaquatique et photographie aérienne*. Saint-Blaise, Editions du Ruau (Archéologie neuchâteloise, 1).

BECKER, B., BILLAMBOZ, A. and SCHMIDT, B. 1984. Dendrochronologische Untersuchungen in der 'Siedlung Forschner' (Federsee) und in Weiteren bronzezeitlichen Siedlungen Südwestdeutschlands, *Berichte zu Ufer-und Moorsiedlungen Südwestdeutschlands I*, 53–63.

BOCQUET, A. 1984. *Archéologie des Lacs et des Rivières*. Musée d'Annecy, Annecy.

BORELLO, M. A., BROCHIER, J.-L., CHAIX, L. et HADORN, P. 1986. *Courtaillod-Est, un village du Bronze final, 4. Nature et environnement*. Saint-Blaise, Editions du Ruau (Archéologie neuchâteloise, 4).

EGLOFF, M. 1981. Versunkene Dörfer der Urnenfelderzeit im Neuenburgersee, *Archäologisches Korrespondenzblatt II*, 55–63.

PERINI, R. 1984. *Scavi archeologici nella zona palafitticola di Fiavé-Carera. Parte I: Campagne 1969–1976*. Servizi o Beni Culturali della Provincia Autonoma di Trento.

— 1987. The typology of the structures on Bronze Age Wetland Settlements at Fiavé and Lavagnone in the Italian Alpine Foothills, in J. M. Coles and A. J. Lawson (eds) *European Wetlands in Prehistory*, 75–93. Oxford University Press.

PÉTREQUIN, P. 1984. *Gens de l'Eau, Gens de la Terre*. Hachette, Paris.

RUOFF, U. 1981. Altersbestimmung mit Hilfe der Dendrochronologie, *Helvetia Archaeologica 45/48*, 89–97.

— 1987. Archaeological Investigations beside Lake Zurich and Lake Greifen, Switzerland, in J. M. Coles and A. J. Lawson (eds) *European Wetlands in Prehistory*, 55–73. Oxford University Press.

SCHLICHTHERLE, H. and WAHLSTER, B. 1986. *Archäologie in Seen und Mooren*. Konrad Theiss Verlag, Stuttgart.

Subsistence and Material Culture Many of the later prehistory references, plus:

BORELLO, M. A. 1982. '"Site catchment analysis" d'Auvernier-Nord (Bronze final) Lac de Neuchâtel', *Jahrbuch der Schweizerischen Gesellschaft für Ur- und Frühgeschichte 65*, 83–91.

BORELLO, M. A. and CHAIX, L. 1983. 'Étude de la faune de Hauterive-Champréveyres (Neuchâtel) (Bronze final) (1979–1980)', *Bulletin de la Société Neuchâteloise des Sciences Naturelles 106*, 159–69. (includes comparisons with other contemporary sites).

CHAIX, L. 1986. La faune, in M. A. Borello, J. L. Brochier, L. Chaix et P. Hadorn *Cortaillod-Est, un village du Bromze final, 4. Nature et environnement*, 47–73. Saint-Blaise, Editions du Ruau (Archéologie Neuchâteloise, 4).

EGLOFF, M. 1980. *Auvernier-ein Dorf aus der Urzeit*, Museum zu Allerheiligen, Schaffhausen.

GREIG, J. 1984. A preliminary report on the pollen diagrams and some macrofossil results from palafitta Fiavé, in R. Perini *Scavi archeologici nella zona palafitticola di Fiavé-Carrera. Parte I: Campagne 1969–1976*, 305–23. Servizio Beni Culturali della Provincia Autonoma di Trento.

HEITZ, A., JACOMET, S. and ZOLLER, H. 1981. 'Vegetation, Sammelwirtschaft und Ackerbau im Zürich-seegebiezur Zeit der Neolithischen und spätbron-zezeitlichee Ufersiedlungen', *Helvetia Archaeologica 45/48*, 139–52.

PERINI, R. 1987. *Scavi Archeologici della zona Palafitticola di Fiavé-Carera. Parte II: Reste della Cultura Materiale*. Servizio Beni Culturali della Provincia autonoma di Trento.

JONES, G. and ROWLEY-CONWY, P. 1984. Plant remains from the North Italian Lake Dwellings of Fiavé (1400–1200 bc), in R. Perini *Scavi archéologici della zona palafitticola di Fiavé-Carrera. Parte I: Campagne 1969–1976*, 323–55. Servizio Beni Culturali della Provincia Autonoma di Trento.

SCHÖBEL, G. S. 1987. 'Ein Flötenfragment aus der spätbronzezeitlichen Siedlung Hagnau-Burg, Boden-seekreis', *Archäologische Nachrichten aus Baden 38/39*, 84–7.

WYSS, R. 1981. 'Kostbare Perlenkette als Zeuge ältesten Fernhandels in Zürich', *Helvetia Archaeologica 45/48*, 242–51.

Away from the Alps

BRADLEY, J. 1983. 'Excavations at Moynagh Lough, Co. Meath, 1980–81', *Riocht na Midhe 7(2)*, 12–32.

— 1984. 'Excavations at Moynagh Lough 1982–83', *Riocht na Midhe 7(3)*, 86–93.

—1986. 'Excavations at Moynagh Lough 1984', *Riocht na Midhe 7(4)*, 79–92.

— 1986. 'Moynagh Lough, Co. Meath, Ireland', *NewsWarp 1*, 4–5.

COLES, B. and J. 1986. *Sweet Track to Glastonbury: the Somerset Levels in Prehistory*. Thames and Hudson, London and New York.

COLES, J. M. 1987. *Meare Village East: The Excavations of A. Bulleid and H. St George Gray 1932–1956*. Somerset Levels Project.

DIXON, N. 1984. 'Oakbank Crannog', *Current Archae-ology 90*, 217–20.

— 1988. 'Survey and excavation of submerged settlement sites in Scotland', *NewsWarp 4*, 1–3.

HALL, D. 1987. 'The Fenland Project, No. 2: Fenland landscapes and settlement between Peterborough and March', *East Anglian Archaeology 35*.

MORRISON, I. 1985. *Landscape with Lake Dwellings: the crannogs of Scotland*. Edinburgh University Press, Edinburgh.

PRYOR, F., FRENCH, C. and TAYLOR, M. 1986. 'Flag Fen, Fengate, Peterborough I: Discovery, Reconnaissance and Initial Excavation (1982–85)', *Proc. Prehist. Soc. 52*, 1–24.

RAJEWSKI, Z. 1970. *Biskupin. A fortified settlement dating from 500 BC*. Wydawnictwo Poznańskie, Poznań.

Riverside and flood plain

BARFIELD, L. 1971. *Northern Italy before Rome*. Thames & Hudson, London.

BOCQUET, A. 1984. *Archéologie des lacs et des rivières. 1984*. Musée d'Annecy, Annecy.

BURNEZ, C. 1987. 'Wetland archaeological research in west-central France', *NewsWarp 3*, 19–21.

NEEDHAM, S. 1985. 'Neolithic and Bronze Age settlement of the buried flood plains of Runnymede', *Oxford Journal of Archaeology 4*, 125–37.

MUNRO, R. 1890. *The Lake Dwellings of Europe*. Cassell & Co., London.

Elsewhere in the world

BELLWOOD, P. 1971. 'Fortifications and economy in prehistoric New Zealand', *Proc. Prehist. Soc. 37(1)*, 56–95.

GIMBUTAS, M. 1965. *Bronze Age Cultures in Central and Eastern Europe*, Mouton & Co., The Hague.

JACKSON, L. 1986. 'Dawson Creek: an Early Woodland Site in S. Ontario', *American Antiquity 51(2)*, 389–401.

PURDY, B. and NEWSOM, L. A. 1985. 'Significance of Archaeological Wet-Sites: a Florida Example', *National Geographic Research 1(4)*, 564–69.

WILSON, J. (ed.) 1987. *From the Beginning. The archaeology of the Maori*. Penguin Books, Auckland.

WINTEMBERG, W. J. 1936. 'The Roebuck prehistoric village site, Grenville County, Ontario', *National Museum of Canada Bulletin 83*. 1936. Ottawa.

6 Reaching the far side

Peatbogs and trackways

CASPARIE, W. A. 1982. 'The Neolithic wooden trackway XXI (Bou) in the raised bog at Nieuw-Dordrecht (The Netherlands)', *Palaeohistoria 24*, 115–64.

— 1984. 'The three Bronze Age footpaths XVI (Bou), XVII (Bou) and XVIII (Bou) in the raised bog of southeast Drenthe (The Netherlands)', *Palaeohistoria 26*, 41–94.

COLES, B. & J. 1986. *Sweet Track to Glastonbury. The Somerset Levels in prehistory*. Thames & Hudson, London.

GORE, A. J. P. (ed.) 1983. *Ecosystems of the World. 4a. Mires: Swamp, Bog, Fen & Moor*. Elsevier Scientific Publishing Co.

HAYEN, H. 1971. 'Hölzerne Kultfiguren am Bohlenweg XLII (1p) im Wittemoor', *Die Kunde 22*.

— 1972. 'Vier Scheibenräder aus Glum', *Die Kunde, 23*, 62–86.

— 1973. 'Räder und Wagenteile aus nordwestdeutschen

Mooren', *Nachrichten aus Niedersachsens Urgeschichte 42*, 129–76.
— 1977. 'Bohlenwege in den grossen Mooren am Dümmer', *Archiv für Deutsche Heimatpflege GMBH 45*, 33–48.
— 1979. 'Der Bohlenweg VI (Pr) im grossen Moor am Dümmer', *Materialhefte zur Ur-und Frühgeschichte Niedersachsens 15*.
— 1983. Handwerklich-technische Lösungen im vor-und frühgeschichtlichen Wagenbau, in H. Jankuhn, W. Janssen, R. Schmidt-Wiegand & H. Tiefenbach (eds), *Das Handwerk in vor-und frühgeschichtlicher Zeit*, 415–70. Vandenhoek & Ruprecht, Göttingen.
— 1987. 'New light on the history of transport', *Endeavour n.s. 11,4*, 209–15.
— 1987. Peatbog archaeology in Lower Saxony, West Germany, in J. M. Coles & A. J. Lawson (eds) *European Wetlands in Prehistory*, 117–36. University Press, Oxford.
JØRGENSEN, M. S. 1988. 'Faerdsel over stenalderfjorden', *Fortidsminder og Kulturhistorie. Antikvariske studier 9*, 157–67.
LUCAS, A. T. 1985. 'Toghers or Causeways: some evidence from archaeological, literary, historical and place-name sources', *Proc. Royal Irish Academy 85, C*, 37–60.
O'CONNELL, C. (ed.) 1987. *The IPCC Guide to Irish Peatlands*. Irish Peatland Conservation Council.
PIGGOTT, S. 1982. *The Earliest Wheeled Transport. From the Atlantic coast to the Caspian Sea*. Thames & Hudson, London.
RAFTERY, B. 1986. 'A wooden trackway of iron age date in Ireland', *Antiquity 60*, 50–53.
VAN DER WAALS, J. D. 1964. *Prehistoric disc wheels in the Netherlands*. Wolters, Groningen.

Transport on water and snow

AALTO, M., TAAVITSAINEN, J.-P. & VUORELA, I. 1980. 'Palaeobotanical investigations at the site of a sledge runner find, dated to about 4900 BP, in Noormarkku, S. W. Finland', *Suomen Museo*, 41–65.
ARNOLD, B. 1985. 'Navigation et construction navale sur les lacs suisses au Bronze final', *Helvetia archaeologica 63/64*, 91–117.
CASTIGLIONI, O. C. & CALEGARI, G. 1978. 'Le piroghe monossili italiane', *Preistori Alpina 14*, 163–72.
JONCHERAY, D. 1986. *Les embarcations monoxyles dans la region pays de la Loire*. Etudes préhistoriques et historiques des pays de la Loire 9.
MILLETT, M. & McGRAIL, S. 1987. 'The archaeology of

the Hasholme logboat', *Archaeol. J. 144*, 69–155.
PARET, O. 1930. 'Die Einbäume im Federseeried und im übrigen Europa', *Praehistorische Zeitschrift 21*, 76–116.
VILKUNA, J. 1984. 'Ancient skis of central Finland', *Fennoscandia archaeologica 1*, 31–41.
— 1986. 'Kaksi muinaisten suksirekien jalasta Keski-Suomesta', *Keski-Suomi 18*, 8–16.
— 1987. 'Prehistoric paddles from Finland', *NewsWarp 3*, 32–4.
WRIGHT, E. V. 1976. *The North Ferriby boats. A guidebook*. National Maritime Museum, Greenwich.

7 Bogs and bodies

BERG, S., ROLLE, R. and SEEMANN, H. 1981. *Der Archäologie und der Tod. Archäologie und Gerichtsmedizin*. Bucher, Munich.
BROTHWELL, D. 1986. *The Bog Man and the Archaeology of People*. British Museum Publications, London.
CLAUSEN, C. J., COHEN, A. D., EMILIANI, C., HOLMAN, J. A. & STIPP, J. J. 1979. 'Little Salt Spring. Florida: a unique underwater site', *Science 203, no. 4381*, 609–14.
DEYTS, S. 1983. *Les bois sculptés des Sources de la Seine*. XLII supp. Gallia. CNRS, Paris.
DIECK, A. 1965. *Die Europäischen Moorleichenfunde*. Neumünster.
EBBESEN, K. 1986. *Doden i mosen*. Carlsen, Copenhagen.
GLOB, P. V. 1969. *The Bog People. Iron Age man preserved*. Faber, London.
HAGBERG, U. 1967. *The Archaeology of Skedemosse*. Almquist & Wiksells, Stockholm.
HAYEN, H. 1985. 'Bergung, wissenschaftliche Untersuchung und Konservierung moorarchäologischer Funde', *Archäologische Mitteilungen aus Nordwestdeutschland 8*, 1–43.
ILKJAER, J. and LONSTRUP, J. 1983. 'Der Moorfund im Tal der Illerup-A bei Skanderborg in Ostjütland (Dänemark)', *Germania 61*, 96–116.
JENSEN, J. 1982. *The Prehistory of Denmark*. Methuen, London and New York.
MACDONALD, G. F. & PURDY, B. A. 1982. 'Florida's wet sites: where the fragile past survives', *Early Man 4(4)*, 4–12.
Ó FLOINN, R. 1988. 'Irish bog bodies', *Archaeology Ireland 2*, 94–97.
RADDATZ, K. 1987. *Der Thorsberger Moorfunde Katalog. Offa-Bücher 65*. Karl Wachholtz Verlag, Neümunster.
STEAD, I. M., BOURKE, J. B. & BROTHWELL, D. 1986. *Lindow Man. The Body in the Bog*. British Museum Publications, London.

Sources of illustrations

Drawings (*redrawn by M. Rouillard)

Albrethsen and Brinch Petersen 1977 *50**
Andersen 1987 *47, 48, 50*, 49* (E. Morville)
Arnold 1983 *87**; 1986 *1, 85*, 86*, 89**
Bellwood 1971 *108**
Billamboz 1985 *70*
Billamboz and Schlichtherle 1984 *67*
Bocquet 1984 *71*
Bocquet et al. 1987 *68*
Casparie *114*
Croes, D. *42*
Cushing 1896 *29*
Darbishire 1874 *25, 26*
Deyts 1983 *129*
Doran *128**
Ebbesen 1986 *135*
Egloff 1980 *11, 91, 93*; 1987 *90*
Feldtkeller and Schlichtherle 1987 *77**
Fenland Archaeological Trust *101* (R. Parkin)
Gilliland 1988 *32*
Gimbutas 1965 *107*
Glob 1969 *138, 146*
Gramsch 1987 *64**
Haarnagel 1979 *58, 60*
Hall 1987 *100*
Hayen 1971 *119;* 1977 *117, 120*; 1981 *131*; 1985 *122*
Hendersen, K. *106*
Jensen 1982 *143*
Joncheray 1986 *123*
Keller 1878 *10, 12, 14, 16, 18, 20, 21, 34*
Larsson 1984 *50**
Louwe Kooijmans 1987 *53*, 54, 55*
Macdonald and Purdy 1982 *127*
Müllerbeck 1965 *73, 76*
Munro 1882 *23, 24*; 1892 *17*; 1912 *15, 99*
Oshibkina 1982 *63**
Perini 1984 *88**, 1987 *94, 95, 96, 98*
Rajewski 1980 *102**
Ramseyer 1986 *75*
Rouillard, M. *9, 19, 22, 40, 41, 45, 46, 51, 52, 53, 57, 62, 66, 80, 81, 83, 110, 128, 130, 140, 147*
Schlichtherle and Wahlster 1986 *35, 65, 72, 74, 82*, 84**
Schmid 1977 *57**; 1982 *59*
Schöbel 1987 *97**
Skaarup 1983 *44*
Somerset Levels Project *title page, 104* (S. Rouillard); *103* (R. Walker)
Speck 1981 *8, 13*
Svendsen, O. *118*
Therkorn et al. 1984 *56*
Van der Waals 1964 *4*
Vilkuna 1984 *124**; 1987 *125**

Wood-Martin 1886 *5, 6, 7*
Wright, E. V. *126*
Wyss 1981 *92**

Photographs

Archäologisches Landesmuseum der Christian-Albrechts-Universität, Schleswig *133, 136, 137, 139, 145*
M. Brooks, Central Excavation Unit, Scottish Development Department *105*
A. Bulleid and H. St George Gray *27*
Centre de Documentation de la Préhistoire Alpine *69*
J. M. Coles *2, 28, 109, 111, 112, 115, 116, 132, 144, 149*
T. Cowell, copyright the British Museum *141*
G. J. Landweer *3*
H. Masurel *79*
National Museum of Denmark *138, 146, 148*
Niedersächsisches Landesinstitut für Marschen und Wurtenforschung *61*
Panstwowe Muzeum Archeologiczne Oddzial w Biskupinie *37, 38*
B. Raftery *113*
R. Schneider *121*
Schweizerisches Landesmuseum Zurich *78*
M. Short, Ozette Project *43*
Silkeborg Museum *134*
National Museum of Natural History, Smithsonian Institution *29–33, 39*
Staatliches Museum, Oldenburg *142*
P. Vouga *36*

Sources in museum archives and collections

Archäologisches Landesmuseum Christian-Albrechts-Universität, Schleswig *2, 130, 132, 133, 136, 137, 139, 140, 144, 145, 149*
British Museum *141*
Florida State Museum *127*
Forhistorisk museum, Moesgård *48, 49*
Keski-Suomen Museo, Finland *124, 125*
Musée cantonale de Neuchâtel *89–91, 93*
Musée municipal d'archéologie, Lons-le-Saunier *79*
Museo provinciale d'Arte, Trento *94–96, 98*
National Museum of Denmark *138, 146, 148*
National Museum of Natural History, Smithsonian Institution *29–33, 39*
Niedersächsisches Landesinstitut *58, 61*
Panstwowe Muzeum Archaeologiczne Oddzia w Biskupinie *37, 38*
Schweizerisches Landesmuseum Zürich *78, 92*
Silkeborg Museum *134*
Staatliches Museum, Oldenburg *115, 119, 142*

211

Index